Aftershock

Aftershock

PROTECT YOURSELF AND PROFIT IN THE NEXT GLOBAL FINANCIAL MELTDOWN

THIRD EDITION

David Wiedemer, PhD

Robert A. Wiedemer

Cindy Spitzer

WILEY

Contents

Executive Summary

What Is a Bubble?

An asset value that temporarily booms and eventually busts, based on changing investor psychology, rather than on underlying fundamental economic drivers that are sustainable over time.

What Is a Bubble Economy?

An economy that grows in a virtuous upward spiral of multiple, rising bubbles (real estate, stocks, private debt, dollar, and government debt) that interact to drive each other up, and that will inevitably fall in a vicious downward spiral as each falling bubble puts downward pressure on the rest, eventually pulling the whole economy down.

What Is the Aftershock?

In Phase 1, the real estate, stock, private debt, and discretionary spending bubbles began to fall.

Next, in Phase 2, just when many people think the worst is over, the dollar and government debt bubbles will pop, bringing on the worldwide Aftershock.

Acknowledgments

The authors thank John Silbersack of Trident Media Group and David Pugh, Laura Gachko, and Joan O'Neil from John Wiley & Sons for their relentless support of this book. We would also like to thank Stephen Mack and Jeff Garigliano for their help in writing this book. We thank Jim Fazone, Jay Harrison, and Nancy McSally for their work on the graphics; Michael Lebowitz for his help on the data; and Beth Gansner for her help in proofreading. We also want to acknowledge Christine Peglar's and Jennifer Schoenefeldt's help in keeping us organized.

David Wiedemer

I thank my co-authors, Bob and Cindy, for being indispensable in the writing of this book. Without them, this book would not have been published and, even if written, would have been inaccessible for most audiences. I also thank Dr. Rod Stevenson for his long-term support of the foundational work that is the basis for this book. Dr. Jeff Williamson and Dr. Lee Hansen also provided me with important support in my academic career. And I am especially grateful to my wife, Betsy, and son, Benson, for their ongoing support in what has been an often arduous and trying process.

Robert Wiedemer

I, along with my brother, want to dedicate this book to our mother, who died late last year. She inspired us to think creatively and see the joy in learning and teaching. We dedicate this to our father, the original author in the family. We want to thank our brother, Jim, for his lifelong support of the ideas behind this book. Chris Ruddy and Aaron De Hoog have been enormous supporters of *Aftershock*. It's been great to have such support. I want to thank early supporters Stan Goldstein, Tim Selby, Sam Stovall, and Phil Gross. I also want to thank Dan Cohen and Michael Calkin for their support of this book. I am most grateful to Weldon Rackley, who helped my father to become an author and who did the same for me. A very heartfelt thanks goes to John R. Douglas for his very special role in making our books a reality.

Of course, my gratitude goes to Dave Wiedemer and Cindy Spitzer for being, quite clearly, the best collaborators you could ever have. It was truly a great team effort. Most of all, I thank my wife, Sera, and children, Seline and John.

Cindy Spitzer

Thank you, David and Bob Wiedemer, once again for the honor of collaborating with you on our sixth book. I look forward to many more. For their endless patience and support, my deep appreciation and love go to my husband, Philip Terbush; our children, Chelsea, Anya, and Zachary; and my dear friend Cindi Callanan. I am also filled with a lifetime of gratitude for two wonderful teachers: Christine Gronkowski (SUNY Purchase College) and two-time Pulitzer Prize winner Jon Franklin (UMCP College of Journalism), who each in their own way helped move me along an amazing path. My appreciation also goes to Christie Chroniger and Beth Goldstein for their ongoing help with all things great and small.

Preface to the Third Edition
of *Aftershock*

Judging from recent media reports in 2013, as well as the forecasts of many investment professionals, it appears we have passed the financial crisis (which we know was caused by the early popping of the bubble economy), and there will be no Aftershock.

That would be welcome and comfortable news—if only it were true.

Instead, what has happened since the 2008 financial crisis is just as we predicted in our earlier books. As the four interacting bubbles (stocks, housing, private credit, and consumer spending) pop, they will put enormous pressure on the two remaining—and much more fundamental—bubbles in our bubble economy: the government debt and dollar bubbles.

That's because there has been an enormous incentive to further inflate the government debt and dollar bubbles in an effort to stall the popping of the other bubbles. And that is exactly what the government has done in two ways. First, it has increased its annual deficit by almost 400 percent from $167 billion in 2007 to almost $1 trillion in 2013, pumping up the government debt bubble. And even more stunningly, it has increased the U.S. money supply by an unthinkable 200 percent (from $800 billion in 2008 to more than $3.6 trillion as of the end of 2013), pumping up the dollar bubble.

By inflating these bubbles even more, we are temporarily preventing the other bubbles from deflating further and, in some cases, such as the stock market, we are actually reinflating the bubble to some extent. This was most clearly shown in late 2010 when Fed Chairman Ben Bernanke announced another round of money printing (via the second round of quantitative easing, QE2), and the stock market not only avoided what would have likely been a 10 to 15 percent decline in the year but also enjoyed more than a 10 percent gain. By early 2011, the market was up more than 30 percent from when Ben made the announcement. Now, with QE3 in place since 2012 (with money printing currently at $85 billion per month in late 2013), the Dow has been hitting new highs.

With great short-term benefits like this, further increases in the government debt bubble and the dollar bubble are likely to continue. Until we actually see inflation or have problems selling our government debt, there is no compelling, immediate reason to face, or even admit, any future problem with inflation or debt. Of course, now that we have shown an enormous willingness to print money in order to buy our own government debt, we will always be able to sell it. So the only real future problem with this scenario comes when concerns over the sustainability and long-term consequences of that money printing become too great for stock market investors.

In fact, we could pump up the government debt and dollar bubbles even more and truly boost the economy into high gear. Double the deficit or triple the money supply again and, no doubt, stocks, housing, and the economy will improve dramatically along with the overall economy. Only if people fear the long-term consequences of these actions will they become a problem. The story of the economy and of financial markets has become less a story about various market forces and increasingly more a desperate fight between investor fantasy psychology and the deeper reality of what's actually happening in the economy.

As long as investors and politicians can ignore the future consequences, there is no short-term reason not to pump up the government debt and dollar bubbles. In fact, there is good short-term rationale for continuing, because if the government were to cut our federal deficit back down to where it was in 2007, before the financial crisis, the government almost certainly would cause a major recession that would immediately pop the stock, housing, private credit, and consumer spending bubbles again. The same is true for the money supply. If we took out all the money we have printed since the financial crisis of 2008, we would certainly cause another bubble-popping recession.

But here's the catch. The only thing worse than the recession that would result from purposely deflating our government debt and dollar bubbles now will be the much, much bigger global depression that will eventually result from pumping them up even further. Deflating these bubbles now would pop our multibubble economy, but continuing to inflate them will eventually cause an even more massive and destructive pop in the future. We can have either pain now or a whole lot more pain later. As it stands, we have chosen a whole lot more pain later.

So we have successfully postponed the Aftershock. How long we can postpone it depends on the government's recklessness and the investment community's continued willingness to believe in the fantasy that nothing but good will come from massively expanding the government debt and dollar bubbles.

We don't think the Aftershock can be postponed much longer, but, as we said in the book, that is largely a matter of governmental decisions and investor psychology. Could it be five years away? We think that is unlikely. Could it be just one year away? We think that is probably equally unlikely. Exactly when the Aftershock will hit is hard to say because there is no easy way to predict governmental actions or investor psychology. Best guess: two to four years.

Whatever happens, it will certainly be interesting to see how this story plays out, even if we already know how the story ends. Too bad it's not just a story.

Introduction:
Your Guide to the Third Edition
of *Aftershock*

T his third edition of *Aftershock* contains a number of important updates and clarifications to the previous book. We have been fortunate to have received lots of excellent feedback and suggestions from our readers, much of which we have incorporated into this new book. Some important changes include the addition of Chapter 1, "This Recovery Is 100 Percent Fake." This chapter will update you on our latest thinking on the Aftershock and how the current recovery in the stock market and economy will affect the Aftershock.

In addition, we have added Chapter 4, "The Market Cliff," which explains in detail how we expect to see the stock and bond markets behave as we head toward the Aftershock.

We have also updated and added new material to Chapter 5 on inflation. In this chapter, we have added actual research from the Federal Reserve itself that shows the high correlation between increases in the money supply and long-term inflation (a correlation of over 90 percent). We have also addressed in more detail the obvious question of why inflation has not yet occurred, despite the massive money printing by the Federal Reserve. We discuss how this will affect the Aftershock and, in Chapter 4, we address the role we see inflation playing in the downfall of the stock and bond markets.

Finally, we want to take this opportunity to thank our readers for the incredible support they have shown us. We couldn't have asked for a better response. Many people have told us how much they enjoyed the book, sometimes reading it multiple times, and even giving extra copies to their friends and relatives. Wow—thank you, thank you, thank you!!! It is deeply satisfying to know we are being read, understood, and even appreciated. It's just fantastic!

It's also great that so many of you are helping us get the word out to help as many people as possible. That is so important to us. Hence, we give away free books, and we also make free presentations to worthy organizations. We want to get the word out as quickly as we can, and as widely as possible. We hope that this updated edition of *Aftershock* will be an important step in our mission to help people better understand what is going on with the economy, so that they can act now to protect themselves and to prosper in these most unusual times. We hope you find this third edition of *Aftershock* helpful in the months and years ahead.

PART

I

THE COMING AFTERSHOCK

CHAPTER 1

This Recovery Is 100 Percent Fake

WHY THE AFTERSHOCK HAS NOT BEEN CANCELED

We open this third edition of *Aftershock* in 2014 with the same first chapter we offered you in our last book, *The Aftershock Investor*, Second Edition, published in November 2013. Not everyone sees every book we write, and this particular chapter is just too important to miss. The economic cheerleaders and bubble-blind "experts" from whom most people get their financial news are simply not going to warn you about what is ahead or tell you what you need to know to protect yourself. If you've already read this chapter, please skip to Chapter 2. Otherwise, begin here.

With the U.S. stock markets hitting new highs, home prices rising, and so much "happy talk" in the media, it's easy to think that all is well or will be soon. The economy, they tell us, is in recovery, and the coming Aftershock, our critics say, has been canceled.

How wonderful that would be—if only it were true. But nothing has happened to change our minds about our earlier forecasts. In fact, current events fall in line pretty well with our previous analysis and predictions, dating back to our earliest books, *America's Bubble Economy* in 2006 and the first edition of *Aftershock* in 2009. From the beginning, we said that massive federal government support would keep the bubble economy going as long as possible. Through massive money printing and massive money borrowing, the stock, real estate, private debt, and consumer spending bubbles have been kept from fully popping. That is the only way to keep this temporary bubble party going, and the government is doing all it can to keep pumping helium into the balloons. However, this effort to support the bubble economy has been pumping up two additional bubbles: the dollar and the government debt bubbles. With the total national debt now more than $17 trillion and the Federal Reserve flooding the economy with $75 billion in newly printed money *every month* (at the time of this writing in early 2014), our predictions are looking pretty spot-on.

We never said the stock market wouldn't rise—in fact, it may go even higher. We never said the economy couldn't temporarily stabilize or that home prices couldn't rise in some areas in the short term. We said this is a bubble economy and that the government will do anything it can to keep the bubbles going—and that is exactly what they are doing. But please don't confuse a temporary, artificially created recovery with the real thing. Any recovery that is created by massive government stimulus and can be maintained only with continued massive government stimulus is a *fake* recovery.

Why? Because the fundamental economic realities have not changed, and even massive government stimulus cannot permanently override the fundamentals. The fact is that since the early 1980s we have been living in a *bubble economy* (see Chapter 2 for why we say so), and bubbles don't last forever. We saw the beginning of the pop with the partial decline of the real estate bubble in 2007, which helped kick off the global financial crisis of late 2008. Since then, we've seen a mammoth effort to partially reinflate and maintain the sagging bubbles with an enormous amount of money printing and money borrowing.

But this huge stimulus has been only marginally successful. It's true that stocks have been pushed up passed previous highs by massive money printing and real estate is rising, but the deeper measures of economic recovery—GDP growth and employment—are not significantly improving. Without strong GDP and employment growth, there is no real recovery. This highly expensive, bubble-maintaining stimulus may work for a while—maybe even years—but it won't work forever. In the long run, the massive stimulus will be forced to end, and it will have made our problems even worse in the future.

So contrary to popular belief, this "recovery" is 100 percent fake and the Aftershock has *not* been canceled.

Isn't a Fake Recovery Better than No Recovery at All?

That seems true, but it really isn't. The massive money printing and borrowing that is creating this fake recovery and delaying the Aftershock will only make the coming crash all the worse later. That's why we say it's nothing to cheer about. A fake recovery may feel good now—like postponing a trip to the dentist with a strong painkiller—but it will only bring us much more pain later.

"Now we just have to sit back and wait for the Fed to bail us out."

Not only will the temporary painkiller eventually wear off, but the medicine itself will later become a poison as the massive money printing eventually causes *dangerous future inflation.* Why is that so dangerous? Because rising inflation will cause rising interest rates, and rising interest rates will cause markets to crash even harder than they would have had we not printed so much money.

And, of course, just like postponing a trip to the dentist, putting off dealing with our underlying problems only increases our future pain because it postpones the fundamental changes we desperately need to make in order to create a real economic recovery. What we need is not more government borrowing and more dollars created out of thin air to keep the party going. What we need is a true economic recovery based on fundamental changes that will boost real productivity (the subject of future books). Real productivity growth would generate real economic growth and real, nonbubble wealth that would not be vulnerable to bubble pops.

The problem is that those changes are difficult. No one wants to hear that we have to make tough choices and endure a lot of pain now to create real economic growth later. It's much easier to let the government borrow and print for now, and kick all the rest of it down the road to deal with later. Politicians might talk about fiscal and monetary responsibility, but the short-term consequences of stopping the current bubble-supporting machine would put their jobs in jeopardy. This is why we have been predicting since 2006 that our bubble economy will continue to be maintained until that maintenance is no longer possible. We will throw everything at it until it no longer works and eventually explodes. While marginally effective in the short term, eventually this strategy will fail. Until then, no one wants to pop the temporary bubble party.

Inflation or Deflation?

Nobel Prize–winning economist Milton Friedman in the 1970s famously said: "Inflation is always and everywhere a monetary phenomenon."

In fact, inflation and deflation are both "monetary phenomena," meaning they both result from changes in the money supply. Inflation results from *increasing* the money supply faster than the economy grows, devaluing the dollar and causing goods and services to cost more. Deflation results from *decreasing* the money supply relative to the economy, pushing up the value of the dollar and causing goods and services to cost less.

The Great Depression gave us deflation, not inflation. Too few dollars relative to the economic needs of the time caused the value of the dollar to rise, and the cost of goods and services to fall.

By sharp contrast, we are printing enormous amounts of new money, increasing the monetary base much faster than the economy is growing, which will bring us future inflation, not deflation.

Those who point to falling prices or the threat of future falling prices, and call it deflation, are making a fundamental mistake. Separate from inflation or deflation, prices also rise and fall because of changes in supply and demand. For example, when an asset bubble pops (such as real estate), falling home prices are not due to deflation; home prices fall because there are more sellers than buyers.

Just before and during the Aftershock, multiple popping bubbles will cause many asset prices (in inflation-adjusted dollars) to fall. That is not deflation; that is a price drop due to a bubble pop!

If the Aftershock Has Not Been Canceled, Why Hasn't It Happened Yet?

While we stand by our past and current predictions for the coming Aftershock, we admit that predicting exactly when the bubbles will fully burst is difficult. What we can do is look at the fundamentals of this economy, and they don't look all that impressive. Given the huge amount of government stimulus (massive money printing and borrowing) for five years, the fact that the economy is only growing slowly is very telling. What it tells us is that this is a falling multibubble economy whose inevitable fall is being temporarily delayed by enormous bubble-supporting efforts that cannot continue forever. If five years of massive, unprecedented money printing and borrowing has only given us the economy we have today, what kind of economy and stock market would we have without that massive stimulus? And, of course, none of the underlying problems that got us into this mess in the first place (see Chapter 2) have gone away.

So while we cannot easily predict the timing of the coming Aftershock, we have no doubt that it will happen. The big multibubble pop and Aftershock cannot be permanently avoided, only delayed.

To understand why the Aftershock hasn't happened yet, let's take a closer look at what is keeping this fake recovery going and how long we think it might last.

The Key to Creating and Maintaining the Fake Recovery: Massive Money Printing

Massive money printing is quickly becoming the key support of our multibubble economy. We are not talking about creating a modest amount of extra money to keep up with a growing economy, like we used to do. We are talking about a truly staggering amount of new money printing, more than we've ever done in U.S. history. If you think we are exaggerating, consider this: since the creation of the U.S. Federal Reserve almost a century ago, we have printed roughly $800 billion from 1913 to 2007. But in 2013, the Fed printed more new money than that *in just one year* (see Figure 1.1) and will likely do the same in 2014. That's more money printing in one year than in nearly 100 years!

Since the financial crisis of 2008, the Fed has increased the monetary base from about $800 billion to more than $4 trillion.

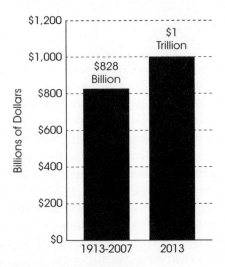

Figure 1.1   Massive New Money Printing
We printed more new money in 2013 than we created in total since the Federal Reserve was formed almost 100 years ago up to 2007.
Source: Federal Reserve.

This is a truly *enormous* increase. By making money so abundant and therefore cheap to borrow, money printing allows the government to run high deficits. And money printing helps boost the stock market and real estate markets as well.

A government can boost the economy by running a large deficit. But, eventually, it will have to pay higher interest on its bonds as investors become more and more skeptical of the government's ability to pay its increasingly large debt obligations. The solution to having to pay higher interest costs: money printing. The central bank uses printed money to buy government bonds in large quantities, thus creating an artificial demand for those bonds and keeping interest rates low.

The artificial demand for government bonds and mortgage bonds carries over to the rest of the bond market as well, where interest rates are often defined by the markup over the rate on Treasury bonds. The low interest rates in the bond market carry over into the mortgage market as well, keeping up demand for easy home loans and propping up the real estate market.

Low yields on bonds leave many investors chasing bigger gains. And what better place to increase their return on investment than the stock market? There's plenty of capital to put into stocks, too. After all, when the Fed prints money to buy bonds, it has to buy those bonds from somebody, and then they have to do something with it. Much of that newly printed money goes right from investors' bank accounts into the stock market, raising demand for stocks and boosting the overall stock market. The rising stock market further encourages the real estate market and general consumer spending, creating the fake recovery we have today.

So if money printing enables the government to run large deficits with little consequence and it boosts the stock, bond, and real estate markets as well, what's the downside? The answer is *future inflation*. Printing many more dollars while economic growth is very slow means they will eventually become less valuable (please see Chapter 5 for more on how this happens). Rising inflation ultimately pushes up interest rates. Higher interest rates in a bubble economy will mean collapsing markets and exploding government debt. Rising inflation is something a bubble economy cannot afford.

When the Fed's first two rounds of quantitative easing (QE1 and QE2) failed to create the economic recovery they wanted, they moved to yet a third round of quantitative easing (QE3). But this time, perhaps losing confidence in the economy's fundamentals, the Fed put no time limits on its money-printing operations, saying only it would commit to $40 billion a month in bond purchases until unemployment figures had reached a satisfactory level. It didn't take long before that $40 billion commitment became a staggering $85 billion per month in November 2012 and continues at a staggering $75 billion per month, as of this writing in January 2014.

That's a lot of artificial government stimulus to keep markets up. So far, it's working. Stocks are up, real estate is rising, and the rest of the bubble economy is holding on (although hardly booming) due to massive money printing. But does anyone really think that endlessly creating new dollars is a path to future prosperity? It's almost silly to believe in such a fantasy, and yet the psychological drive to accept this as a safe and effective cure for our problems generally overrides logic. Investors love the easy-money fantasy that money printing supports, and they want it to go on forever.

We are not saying that if we stopped the stimulus today, all would be fine. Just the opposite, ending the stimulus entirely would quickly throw the economy into severe recession. But our economic problems are not due to a lack of stimulus; therefore, the stimulus, no matter how massive, will not save us; it will only delay the inevitable economic pain and will make it all the worse when the Aftershock happens later. This is a falling bubble economy (see Chapter 2 for details) and the money-printing and money-borrowing stimulus is simply delaying its further fall. But the more stimulus we throw at it now, the harder the crash will be later because inflation and interest rates will be that much higher.

In a Supporting Role: Cheerleading

Cheerleaders root for the home team. They won't tell you the quarterback has a weak arm, or that the offensive line is outmatched, or that the head coach is inexperienced. Their job is to be positive and cheer for the home team!

In recent decades we've seen the financial world take on a "home crowd" type of atmosphere, with financial pundits and economists assuming roles as cheerleaders rather than analysts. They won't tell you about the fundamental problems in the economy. They'll only assure you that everything is bound to get better, that recovery is right around the corner, or that it's already here. The cheerleading mind-set is a big reason we ended up with a bubble economy in the first place. Brokerage firms needed to sell stocks in order to make money. Fundamentals didn't matter, as long as everyone played along. They cultivated a deep belief that stock prices were always going to go up, up, up. Remember how optimistic all the experts were before the 2008 financial crisis?

The cheerleading mind-set persists, as the analysts hype every little positive and ignore or downplay every important negative. They say we can't possibly have future inflation. It doesn't matter how much money the Fed prints. The unemployment rate is falling. It doesn't matter how many people leave the workforce. New home sales are on the rise. It doesn't matter how low they are compared to a few years ago.

Oh, but if gold prices drop, that's a "rational correction" on a fundamentally bad investment, even though gold has generally been on the rise for more than a decade and is in high demand worldwide.

The cheerleaders always root for the home team based on selective data, no matter what other data is available for consideration. Anything that supports their cause is automatically true and highly significant, while the rest of the facts are considered insignificant or entirely ignored.

Ammo for the Cheerleaders: Inflation Appears Low

Our critics like to point to the current absence of rising inflation to show that we are wrong about money printing causing rising future inflation and interest rates, which are key to our predictions for the coming Aftershock. They say if we need inflation to push interest rates up and kick off the Aftershock and we have no inflation, then clearly the Aftershock has been canceled.

We disagree. To a large extent, the reason we haven't seen significant inflation yet in spite of massive money printing is that, as we'll explain in more detail in Chapter 5, there are "lag factors" that create a delay between when money is printed and when inflation sets in.

But also keep in mind that we have seen *some* inflation. While inflation may not be 10 or 20 percent yet, the government's sub–3 percent figures are difficult to believe. Anyone who buys food or puts gas in their car knows that prices of many things have gone up in the past few years. So why doesn't the government's measure of inflation seem to more fully reflect this?

One important reason has to do with the way the government measures inflation, which they have purposely changed in the past couple of decades in order to downplay the inflation rate. While manipulation of economic statistics is expected and accepted as an everyday occurrence in some other countries, the United States is not known for regularly manipulating our statistics. However, that doesn't mean it doesn't happen, albeit in subtle ways.

One of the easiest and most convenient statistics to manipulate is the inflation rate, and the United States is almost certainly massaging its chief measure of inflation, the Consumer Price Index (CPI). This figure can easily be manipulated by making changes to the basket of goods and services measured over time and making subjective judgments about product substitution. For example, a $2,000 computer in 2014 has about 10 times the power of a $2,000 computer in 1990. We can say there has been no change in cost, but these are hardly the same computers.

We are not at all surprised that the government is taking steps to hide the real inflation rate. The stakes are very high, and the people generating inflation statistics are likely under a certain amount of subtle pressure to produce statistics that are more supportive of current economic policy. Aside from the danger that inflation leads to higher interest rates that can hurt the markets, inflation also puts a big strain on the government budget. The government has to make higher and higher payments for any inflation-indexed programs, including pensions and Social Security, and higher interest rates mean the government has to offer higher rates to finance its debt.

Inflation also eats away at gross domestic product (GDP) growth figures. If inflation reaches 4 or 5—let alone 10 or 20—percent, any growth in GDP has to be adjusted accordingly. With our economy right now *officially* growing by only about 2 percent annually (and likely the real number is less than that), it's very much in the government's interest to report low CPI inflation figures. That has no doubt played a role in the shifting standards for measuring inflation over the past couple of decades.

The unreliability of government statistics makes it difficult for us to say exactly what the inflation rate really is right now. But we don't see any reason to believe that the government's "new and improved" measure of inflation is more accurate than the measure they used 30 years ago. In fact, it is probably less accurate. It seems that the changes in the way they calculate the CPI were made out of self-interest, not a concern for accuracy.

More Ammo for the Cheerleaders: Relatively Low Unemployment Rate

When you combine the inflation rate with the unemployment rate, you get the *misery index*. Generally speaking, the higher this number is, the more economic and social woes we face. So unemployment is another figure the government has a keen interest in understating. And while employment statistics are not as easy to manipulate as the CPI, that doesn't mean we should take them all at face value.

More jobs were lost from 2007 to 2009 (almost 9 million) than were gained in the housing boom. So employment statistics are important numbers for the media and the cheerleaders.

To be counted in the official "unemployment rate" a person has to be out of work entirely and actively seeking a job. This means those who have given up searching and whose unemployment benefits have lapsed—referred to as the *discouraged unemployed*—are not counted in the popular unemployment rate that gets reported so much in the news.

Also not counted in the typically reported unemployment rate are those working part time when they would rather work full time, or who are working well below their education and skill levels. In July 2013, Gallup reported that more than 17 percent of the workforce characterizes itself as "underemployed." Many previous full-time workers have been forced to take part-time work while they continue to look for better employment. When the media and cheerleaders tell us to feel good about the creation of new jobs, they don't often mention that most of those new jobs are only part time.

While the typical unemployment rate reported in the media has recently held steady around 7 or 8 percent, it doesn't tell the whole story. For that, we need to look at what is called the U6 unemployment rate, which conveniently the government and the media avoid discussing too much. The U6 rate, which includes discouraged unemployed and those working part time when they'd rather work full time, is officially 13.2 percent, as of November 2013. When you also add in those who left the workforce, the number is even higher (see Figure 1.2).

Nonetheless, it has become an increasingly common phenomenon to see the official unemployment rate figure remain flat or even go down slightly while the number of people dropping out of the workforce goes up. In fact, according to the Bureau of Labor Statistics, the number of *working-age* Americans who have now dropped out of the workforce is about 3 to 4 million. The majority of these folks are under 50 years old, so they aren't retiring. They are just giving up. There are typically some working-age Americans out of the workforce—such as full-time parents—but this is an exceptionally high number. Recently, the employment-to-population ratio (in which "population" counts anyone 16 years of age and older) is down to 58.5 percent, when it had hovered around 63 percent for much of the previous decade.

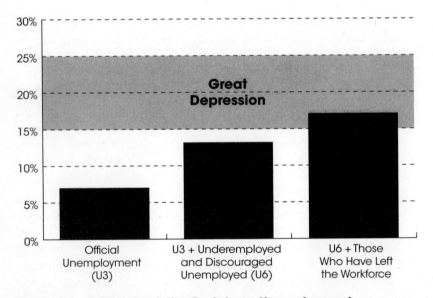

Figure 1.2   Pulling Back the Curtain on Unemployment
The official unemployment figure (U3) is about 7 percent. However, adding in the underemployed and discouraged unemployed (U6) puts the true unemployment rate near Depression-era levels, which peaked briefly at 25 percent.
Source: Bureau of Labor Statistics.

And if you think job growth is bad, *wage growth* is in even worse shape. In fact, according to Commerce Department data, real wage growth (adjusted for inflation) is worse now than it was during the Great Depression. In fact, the growth of household incomes has been essentially flat in the past few years (see Figure 1.3).

Between the underreported unemployment figures and the lack of income growth, much of the pain in the economy is quiet pain—meaning that it doesn't get much media coverage and few people are discussing it. But its impacts are widespread. Perhaps some of our readers know people who have lost their jobs and are looking for work, or who have dropped out of the workforce entirely, with little or no hope of finding a job. Or you might know some who have seen their wages or income fall or their business suffer. In spite of these realities we all see right in front of us, the government will still claim we are in a "recovery," trying to distract us with numbers that don't tell the true story. If this really were a recovery, we'd be seeing more jobs and higher incomes by now.

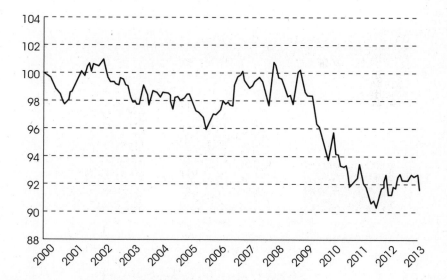

Figure 1.3   Household Incomes Are Languishing
Median household incomes, adjusted for inflation, have declined and not recovered much since the financial crisis of 2008.
Source: Sentier Research and the *Wall Street Journal.*

Money Printing = No Inflation = No Taxes! We Are Fooling Ourselves—and We Know It

One of the craziest ideas that the cheerleaders promote can be summarized as "Don't worry, massive money printing is always perfectly safe!"

Really? If it's really so safe, why are we doing it only on an "as-needed" basis? Why not do it all the time, not just in a crisis? If it's really so safe, why ever stop?

And if it is really so safe, why not do a whole lot more of it? After all, if massive money printing doesn't cause future inflation, why are they so afraid of doing more? Surely, if $75 billion of new money per month is good, then $100 billion per month would be even better, right?

What the heck, if there's no downside to massive money printing, why not go for *$200 billion* per month? Think of how much that would boost the markets and the economy. It would be great! Why aren't we doing that right now? In fact, why do we need to pay any taxes at all? Let's just print all the money we will ever need, whenever we need it!

But you'll notice we don't actually do that, do we? How come? Because everyone knows that it can't work. If we didn't know, we'd be doing it, so obviously, we know. People know that massive money printing comes with a nasty future price tag (inflation). If it didn't, why should we limit it and why should we ever stop? Like smoking crack, we know darn well that this is a dangerous drug; we just can't kick our addiction to its short-term high.

How much crack can we smoke before we scare ourselves by the sheer quantity? Well, if we start out slowly and get ourselves used to it, our love of the short-term high can convince us that we are always printing the "just right" amount of new money. When we first started with limited quantitative easing (QE1) in early 2009, the idea of printing $75 billion/month without an end date would have seemed irresponsible. But by raising the amount of money printing gradually over time to create and maintain the fake recovery, each new round of QE was welcomed as perfectly safe and perfectly sized. Now $75 billion/month seems "just right."

If we lower the amount of money printing for a while, it will only be to make the insane appear more sane.

Still Not Sure This Recovery Is 100 Percent Fake?

We've explained why this recovery is entirely fake and the coming Aftershock has not been canceled, but maybe you're still not convinced. Maybe you think the economy really is turning around, that employment will pick up or that China will carry the rest of the world out of this malaise. If we haven't made the case yet that the fundamentals of the economy are not improving, and in fact are only getting worse, here are a few more facts to wake you up.

If This Recovery Is Real, Why Is Government Borrowing Outpacing GDP Growth?

While many people seem to cheer every little positive sign of growth in the economy (and ignore or downplay any negative news), what's really astonishing is just how little economic growth we've seen in spite of all the massive government intervention. Between 2008 and 2013, the government borrowed $4.7 trillion, yet over that same period the cumulative increase in GDP in the United States was only $2.8 trillion (see Figure 1.4). That's a whole lot of borrowing for not much growth.

Such huge government borrowing relative to GDP shows just how fragile the U.S. economy really is. It also shows how ineffective government intervention has been at turning a falling bubble economy into a healthy, growing economy. Pro-intervention pundits and academics like to think of government intervention as a parent holding up a young child's bicycle, ready to pull the hand away as soon as the child can stay upright. In truth, the government is more like pushover parents who keep giving their children barrels of money well into their adult years, seeing less and less return on their investment as the kids become increasingly dependent. If the parents cut them off, they would be out on the streets immediately.

It's the same for this economy. If you took away the huge money borrowing, we'd be thrown into an instant recession. At this point, the massive money printing and massive money borrowing are keeping the economy on temporary life support. In order to get real and sustainable economic growth, we need something more than massive temporary stimulus; we need significant increases in real productivity growth, which we have not had for decades. Understanding the real cause of our economic problems is the first step in solving those problems (see Chapter 11).

After Five Years of Emergency CPR, the Patient Is Not Recovering

If the global financial crisis of 2008 was like a heart attack for the U.S. economy, then the massive stimulus (massive money printing and borrowing) needed to jump start this patient has kept the patient alive, but it certainly hasn't restored full health. Even after five years of massive stimulus, we are still getting nowhere.

If GDP is growing by 2 percent (the equivalent of $300 billion), even assuming that deficit spending is reduced to $700 billion this year, we are in fact buying very little GDP growth with a huge amount of debt. We are borrowing much more than the amount of GDP growth we get for the borrowing (see Figure 1.4 and Figure 1.5).

That means with all this stimulus, we are stimulating nothing. It is all just fake bubble maintenance and no real growth. The only recovery has been in asset prices, not the economy. Only the assets (especially stocks) are up, while the economy is not.

Five years of CPR may keep some vital signs going, but the patient is not recovering. And with so much money printing and borrowing weighing heavily on our future, this patient will be sicker than before.

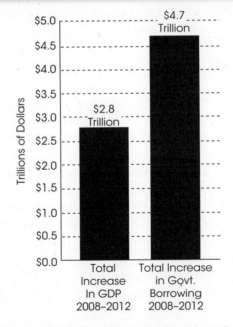

Figure 1.4   Increase in GDP Growth versus Increase in Government Borrowing
We are borrowing far more than the economy is growing.
Source: Bureau of Economic Analysis.

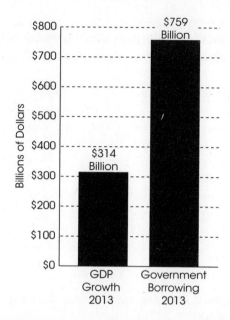

Figure 1.5   GDP Growth versus Current Government Borrowing
We are borrowing at a rate that is more than double our current growth rate. Apparently, we are not getting much of a bang for our borrowed buck.
Source: White House (projected debt 2013), Bureau of Economic Analysis (GDP, calculated assuming 2 percent annual growth).

If This Recovery Is Real, Why Are Stock Prices Growing Much Faster than Company Earnings?

Lately, we have relied on the stock market for optimism. And while anyone can appreciate some healthy optimism, the kind of blind optimism we're seeing in the stock market right now helps no one.

A big reason for the stock market's record highs in 2013 was investors' outlandish expectations for future earnings. According to FactSet, industry analysts in spring 2013 expected record earnings for the Standard & Poor's (S&P) 500 in the third and fourth quarters of 2013. In fact, projections for the fourth quarter of 2013 were more than 15 percent above the fourth quarter of 2012. That would be an impressive rise for any period and a great reason for people to want to own stock in these companies. However, earnings barely rose 2 percent in the third quarter of 2013. Did the market care that earnings were so far below expectations? Of course not! This is a fantasy market, not a real market driven by real earnings.

In addition, revenue growth is poor. S&P revenues grew only 1 to 2 percent for most of 2013. This is no surprise given that U.S. GDP growth was only 2 percent in 2013 and most major world markets aren't growing much faster. But despite this, the market is still rising.

This kind of freakish optimism isn't just calling the glass half full. This is like saying the glass is overflowing when there's barely a drop of water! Company earnings are not growing at nearly the rate that stock prices are growing; therefore, you are paying more for the same earnings you could buy for less before. That's nothing to cheer about.

If This Recovery Is Real, Why Are Stock Prices Growing Much Faster than GDP?

It won't take you more than a quick look at Figure 1.6 to see that stock prices are far outpacing lackluster economic growth. What does that tell you about the short-term power of positive investor psychology fueled by massive money printing?

Can this kind of divergence between stock prices and GDP growth continue for a while longer? Yes, it probably can. Can it continue indefinitely? Even our biggest critics would have a hard time justifying that fantasy. Without greater GDP growth, job growth, and company earnings growth eventually kicking in, positive investor psychology and massive money printing cannot sustain this kind of stock growth forever. Eventually, some investors will look around and notice the glaring lack of overall economic growth, despite the Happy Talk and the massive stimulus that is temporarily supporting stocks today.

If This Recovery Is Real, Why Is the Global Economy Slowing?

One reason for slow earnings growth in the United States is the slowing global economy. For multinational corporations, like those that make up the S&P 500 and the Dow, a significant portion of their revenues comes from overseas operations. And the news from overseas has been pretty bleak.

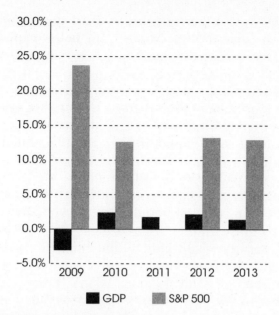

Figure 1.6   Assets Up, Economy Flat
Only asset prices are up, not the overall economy. By definition, that makes it a bubble.
Source: Standard & Poors and the U.S. Department of Commerce.

In Europe, the north is in recession, while the south is in depression. Unemployment numbers in Spain, Italy, and Greece are staggering. In the north, even Germany is suffering from a slowdown, with big companies like Daimler abandoning their profit forecasts due to falling demand. France and the United Kingdom, Europe's second- and third-largest economies, are flirting with recession. In fact, the entire Euro Zone grew only 0.1 percent in the third quarter of 2013.

China, the engine many thought would pull the rest of the world out of this mess, is experiencing a slowdown in growth even by its own admission. The truth is likely even worse than the Chinese government lets on, as the enormous construction bubble that was built up in response to the 2008 financial crisis is becoming increasingly unsustainable. A *60 Minutes* report in March 2013 showed entire cities being built—high-rise luxury condominiums, expansive malls—with *no one living in them*. So much for the world's growth engine.

China's slowdown is taking a toll on the rest of the world, too. Brazil's impressive growth has slowed to a crawl (and possibly contraction if inflation is properly accounted for). Turkey, another country that seemed to be flying above the global earthquake, saw just 2 percent growth in 2012—down from about 9 percent in 2010 and 2011. Japan's economic growth has been so poor that the government began a money-printing campaign in 2013 that would make even Ben Bernanke blush—printing $75 billion a month in an economy that is only about a third of the size of the United States.

And while there's been a lot of talk about "emerging markets," it's becoming increasingly apparent that those markets were fueled largely by China's rise, and thus are suffering now that China is struggling to keep pace with its earlier gains.

This is important because the global slowdown has a direct impact on the U.S. economy and U.S. stocks, particularly those that collectively make up the S&P 500. That's because in this global economy, no country is an island. Some countries may fare better than others, but trends around the world operate as a large feedback loop. When the United States falters, Europe slows down. When demand in Europe drops, exports in China drop. When China slows down, Europe sinks further, and other economies can't keep up their previous pace. In the global economy, every economy really does depend on other economies, and the United States is not exempted from that.

How Do You Define a Bubble? Assets Up, Economy Flat

The only thing we are getting from all this massive government stimulus is more support for the bubbles, not real economic growth. This can clearly be seen in Figure 1.6. Only asset prices have been significantly rising, not GDP.

How Do You Define Insanity?

The classic definition of *insanity* is doing the same thing and expecting different results. That's exactly what we've been doing: applying the same stimulus (massive printing and massive borrowing) and expecting different results. More money printing, more money borrowing, more cheerleading, and more statistical smoke and mirrors are not going to give us the needed productivity improvements that can lead to significant GDP growth, more quality jobs, rising wages, or anything else that comes with real economic recovery and growth.

The only thing we are buying with this all this ongoing stimulus is temporary asset bubble maintenance—that's all.

Don't Believe the Stimulus Has to Eventually End? There Is a Limit to What the Government Can Do

While the federal government does have much more power to affect markets and the overall economy than any private investor or company, even the federal government has its limits.

The limit to continuing the stimulus of massive money borrowing is the government's ability to find investors willing to continue to buy our debt. In a way, we've already hit that limit. The fact that the Fed started printing massive amounts of money in 2009 to buy our debt was a clear indicator that the government's borrowing ability at low interest rates had essentially come to an end. We had to print the money to enable the government to keep borrowing at low interest rates. As we said before, the Federal Reserve had to begin massive money printing in 2009 in order to keep us from falling into a much deeper recession. When each round of money printing wasn't enough to create a full recovery, they had to increase the printing even more. If there were enough of a real economic recovery occurring, the money printing would have ended.

Not only has it not ended, it has exploded. At this point, the Fed is now printing almost $1 trillion a year—money it uses to buy government bonds, creating artificial demand and keeping interest rates low. That's much more money than the $744 billion that the government is projected to borrow in 2014. That means the government's ability to continue borrowing is being entirely supported by the Fed's money printing. Would anyone be able to buy Treasuries at very low interest rates today if they weren't backed by the Fed's massive money-printing machine?

So, what is the limit to the Fed's massive money printing? Theoretically, there isn't any. But history and the laws of economics tell us that the stimulating effect of money printing becomes increasingly ineffective over time. That's because, in time, people do begin to notice that the massive stimulus is not buying all that much growth.

In the early stages, investors may be slow to notice this because powerful group psychology of denial is so strong. But in time, a small but growing group of increasingly skeptical investors will want to be a bit more cautious, exiting some of their stocks and bonds.

That, too, will go mostly unnoticed at first, but as more investors become more cautious, others will begin to notice and become somewhat anxious, too. Once investor psychology turns negative enough, a critical threshold of anxiety will be reached and a series of mass exits out of bonds and stocks will occur—pushing us over what we call the Market Cliff (see Chapter 4).

With stocks and bonds falling and investor and consumer psychology falling, too, the ugly price tag of all that earlier money printing will begin to show up, namely, rising inflation (see Chapter 5). Rising inflation will naturally eventually lead to rising interest rates, crippling the economy and ultimately canceling out the earlier positive effects that the stimulus originally provided.

The fact that there are lag factors between money printing and inflation is the only reason money printing can be so effective in the short term. After that, the long term negative consequences of money printing (rising inflation and high interest rates) will kick in. That would be bad news for any economy, even a strong economy in a real recovery and with real growth. However, for a sagging multi-bubble economy in a fake recovery with almost no growth, the consequences will be very bad, indeed.

It's only a matter of time.

Wondering Why the Aftershock Hasn't Happened Already? "Animal Spirits" Are Keeping Us Going

For some of our biggest fans, the question isn't "Has the Aftershock been canceled?" but "What the heck is taking it so long?!" You might think, given the staggering amounts of money printing and borrowing, lack of jobs, overvalued assets, and low GDP growth, that the bubbles would have popped by now. Why hasn't the Aftershock happened yet?

The reason that the Aftershock has not happened yet is that our economy is not simply a bunch of statistics, facts, and mathematical equations. Our economy is also the direct result of collective group behavior, and group behavior is highly driven by collective group psychology.

Without ongoing positive investor psychology, no amount of money printing, cheerleading, or massaged statistics would be very effective at maintaining the fake recovery. Just as for a rising bubble, for a fake recovery to continue, you need people to continue to believe in it.

Sometimes the term *animal spirits* is used to refer to the emotional component of the economy, represented by consumer and investor confidence. Without positive animal spirits, the rest of the fake recovery maintenance activities simply would not work. But as long as the animal spirits stay positive, the activities to maintain the fake recovery will work for a while longer. People have to believe this recovery is real or all efforts to keep it going will fail. Once enough people stop having faith in the economy—once they stop believing in the strength of the dollar, the soundness of the markets, the good faith of the government, and the financial system—the game is over and the bubbles will pop.

At that point, any additional money printing would translate immediately into inflation, with no beneficial effect. Cheerleading will fall on deaf ears. Currency and market manipulations will fail to make people invest. And no amount of dumping gold on the market to lower its price will turn investors away from its perceived safety.

So when you ask, "When will the Aftershock hit?," you are really asking: "When will positive psychology turn negative enough to pop the bubbles?" In the end, the timing of the turning point comes down to how people *feel*, not to economic statistics or sophisticated financial analysis.

While the final trigger won't be about numbers directly, in the buildup to the change in investor psychology, some numbers will matter because they will begin to weigh heavily on investor optimism. One of these important, psychology-changing numbers will be the continued low growth in GDP and good jobs after more than five years of tremendous stimulus since the 2008 financial crisis.

The lack of growth will turn investor psychology more negative, eventually pushing stocks and bonds over the Market Cliff (see Chapter 4). Once those bubbles have popped, *inflation* will begin to rise (see Chapter 5) due to all that money printing we've been doing since 2008.

And our troubles won't stop at rising inflation. When inflation moves up, *interest rates* will naturally move up as well. For example, if inflation goes to 5 percent, interest rates would have to rise to 6 percent just to bring lenders a 1 percent return after inflation. Higher interest rates certainly would be a big downer for stocks, bonds, real estate, and the overall economy.

How high will inflation go? We will cover that in much more detail in Chapter 5, but for now please know this. According the Federal Reserve's own research, it is reasonable to expect about the same amount of inflation as the money supply is increased. In other words, if we increase the money supply by 10 percent, we can expect roughly about 10 percent future inflation. If we increase it by 15 percent, we eventually will get about 15 percent inflation, and so on.

So far, since we started this massive money printing in early 2009, we've increased the U.S. monetary base by more than 400 percent. That means, based on the Fed's own extensive research, we can expect about 400 percent inflation. But even if the actual number is lower than that, certainly rising inflation and even higher interest rates won't be good for economic recovery and growth. Instead, all the bubbles will pop and the Aftershock will begin.

The sequence leading to the Aftershock will likely be:

1. Continued slow economic growth and continued lack of high-paying full-time jobs.
2. Gradual decline of positive investor psychology.
3. Increasing negative investor psychology.
4. The bond and stock markets fall in the Market Cliff (see Chapter 4 for details).
5. Rising inflation.
6. Rising interest rates.
7. The multibubble economy fully pops.
8. The Aftershock begins.

At that point, the bubble economy will be no more. Remember: bubbles go up because of irrational exuberance based on irrational thinking, but they come down because of rational fear based on rational thinking.

It is hard to time the triggering events with precision, but they have no choice but to eventually occur. In the end, the final trigger will be the damning facts themselves.

The Fierce Fight to Save the Bubbles

In the meantime, as long as investor psychology is still good, it is in the government's and the financial system's best interests to keep animal spirits up *at all costs*. There is even some evidence that there may already be some government intervention in the stock and gold markets (see Appendix). The motivations for this are strong because the stakes are so high. As long as the powers that be can convince people that the economy is recovering, that the markets will continue to fly high, that the dollar is strong, and that real job growth is just around the corner, they can continue to keep the asset bubbles going.

Of course, all of this works only because most people are all too willing to believe the good news. Just like the government, they also have plenty to lose by facing reality. Jobs, careers, businesses, and lifestyles are in jeopardy. No one wants to face that our beloved age of easy bubble money cannot go on and on.

Could additional money printing and borrowing maintain the asset bubbles and positive investor psychology for a while longer? Most definitely, yes. Will more money printing and borrowing be able to keep the party going for another decade or more? Absolutely not.

Over time, as the economy continues to have minimal or negative growth despite massive government stimulus, people will start to wake up. That will mean changes in what they buy, save, sell, and invest in. Increasing negativity (just like positivity) will become self-fulfilling for the economy. As more and more investors become anxious enough to exit their bubble-pumped investments, other investors will want out, too (see Chapter 4 for details about each stage of the coming Market Cliff). Once enough investors try to exit, the U.S. bubbles will pop, and the global Aftershock will begin, impacting economies around the world.

When Will It Happen?

Our best guess about when the bubbles will pop and the global Aftershock will begin:

2–5 years	Probably
5–10 years	Possibly, but much less likely

Even if the bubbles don't all pop in the next 2 to 5 years, they certainly won't last another 10.

Please Prepare Now

So let's review. Right now, massive money printing (and the low interest rates it creates) are boosting the stock market, protecting the bond market, supporting the overall economy, and allowing the government to borrow massively. We like to tell ourselves it's all risk free, but we know that's a lie. Massive money printing will eventually cause rising future inflation, which will push up interest rates, which will pop our multibubble economy (hurting stocks, bonds, and real estate).

No one enjoys thinking the current recovery is entirely fake—not even us. We are not "permabears" always predicting the economy will get worse. In the future, we look forward to writing about what can be done to bring about real productivity improvements and how to cash in on the real economic growth that will create. We just aren't there yet.

We're not writing this book to cheer the collapse of the economy, nor are we trying to rub it in that we were right in the past. We know it is uncomfortable to face these facts and it is uncomfortable to have to go against conventional wisdom in order to prepare correctly. Group denial will certainly delay the Aftershock for a while, but please don't count on that to last forever. People eventually do smell fire in a burning building, even when they initially didn't want to. As group denial turns into growing group awareness, conditions can change very quickly. At that point, the bubbles will pop and no amount of additional money printing or other stimulus will be able to stop it. In fact, additional money printing at that point will only fan the flames, not put out the fire.

Please prepare now, while you still can.

It may not be necessary to run and sell off all your investments today or tomorrow. But it is necessary that you pay attention to the fundamentals of the economy so that you can protect yourself and your investments before it's too late. In this updated third edition of *Aftershock*, that continues to be our goal.

Remember, we saw these problems coming prior to publishing our first book in 2006, back when many experts expected that home prices would rise forever. The fundamentals of our macroeconomic point of view were correct then and are still correct today. All we ask is that you listen to what we have to say and decide for yourself. The popping of America's bubble economy and the coming Aftershock will be like nothing we've seen before. The good news is that there's still time to prepare.

Along the way, if you're ever tempted to think that all is well, just remember these four damning facts:

1. *Massive money printing.* We've *quintrupled* the monetary base and are printing $75 billion per month more, keeping the stock, bond, and real estate bubbles afloat.

2. *Massive money borrowing.* We owe a staggering $17+ trillion in total debt, and are borrowing another $700 billion this year—four times more than what we borrowed in 2007.
3. *Paltry GDP growth.* We're growing at only 1 to 2 percent per year, which means we are borrowing almost three times more than the economy is growing.
4. *Pitiful job growth.* New jobs are barely keeping up with population growth and not even close to replacing the more than 7 million jobs lost from September 2008 to February 2010. Also, a very large number of the newly created jobs are only part time.

This recovery is 100 percent fake and the Aftershock has not been canceled. Please don't stay asleep with the sheep. If you want to protect yourself, you have to wake up before everyone else does. Chapters 2 through 7 will show you how we got ourselves into this mess, and Chapters 8 through 12 will help you prepare for and even profit from it.

CHAPTER 2

America's Bubble Economy

UNDERSTANDING HOW WE ACCURATELY PREDICTED THE FINANCIAL CRISIS OF 2008 IS KEY TO UNDERSTANDING WHY OUR LATEST PREDICTIONS ARE ALSO CORRECT

When our first book, *America's Bubble Economy*, came out in 2006 (the book proposal was actually submitted 18 months earlier), we were right and almost everyone else was wrong. We don't say this to brag. We say it because it's important for understanding why you should bother to pay attention to us now.

America's Bubble Economy (John Wiley & Sons, 2006) accurately predicted the popping of the real estate bubble, the collapse of the private debt bubble, the fall of the stock market bubble, the decline of consumer spending, and the widespread pain all this would inflict on the rest of our vulnerable, multibubble economy. We also predicted the eventual bursting of the dollar bubble and the government debt bubble, which are still to come. Of course, back in 2006, our predictions were largely ignored. Two years later, they started coming true: the housing, private debt, and stock bubbles fell dramatically, causing the global financial crisis in late 2008.

How did we see it coming? Certainly not by looking only at current conditions, which, at the time we wrote the first book, still looked pretty darn good. In fact, real estate prices in 2006 were close to their record highs. And with home values high and credit flowing, American consumers were still happily tapping into their home equity and credit cards to buy all manner of consumer products, from designer diapers to flat-screen TVs, importing goods from around the world, and boosting the economies of many nations. Businesses and banks appeared to be in good shape (very few banks were even close to failing), unemployment was relatively low, and Wall Street was still on an upward climb toward its record closing high (Dow 14,164) a year later on October 9, 2007.

With so much seemingly going so well back in 2006, how could we have been so sure that the housing bubble would pop, private credit would start drying up, the stock market would begin to fall, and the broader multibubble economy, here and around the globe, would begin a dramatic decline in 2008 and beyond?

Our accurate predictions were not a matter of blind luck, nor were they merely a case of perpetual bearish thinking finally having its gloomy day. In 2006, we were able to correctly call the fall of the U.S. housing bubble and its many consequences because we were able to see a *fundamental underlying pattern* that others were—and still are—missing.

In this pattern, we saw bubbles. Lots of them. We saw six big economic bubbles linked together and holding up one another, all supporting a seemingly prosperous U.S. economy. And we also saw that each conjoined bubble was leaning heavily on the others, each poised to potentially pull the others down if any one of these economic bubbles were to someday pop.

Why would they ever pop? We knew they would eventually pop because we saw that the evolving economic facts on the ground did not justify the volume or height of the bubbles; therefore, we knew they would have to burst sooner or later. In the next chapter, we will tell you more about these six big economic bubbles (the first four have already begun to burst and the other two will shortly) and how we knew they were bubbles. For now, the point is that economic bubbles, by nature, do not stay afloat forever. Sooner or later, economic reality, like gravity, eventually kicks in, and bubbles do fall. After they burst, they never are able to reinflate fully and lift off again. In time, new bubbles may grow, but old popped bubbles generally do not take off again. When the party is over, it's over.

Most people, even most "experts," find it much easier to recognize a bubble (like the Internet bubble of the 1990s) *after* it pops. It is a lot harder to see a bubble *before* it bursts, and much harder still to see an *entire multiple-bubble economy* before it bursts. A single, not-yet-popped bubble can look a lot like real asset growth, and a collection of several not-yet-popped bubbles can look a whole lot like real economic prosperity.

We wrote our first book, *America's Bubble Economy*, in 2006 because, based on our unique analysis of the evolving economy, the facts on the ground did not support the bubbles in the sky. By that we mean high-flying asset growth that is not firmly pinned to real underlying economic drivers is not sustainable. For example, real estate prices are typically driven higher by a growing population (increasing demand) and the growing incomes of home buyers (increasing ability to buy). When populations increase and incomes increase, home prices also increase. However, if you see home prices increasing, let's say, twice as fast as incomes, then that could mean something unsustainable is happening to the value of real estate. Why? Because home prices that high are not sustainable without a similar rise in the ability of buyers to keep paying those prices.

Asset bubbles are not always bad. On the way up, they can lift part or all of an economy and spur future economic growth. This certainly was the case with the housing bubble. On the way down, however, they can cause real problems. In fact, the bigger the bubble, the harder the fall.

America's Bubble Economy identified several economic bubbles that were once part of a seemingly *virtuous upward spiral* that first lifted and supported the U.S. economy over many decades, and are now part of a *vicious downward spiral* that will inevitably harm the U.S. and world economies as these sagging, co-linked bubbles weigh heavily on each other and ultimately burst.

We have been making this point as clear as we can in multiple books. After publishing *America's Bubble Economy* in 2006, we released *Aftershock* in 2009; *Aftershock*, Second Edition, in 2011; *The Aftershock Investor* in 2012; *The Aftershock Investor*, Second Edition, in 2013; and now, in 2014, we offer you this updated and revised third edition of *Aftershock*.

The six big bubbles we have been warning about include the real estate bubble, stock market bubble, private debt bubble, discretionary spending bubble, dollar bubble, and government debt bubble. Despite how well the economy appeared to be doing in 2006, we predicted it would be only two or three years before America's multiple bubbles would begin to decline and eventually even burst.

And that is just what happened.

By the third quarter of 2008, home prices and sales had fallen significantly, mortgage defaults and home foreclosures were skyrocketing, commercial and investment banks were going under, unemployment was rising, and the stock market bubble had fallen from its peak of 14,164 in October 2007 to under 7,000 on the Dow Jones Industrial Average (DJIA) not much more than a year later.

Unlike any other moment in our history, there is something *fundamentally different* going on this time. Even people who pay no attention to the stock market or the latest economic news say they can just feel it in their gut. Experts keep saying we are in a recovery, but something feels different this time.

The difference that many of us feel but few can define is this: We are not in a typical "down market cycle" this time, awaiting an inevitable "up cycle." The difference this time is that we are in an evolving *multibubble economy*. Falling bubbles cannot be reinflated by an "up cycle." With so many linked bubbles now vulnerable, the impact of their combined future fall will be far more dangerous than any downturn or recession we've experienced in the past. Unlike in a healthy economy, in this falling multibubble economy, the usual strategies for returning to our previous prosperity no longer apply. We have, in fact, entered new territory.

In Phase 1 of this multibubble pop, the real estate, credit, and stock market bubbles started to fall, bringing on the global financial crisis of 2008. We say "started to fall" because there is still much more falling to come, not only for the real estate bubble but for the rest of the co-linked multibubble economy, including the stock market bubble and others (see the next chapter for details).

Next, in Phase 2, comes the Aftershock. Just when most people think the worst is behind us, we are about to experience the cascading fall of several co-linked bursting bubbles that will rock our nation's economy to its core and send deep and destructive financial shock waves around the globe. The fall of the housing, credit, consumer spending, and stock bubbles significantly weakened the world economy. But the coming Aftershock will be far more dangerous. Despite massive efforts by the federal government and the Federal Reserve to hold up the falling bubbles with borrowing and massive money printing, the fall of a multibubble economy can be (and is being) delayed, but it cannot be reinflated. Rather than the U.S. economy's recovering fully, as many "experts" want you to believe, we see serious, groundbreaking new troubles ahead. In fact, the worst is yet to come.

That's the bad news. The good news is the worst is yet to come (with emphasis on the word *yet*). There is still time for individuals and businesses to cover their assets and even find ways to profit in the multibubble pop and Aftershock.

But first you have to see it coming.

Prescient Quotes from Our First Book, *America's Bubble Economy*, in 2006

On the Stock Market

"The idea that the stock market at any time is risk free is completely false. Every market has downside risk. Back in the 1950s, 1960s, and 1970s that was understood. It's been a very long time since the experts have tried to tell us there is no risk in the stock market. Guess when it happened before? The last time market cheerleaders tried to get Americans to think of the stock market as risk-free was just before the big 1929 stock market crash that led to the Great Depression. Coincidence? A bloated overvalued market (Dow up ten-fold in 20 years), now "stable" from mid 2000 to 2005 (also known as stagnant), plus cheerleaders telling us that there is no downside risk, all add up to one thing: a Stock Market Bubble on the edge." (p. 110)

"Bottom line: Most stocks are overvalued and on their way down. Will there be some ups and downs? Of course. Is it worth taking a chance on it? We think not. As with real estate, although there may be some potential growth left in the stock market, the timing is very tricky and it's not worth taking the risk. In the short run, you are about as likely to lose as gain. And in the long run, all you will do is lose significantly when stock values begin to seriously plummet. Again, we will show you much better places to put your money." (p. 139)

Fact: The Dow was at 12,100 when the first edition of this book was published in October 2006.

On Real Estate

"In the near term, the slow collapse of the Real Estate Bubble (in some markets it won't be so slow) will weigh heavily on the

(Continued)

stock market. The loss of housing construction jobs, plus the factory and service jobs that support housing construction, will further slow the economy, putting more downward pressure on the stock market." (p. 73)

Fact: The housing price index was at 205 according to Case-Shiller Top 20 Cities Index when our first book was published, and fell to as low as 137 in 2012.

On Private Credit

"All adjustable rate loans, credit cards, and adjustable or variable mortgages will become an absolute disaster when the bubbles burst. Interest rates will rise dramatically and so will your mortgage and other payments if you don't get out of these soon. Now is a great time to lock in your low long-term interest rates. Don't take a chance; get rid of your evil variable rate mortgage and other big debts now!" (p. 141)

Fact: Adjustable-rate mortgages helped kick off the housing price collapse and are still a leading significant cause of mortgage default and foreclosure.

Because Our Earlier Books Were Right, Now You Can Be Right, Too

Most people think the economy is in a recovery and will only improve from here. Unfortunately, this just is not true. We can tell you what you want to hear, or we can help you enormously by showing you how to prepare and protect yourself while you still can, and find opportunities to profit during the dramatically changing times ahead. We may not give you news you like, but it will definitely be news you can do something about.

Now is not the time to look for someone to cheer you up. Now is the time to get it right because you won't care in five years if someone cheered you up today. What you will care about is that you made the right financial decisions. It matters more now than ever before that you get it right today. Please remember this important point as you go through the rest of the book: *It is bad news for your personal economy only if you don't do anything about it.*

And you can do something about it. You can actively and correctly manage your investments and protect your assets now, before it's too late, and you can begin to position yourself to cash in on some really big profit opportunities in the longer term. This is a tricky time and it will only get trickier, which is why we want to help you come through each stage of the coming Aftershock (before, during, and after) in the best shape possible.

Later in the book, we will give you some practical advice for protection and profits. Much more detail about how to invest in this challenging and evolving economy can be found in our recent book, *The Aftershock Investor*, Second Edition (Wiley, 2013).

Before we go on, we should take a moment to assure you that we are neither bulls nor bears. We are not gold bugs, stock boosters or detractors, currency pushers, or doom-and-gloom crusaders. We have no particular political ideology to endorse and no dogmatic future to promote. We are simply intensely interested in patterns—big, evolving changes over broad sweeps of time. And because we look for patterns, we are willing to see them—often where others do not.

At the time we wrote *America's Bubble Economy*, we saw, and still continue to see, some patterns in the U.S. and world economies that others are missing. We see these patterns, in part because we are very good at analyzing the larger picture. In fact, co-author David Wiedemer has developed a fascinating new "Theory of Economic Evolution" (introduced briefly in Chapter 8 of the first edition of *Aftershock*, although not repeated in this updated third edition of the book) that helps explain and even predicts large economic patterns that most people simply don't see.

But there's more to it than that. We can see things happening in the economy right now that many others do not because, at this particular moment in history, it's very hard for most people—even most experts—to face what is actually going on. The U.S. economy has been such a strong and prosperous powerhouse for so long, it's difficult to imagine anything else. When there is so much at stake, it's hard to face reality and oh so easy to stay in denial.

Our goal is not to convince you of anything you wouldn't conclude for yourself, if you had the right facts, based on objective science and logical analysis. Most people don't get the right facts because most financial analysis today is based on preconceived ideas about a hoped-for positive outcome. People want analysis that says the economy will improve in the future, not get worse. So they look for ways to create that analysis, drawing on outdated ideas like repeating "market cycles," to support their case. Such is human nature. We all naturally prefer a future that is better than the past, and luckily for many Americans, that is what we have enjoyed.

Not so this time.

Again, just to be clear, we are not intrinsically pessimistic, either by personality or by policy. We're just calling it as we see it. Wouldn't you really rather face the truth?

At an April 2008 presentation about *America's Bubble Economy* to Hogan & Hartson, one of the nation's largest law firms, co-author Robert Wiedemer said he wished people would treat economists and financial analysts as doctors rather than people trying to cheer you up. What if you had pneumonia and all your doctor did was slap you on the back and say, "Don't worry about it. Take two aspirin, and you'll be fine in a couple of days." Instead, wouldn't you prefer the most honest diagnosis and best treatment possible? But when it comes to the health of the economy, most people want only good news. Even in the face of some very damning economic facts, people still want convincing analysis of why the economy is about to turn around and get better soon. The vast majority of financial analysts and economists are simply responding to the market. That's what people want, and that's what they get.

Despite this universal desire for good news, and despite the fact that the housing and stock markets were both near their peaks in 2006, our first book did remarkably well. In fact, *America's Bubble Economy* was discussed in articles in *Barron's*, Reuters, *Bottom Line*, and the Associated Press. The book was also selected as one of the 30 best business books of 2006 by Kiplinger's. And coauthor Robert Wiedemer was invited to speak before the New York Hedge Fund Roundtable, the World Bank, and on CNBC's popular morning show *Squawk Box*. So, clearly, people are interested in unbiased financial analysis, even when that analysis says there are fundamental problems in the economy that won't be resolved easily or soon.

Then, with the release of *Aftershock* in late 2009, support for our analysis and predictions grew considerably. Dozens of newspapers, magazines, radio broadcasts, and television programs have featured and quoted from the book, and interviewed coauthor Bob Wiedemer, including the *New York Times, Financial Times, Wall Street*

Journal, Associated Press, CNBC, *Fox Business News*, and many more. And within weeks of the release of *Aftershock*, Second Edition, in 2011, the book hit the New York Times Bestsellers list. Yet even within this supportive audience, and even among our most devoted fans, there is still a wish for optimism, a deep-down feeling that the future couldn't possibly be as bad as we say. We understand that. All we can offer is realism, based on facts and logical analysis. In the end, that is what's best for all of us.

Although much of what we predicted has come true, much that we forecasted in our books hasn't happened yet, because most of the impact of the multibubble collapse is still to come. This is good news because it means you still have time to prepare.

Didn't Other Bearish Analysts Get It Right, Too?

Not really. Back in 2006, there was a small group of more bearish financial analysts and economists who correctly predicted some slices of the problems. We say hats off to them for having the courage and insight to make what they felt were honest, if not popular, appraisals of the economy. It takes guts to yell "fire" when so few people believe you because they can't even smell the smoke.

However, there are times when smart people make the right predictions for the wrong reasons, or for incomplete reasons, and that makes them less likely to be right again in the future. In this case, there are important differences between our way of thinking and the typical "bear" analysis, which we think you ought to know about. For one thing, a lot of bear analysis tends to be apocalyptic in tone and predictions, sometimes going so far as to call for drastic survivalist measures, such as growing your own food. Unlike these true doom-and-gloomers, we see nothing of the kind occurring.

Another important difference is that so much bear analysis seems to carry moralistic overtones, implying that, individually and collectively, we have somehow sinned by borrowing too much money, and we will eventually have to pay a hefty price for our immoral ways. We certainly disagree that borrowing money is morally wrong. In fact, depending on the circumstances, borrowing money can be the best course of action for an individual, a business, or a government. Without the leveraging power of credit, it's very difficult to start a business, go to medical school, build a bridge, or lift an economy.

Borrowing is not intrinsically "wrong." The real issue here is that some debts are a lot smarter than others. For example, borrowing money to go to college for four years en route to a lucrative career is smart. Borrowing the same amount to spend four years at Disney World is not. (More on "smart" versus "dumb" debt in the next chapter.) For now, the point is that borrowing money, in and of itself, is not the biggest problem—*stupidity* is. Other bearish analysts who complain about too much borrowing tend to miss this vital distinction entirely.

An even more important difference between our predictions and other bearish analyses is that they tend to ignore the bigger picture of our *multibubble economy*. Even the most realistic bearish thinkers fail to see all the bubbles in today's economy, and they certainly miss the critically important *interactions* between them. Instead, if they mention any bubbles at all, they often focus on one singular bubble—like consumer debt, the housing bubble, or the growing federal debt. They are right to point out that all is not well, but they generally don't connect the dots from their single complaint to the larger multibubble economy. More important, they don't see how the co-linked bubbles interact or will eventually pull the economy down.

Honestly, if all we had was a consumer debt or housing bubble, our economy could get past it fairly unscathed. Unfortunately, our multibubble problem is much bigger than one or two of its parts. As we discuss in more detail in the next chapter, these bubbles worked together in a seemingly *virtuous upward spiral* to lift the economy up in the longest economic expansion in U.S. history, and together these linked bubbles will work together in a *vicious downward spiral* to pop our multibubble economy and bring on the global and Aftershock.

Partly because of their single-bubble focus and partly because people want to hear more optimism about the future, many bears were predicting a strong rebound in the economy as early as 2010. Grumpier bears said it could take several years, but most saw a fairly quick turnaround ahead.

Unfortunately, a full economic rebound has not occurred. Yes, the stock market recovered due to massive money printing, and that has helped spur more consumer spending and some rebound in home prices. But in terms of key recovery areas such as jobs and gross domestic product (GDP) growth, the economy isn't exactly booming.

The economy has not fully recovered because what we have this time is not a normal economic downturn on its way to an upturn. What we have this time is a multibubble economy on its way down. Multibubble economies certainly cannot stay afloat forever. There are real forces that push economies up and real forces that push economies down. These forces are not static, like repeating market cycles, but evolve over time. Based on our science-backed analysis of the evolving economy, which is neither bullish nor bearish, but simply realistic, the U.S. economy is in the middle of a long-term fundamental change. It is *evolving*, not merely cycling back and forth between expansion and contraction. Therefore, the multibubble economy will not automatically turn around and go back up again in the next few years. The idea that the economy is evolving, not merely expanding and contracting and expanding again, is a key difference between us and other bearish analysts; and it is certainly a huge difference between us and the bullish "experts."

Another reason that many "experts" did not (and still don't) see what is really occurring in the economy is that they don't fully understand the short-term power of the federal government to make it *look* as if we are having a recovery when we are not. They see a financial crisis in late 2008, and then they see the short-term positive impact of massive federal government borrowing and money printing on the stock market, helping to create a big stock rally, and from there the experts conclude that the economy is getting back on track.

It isn't.

How the "Experts" Got It So Wrong

We enjoyed an article in the January 12, 2009, issue of *BusinessWeek* magazine so much that we thought we'd include some of it for you here. What follows are observations and predictions about the economy in 2008 by well-known and highly trained financial professionals, writers, investors, and economists. It is interesting to note that, in the course of our research for this book, we kept a file of predictions and observations that well-known analysts, investors, and economists make. In reviewing the file for this section of the book, we noticed that it is very hard to find *anyone* who will predict economic movements beyond a year. Hence, it limits just how wrong they can be. It also makes it very hard to compare our long-term predictions that were made in October 2006 with anyone else's predictions, since so few people in 2006 made predictions for 2008 or 2009. That we can show the accuracy of our long-term predictions against others' short-term predictions, which are much easier to make, shows the power of our financial and economic analyses in understanding the economy. For most investors, long-term predictions are really the most important because most investors are investing for the long term, whether it be for capital appreciation, capital preservation, or for retirement. Financial analysis has to be accurate long term to really be valuable.

Here are the statements of interest from the January 12, 2009, issue of *BusinessWeek:*

Stock Market

"A very powerful and durable rally is in the works. But it may need another couple of days to lift off. Hold the fort and keep the faith!" Richard Band, editor, *Profitable Investing Letter*, March 27, 2008.

What actually happened: At the time of Band's comment, the Dow Jones industrial average was at 12,300. By December 2008 it was at 8,500.

AIG

AIG "could have huge gains in the second quarter." Bijan Moazami, distinguished analyst, Friedman, Billings, Ramsey, May 9, 2008.

What actually happened: AIG lost $5 billion in the second quarter 2008 and $25 billion in the next. It was taken over in September by the U.S. government, which will spend or lend $150 billion to keep it going.

Mortgages

"I think this is a case where Freddie Mac and Fannie Mae are fundamentally sound. They're not in danger of going under. . . . I think they are in good shape going forward." Barney Frank (D-Mass.), House Financial Services Committee chairman, July 14, 2008.

What actually happened: Within two months of Rep. Frank's comments, the government forced the mortgage giants into conservatorships and pledged to invest up to $100 billion in each.

GDP Growth

"I'm not an economist but I do believe that we're growing." President George W. Bush, in a July 15, 2008, press conference.

What actually happened: GDP shrank at a 0.5 percent annual rate in the July–September quarter. On December 1, the National Bureau of Economic Research declared that a recession had begun in December 2007.

Banks

"I think Bob Steel's the one guy I trust to turn this bank around, which is why I've told you on weakness to buy Wachovia." Jim Cramer, CNBC commentator, March 11, 2008.

What actually happened: Within two weeks of Cramer's comment, Wachovia came within hours of failure as depositors fled. Steel eventually agreed to a takeover by Wells Fargo. Wachovia shares lost half their value from September 15 to December 29, 2008.

Homes

"Existing-Home Sales to Trend Up in 2008." From the headline of a National Association of Realtors press release, December 9, 2007.

What actually happened: NAR said November 2008 sales were running at an annual rate of 4.5 million—down 11 percent from a year earlier—in the worst housing slump since the Depression.

Oil

"I think you'll see [oil prices at] $150 a barrel by the end of the year," T. Boone Pickens, one of the wealthiest and most respected oilmen today, June 20, 2008.

What actually happened: Oil was then around $135 a barrel. By late December it was below $40.

Banks

"I expect there will be some failures. . . . I don't anticipate any serious problems of that sort among the large internationally active banks that make up a very substantial part of our banking system." Ben Bernanke, Federal Reserve chairman, February 28, 2008.

What actually happened: In September 2008, Washington Mutual became the largest financial institution in U.S. history to fail. Citigroup needed an even bigger rescue in November.

Bernard Madoff

"In today's regulatory environment, it's virtually impossible to violate rules." Famous last words from Bernard Madoff, money manager, October 20, 2007.

What actually happened: About a year later, Madoff—who once headed the Nasdaq Stock Market—told investigators he had cost his investors $50 billion in an alleged Ponzi scheme.

More Wrong Predictions

Following is another collection of predictions made about 2008 that was published in *New York* magazine. Again, these are all professional financial analysts who represent the opinions of many, many others, even if they are not quoted directly.

Stock Market

"Question: What do you call it when an $8 billion asset write-down translates into a $30 billion loss in market cap? Answer: an overreaction. . . . Smart investors should buy [Merrill Lynch] stock before everyone else comes to their senses." Jon Birger in *Fortune's Investors Guide 2008*.

What actually happened: Merrill's shares plummeted 77 percent, and it had to be rescued by Bank of America through a deal brokered by the U.S. Treasury.

Housing

"There are [financial firms] that have been tainted by this huge credit problem. . . . Fannie Mae and Freddie Mac have been pummeled. Our stress-test analysis indicates those stocks are at bargain basement prices." Sarah Ketterer, a leading expert on housing, and CEO of Causeway Capital Management, quoted in *Fortune's Investors Guide 2008*.

What actually happened: Shares of Fannie and Freddie have lost 90 percent of their value, and the federal government placed these two lenders under "conservatorship" in September 2009.

Stock Market

"Garzarelli is advising investors to buy some of the most beaten-down stocks, including those of giant financial institutions such as Lehman Brothers, Bear Stearns, and Merrill Lynch. What would cause her to turn bearish? Not much. 'Our indicators are extremely bullish.'" Elaine Garzarelli, president of Garzarelli Capital and one of the most outstanding analysts on Wall Street, in *BusinessWeek's Investment Outlook 2008*.

What actually happened: None of these firms still exist. Lehman went bankrupt. JPMorgan Chase bought Bear Stearns in a fire sale. Merrill was sold to Bank of America.

General Electric

"CEO Jeffrey Immelt has been leading a successful makeover at General Electric, though you wouldn't know it from GE's flaccid stock price. Our bet is that in a stormy market investors will gravitate toward the ultimate blue chip." Jon Birger, senior writer, in *Fortune's Investors Guide 2008*.

What actually happened: GE's stock price fell 55 percent, and it lost its triple-A credit rating.

Banks

"A lot of people think Bank of America will cut its dividend, but I don't think there's a chance in the world. I think they'll raise it this year; they have raised it a little in each

of the past 20 to 25 years. My target price for the stock is
$55." Archie MacAllaster, chairman of MacAllaster Pitfield
MacKay, in *Barron's 2008 Roundtable.*

What actually happened: Bank of America saw its stock drop
below $10 and cut its dividend by 50 percent.

Goldman Sachs

"Goldman Sachs makes more money than every other brokerage firm in New York combined and finishes the year at
$300 a share. Not a prediction—an inevitability." James
J. Cramer in his "Future of Business" column in *New York*
magazine.

What actually happened: Goldman Sachs's share price fell to $78
in December 2008. The firm also announced a $2.2 billion
quarterly loss, its first since going public.

Despite the hit to its stock, which has increased from $78 to
nearly $150 (still about half the predicted price of $300), Goldman
has by far the best management and skills on the Street and will
have a consistently better performance than any other major firm.

Predictions from Ben Bernanke and Henry Paulson—We Trust These Officials with Our Economy

Federal Reserve Chairman Ben Bernanke and former Treasury
Secretary Henry Paulson unfortunately make an incredible team
for wrong forecasts. With the performance shown here, you have to
wonder why they are given so much credibility.

March 28, 2007—Bernanke: "At this juncture . . . the impact on
the broader economy and financial markets of the problems in the subprime markets seems likely to be contained."

March 30, 2007—Dow Jones @ 12,354.

April 20, 2007—Paulson: "I don't see [subprime mortgage market troubles] imposing a serious problem. I think it's going
to be largely contained." "All the signs I look at" show "the
housing market is at or near the bottom."

July 12, 2007—Paulson: "This is far and away the strongest global economy I've seen in my business lifetime."

August 1, 2007—Paulson: "I see the underlying economy as being very healthy."

October 15, 2007—Bernanke: "It is not the responsibility of the Federal Reserve—nor would it be appropriate—to protect lenders and investors from the consequences of their financial decisions."

February 28, 2008—Paulson: "I'm seeing a series of ideas suggested involving major government intervention in the housing market, and these things are usually presented or sold as a way of helping homeowners stay in their homes. Then when you look at them more carefully what they really amount to is a bailout for financial institutions or Wall Street."

May 7, 2008—Paulson: "The worst is likely to be behind us."

June 9, 2008—Bernanke: "Despite a recent spike in the nation's unemployment rate, the danger that the economy has fallen into a 'substantial downturn' appears to have waned."

July 16, 2008—Bernanke: "[Freddie and Fannie] . . . will make it through the storm." "[are] . . . in no danger of failing.", ". . . adequately capitalized."

July 31, 2008—Dow Jones @ 11,378

August 10, 2008—Paulson: "We have no plans to insert money into either of those two institutions" [Fannie Mae and Freddie Mac].

September 8, 2008—Fannie and Freddie nationalized. The taxpayer is on the hook for an estimated $1 trillion to 1.5 trillion. Over $5 trillion is added to the nation's balance sheet.

Where *We* Have Been Wrong

In the first and second editions of *Aftershock*, we admitted that there is one area in which we have been wrong before, and likely we will be wrong again. Now in this third edition of the book, we have to repeat that admission again.

Timing exactly when each bubble will pop and the Aftershock will begin has been and remains nearly impossible to accurately predict. For example, in the first *Aftershock* book we said the coming

Aftershock could begin as early as 2011. In the second edition of *Aftershock*, we revised that to 2013. But since we wrote the last book, the U.S. government has intervened massively to delay the coming economic collapse. For example, they enormously increased their borrowing, bailed out many of our largest financial institutions, bailed out our auto companies, gave significant tax credits to home buyers, put less pressure on banks to foreclose on defaulted mortgages, and began a program of massive money printing—all of which helped temporarily support the sagging multibubble economy and delayed the inevitable fall ahead. (All this economic stimulus, by the way, is only going to make matters worse later, by putting more pressure on the debt and dollar bubbles, as you will see in Chapters 3 through 6.)

In addition to huge government stimuli of various kinds, there is possibly some degree of manipulation of the markets for the purposes of keeping investors' psychology from turning too negative (for more on this, please see the Appendix). Keeping the group psychology as positive as possible for as long as possible is vital to keeping the party going and the bubble economy afloat. Government stimuli, market manipulation, and group denial are working together to delay the inevitable, for now. Ultimately, none of these are sustainable, but they do work well enough in the shorter term.

Timing is always tricky when making any forecast, but if you know what to look for, the *overall trends* of each phase are predictable, even if the exact moments when specific triggers that will activate them are not. That's why we try to give general time ranges for our ideas about future events, and we attempt to link these to other signs and events, rather than trying to predict specific dates. Knowing the overall trend is absolutely essential. If you know winter is coming, you can prepare yourself without knowing exactly when and where the first snowflake will fall. However, if you are expecting spring, that first winter storm is really going to hit you hard.

An old stock market saying is "the trend is your friend." We say "the trend is your best way to defend" against the dangers of trying to time the Aftershock. If you know the general trend, your asset protection and investment timing will, on average, be fine (see Chapters 8 through 10). Even if the trend seems to go against you for a while, if you follow a fundamental trend that you know may take years to play out, you will do fine. This type of fundamental, long-term trend thinking is key for success during each stage of the falling bubbles and their Aftershock.

Within an overall trend, there will be moments, or trigger points, when dramatic shifts occur. For example, in the fall of 2008, the stock market dropped more than 20 percent within a few weeks of Lehman Brothers going bankrupt. Predicting the occurrence or the timing of that kind of specific event is essentially impossible. What we did predict with complete accuracy was the overall trend of an overvalued stock market bubble poised for a fall.

Specific trigger points are so hard to predict because their activation usually involves a high psychological component, and try as we might, the timing of human psychology is not especially predictable. For example, if you objectively analyzed the Internet stock bubble prior to its fall, you'd know that it was bound to pop at some point, but you'd be hard-pressed to know precisely when and specifically what would kick it off. Even today, well *after* the fact, it is hard to figure out exactly what triggered the pop of the dot-com bubble in March 2000. Was it the collapse of Microstrategy's stock price due to the restatement of earnings forced on it by PricewaterhouseCoopers in March? That's a good guess, but not necessarily correct. Other people have their own guesses, but in talking to many investment bankers and venture capitalists, we have found no unified identification of the actual trigger point, even though they are experts in this area, and this was a major economic event that affected each of them quite personally. All we know with certainty is that we had a bubble in Internet-related stock prices, and in March 2000 investor psychology dramatically changed.

When thinking about how bubbles in general tend to burst, it's interesting to note that during the fall of the Internet bubble, Nasdaq didn't just collapse and go straight down. Over the course of nine months, it fell and recovered, at one point rising not too far from its peak, before its eventual final fall. Even right in the middle of the dot-com crash, most people didn't see it. In fact, the mantra among investors at the time was that we were simply moving away from a business-to-consumer model toward a business-to-business model, and then to an infrastructure play. The infrastructure play begat the rise of the fiber-optic companies in the summer of 2000, most notably JDS Uniphase, before it, too, collapsed. Ultimately, Nasdaq would rise and fall again many times, until it had fallen 75 percent from its all-time high of nearly 4,700 in early 2000, finally hitting its low point of 1,170 in September 2002.

The moral of the story is that it's hard to predict specific triggers before they happen. Even *after* the fact, it can be hard to understand the timing of specific events. Why did investors change their psychology in March 2000 instead of in August 1999? After March 2000, why did people think that infrastructure was the next big thing? Did they just want to keep the old Internet boom alive, or were they really sold on infrastructure? Most investor decision making turned out to be based on psychology, not real analysis of the underlying trends. Eventually, all the stocks in the infrastructure play collapsed. Even wishful thinking can't grow a bubble forever.

So when people challenge us to tell them exactly when each phase of the Aftershock will begin, we don't take the bait. All we can say with certainty is that the transitions from each phase to the next will involve triggering events, the timing of which will be as hard to predict as the popping of the Internet bubble.

We do know that trends can take years to assert themselves fully, and along the way, long-term trends can be temporarily delayed, even briefly reversed, by a countering short-term trend. For example, the long-term trend of a falling stock market bubble was temporarily delayed by the short-term trend of the rise of the private equity company buyout bubble. With easy credit at very low interest rates, private equity and hedge funds raised enormous amounts of money and went on a company buying spree the likes of which we've never seen. Total merger and acquisition transaction values went from $441 billion in 2002 to $1.4 trillion in 2006 and $1.3 trillion in 2007, according to Mergerstat. This, plus generally good investor psychology, drove stock prices higher, helping to boom the Dow above 14,000 in 2007. Of course, it also made the stock market bubble much bigger and therefore much more vulnerable to the credit crunch, caused by the fall of the housing bubble and the private debt bubble (see Chapter 3).

In another example, the potential full negative impact of the collapse in home prices on the economy and stock market in 2008 was blunted, or at least delayed, by the short-term trend of lenders making much riskier loans in 2006. Historically, in July 2005, home prices stopped going up in many places or slowed their growth dramatically. They weren't falling, but they weren't rising rapidly anymore, thus setting the stage for the subprime and adjustable-rate mortgage collapse. Lenders' willingness to participate in riskier home loans in 2006 and early 2007 to some extent slowed the fall of the housing bubble and delayed its impact on the economy and the stock market for a while. In our first book, we couldn't give the exact timing of the housing bubble fall because it was hard for us to predict just how crazy lenders would get. We did know they could not keep it up forever, and in fact they didn't. Lenders pulled back on their risky loans very dramatically in 2007, triggering an even bigger collapse in real estate prices.

Thus, our 2006 prediction of the long-term trend of falling housing and stock market prices began to emerge with a vengeance by the end of 2007 and early 2008. And if it were not for emergency measures by the Federal Reserve to print massive amounts of money combined with a massive increase in government borrowing, which were unprecedented, the stock market would have fallen much farther.

"These projected figures are a figment of our imagination.
We hope you like them."

But the dramatic government intervention only served to temporarily blunt (not stop) the effects of the underlying fundamental trend. In time, these trends will also include a major Aftershock that few others are anticipating: the bursting of the dollar and government debt bubbles.

When will that happen? As of this writing in January 2014, we believe the conditions necessary to bring on the multibubble pop and Aftershock (namely, a shift toward negative investor psychology, coupled with rising inflation and rising interest rates) will likely begin in the next two to four years. As we will explain in more detail later, it all depends on a change in investor psychology.

So while precise timing is very tricky because there are always so many intervening, complex factors, our predictions regarding the *overall trend* are well intact and still on track.

Love us or hate us, the fact is we got it right before, while others got it wrong. And, unfortunately, we will be right again, for the very same reasons. As Paul Farrell, senior columnist for Dow Jones *MarketWatch*, said about our first book in February 2008, "*America's Bubble Economy*'s prediction, though ignored, was accurate."

CHAPTER 3

Phase 1: The Bubbles Begin to Burst

POP GO THE HOUSING, STOCK, PRIVATE DEBT, AND SPENDING BUBBLES

What in the world happened? There we were, with the Dow over 14,000, U.S. home prices close to their all-time highs, and consumer and commercial credit flowing as freely as honey on a hot summer day. Then, seemingly overnight, things weren't so sweet. It may feel like the proverbial rug was randomly pulled out from under us, but in fact, we've been setting ourselves up for this multibubble fall over many years. Beginning with our decision in the early 1980s to run large government deficits, six co-linked bubbles have been growing bigger and bigger, each working to lift the others, all booming and supporting the U.S. economy:

1. The real estate bubble
2. The stock market bubble
3. The private debt bubble
4. The discretionary spending bubble
5. The dollar bubble
6. The government debt bubble

The first four of these bubbles have already begun to burst, leading to the global financial crisis in late 2008 and 2009. Next, while most people think the worst is over, the coming Aftershock will bring down all six bubbles in the next two to five years.

We know this is hard to believe, and we wish it weren't true, but as you will see in this and the next chapter, all the evidence is right there, plain as day. You just need to know what to look for.

Bubbles "R" Us: A Quick Review of America's Bubble Economy

What is a bubble? This should be an easy question to answer but there is no academically accepted definition of a financial or economic bubble. For our purposes, we define a bubble as an asset value that temporarily booms and eventually busts, based on changing investor psychology rather than underlying, fundamental economic drivers that are sustainable over time.

For quite a few years, America's multibubble economy has been growing because of six co-linked bubbles, some of which you may find easier to believe in than others. These six bubbles are outlined next.

The Real Estate Bubble

Now that it's popped, the housing bubble is easy to see. As shown in Figure 3.1, from 2000 to 2006, home prices almost doubled.

If nothing else, just looking at Figure 3.2 on inflation-adjusted housing prices since 1890, created by Yale economist Robert Shiller,

Income Up 2%   Housing Prices Up 80%

Figure 3.1   Income Growth versus Housing Price Growth, 2001–2006
Contrary to what some experts say, the earlier rapid growth of housing prices was not driven by rising wage and salary income. In fact, from 2001 to 2006, housing price growth far exceeded income growth.
Sources: Bureau of Labor Statistics and the S&P/Case-Shiller Home Price Index.

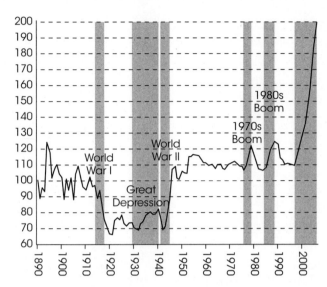

Figure 3.2   Price of Homes Adjusted for Inflation since 1890
Contrary to popular belief, housing prices do not ordinarily rise rapidly. In fact, until recently, inflation-adjusted home prices haven't increased that significantly, but then they just exploded after 2001.
Source: Robert J. Shiller, *Irrational Exuberance*, Second Edition (Princeton, NJ: Princeton University Press, 2005).

should make anyone suspicious that there was a *very* big housing bubble in the making. Note that home prices barely rose on an inflation-adjusted basis until the 1990s and then just exploded in 2001.

However, while home prices exploded, the inflation-adjusted wages and salaries of the people buying the homes went up only 2 percent for the same period (according to the Bureau of Labor Statistics). The rise in home prices so profoundly outpaced the rise of incomes that even our most conservative analysis back in 2005 led us to correctly predict that the vulnerable housing bubble would be the first to fall. We have a lot more to say about what's ahead for the housing market later in this chapter. (*Hint:* It's not what they tell you to think.)

The Stock Market Bubble

This one was almost as easy for us to spot as the housing bubble, yet many times harder to get other people to see. Stocks can be analyzed in many different ways. We find the state of the stock market is easier to understand by looking at Figure 3.3. After decades of growth, the Dow had risen 300 percent from 1928 to 1982

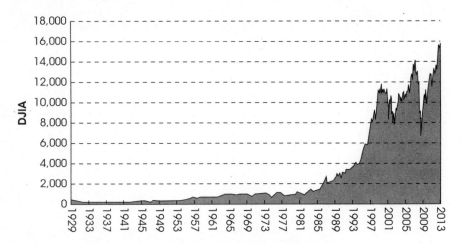

Figure 3.3   Dow Jones Industrial Average, 1928–2009
Despite massive growth in the U.S. economy between 1928 and 1981, the Dow rose only about 300 percent. But, after 1981, it rose an astonishing 1,400 percent.
Source: Dow Jones.

(54 years). Yet in the next 20 years the Dow increased an astonishing 1,200 percent, growing four times as much as before in 70 percent less time. But that growth came without four times the growth in company earnings or our gross domestic product (GDP). We call that a stock market bubble. It looks even more out of line when you consider that the population of the United States more than doubled in that previous period (1928 to 1982), and personal income more than doubled between 1950 and 1970 alone. In comparison, since 1980, our population has grown only 25 percent, and personal income barely has grown 10 percent. Population growth and personal income growth are the key drivers of GDP growth, and GDP growth is the fundamental driver of corporate earnings growth and therefore stock prices.

Shown in a different way in Figure 3.4, the value of financial assets as a percentage of GDP has held relatively steady at around 450 percent since 1960. But, starting in 1981, it rose to over 1,000 percent in 2007, according to the Federal Reserve. We call that prima facie evidence of a stock and real estate bubble.

The Private Debt Bubble

The private debt bubble, like all bubbles, is complex. But we will simplify it a bit by saying it is essentially a derivative bubble that was driven by two other bubbles: the rapidly rising home price bubble

Figure 3.4   Rise of the Financial Assets Bubble
Financial assets as a percentage of GDP: The exploding value of financial assets as a
percentage of GDP is strong evidence of a financial bubble.
Sources: Thomson Datastream and the Federal Reserve.

and the rapidly rising stock market bubble, which combined to
make for a strong and growing economy. In both cases, lenders
of all forms (not just banks) began to feel very comfortable with
the false belief that the risk of a falling economy had been essentially eliminated, and the risk of any lending in that environment
was minimal. This fantasy was supported for a time by the fact that
very few loans went into default. Certainly, at the time we wrote our
first book, commercial and consumer loan default rates were at
historic lows.

The problem was not so much the amount of private debt
that made it a bubble, but taking on so much debt under the
false assumption that nothing would go wrong with the economy.
Lenders felt very comfortable increasing the amount they lent for
consumer credit card loans, home mortgages, home equity loans,
commercial real estate loans, corporate loans, buyout loans, and,
in fact, just about every kind of loan, due to increasing asset values
and a healthy economy that no one thought would change.

For us, it was easy to see in 2006 that if the value of housing or
stocks were to fall dramatically (as bubbles always eventually do),
a tremendous number of loan defaults would occur. The private debt

bubble was an obvious derivative bubble that was bound to pop when the housing and stock market bubbles popped.

The Discretionary Spending Bubble

Consumer spending accounts for about 70 percent of the U.S. economy (depending on exactly how you define *consumer spending*). A large portion of consumer spending is discretionary spending, meaning it's optional (how big a portion depends on exactly how you define *discretionary*). Easy bubble-generated money and easy consumer credit made lots of easy discretionary spending possible at every income level. Now, as the housing, stock market, and private debt bubbles pop and people lose their jobs, or are concerned they might, consumers are reducing their spending, especially unnecessary, discretionary spending.

This is typical in any recession, but this time the effect is much more profound for two key reasons. First, the private debt bubble allowed consumers to spend like crazy because of huge growth in housing prices and a growing stock market and economy, which gave them more access to credit than ever before, via credit cards and home equity loans. As the bubbles pop, that credit is drying up, and so is the huge consumer spending that was driven by it.

Second, much of our spending on necessities has a high discretionary component, which is relatively easy for us to cut back. We need food, but we don't need Whole Foods. We need to eat, but we don't need to eat at Bennigan's or Steak & Ale (both now bankrupt). We need refrigerators and countertops, but we don't need stainless steel refrigerators and granite countertops. The list of necessities that can have a high discretionary component, complete with elevated prices, goes on and on. And all that discretionary spending is on top of completely discretionary spending, such as entertainment and vacation travel.

The combined fall of the first four bubbles (housing, stock market, private debt, and discretionary spending) has already begun. But, unfortunately, our troubles don't end there. Two more giant bubbles are about to burst in the coming Aftershock.

The Dollar Bubble

Perhaps the hardest reality of all to face—the once mighty greenback—has become an unsustainable currency bubble. Due to a rising bubble economy, investors from all over the world were getting huge returns on their dollar-denominated assets. This made the dollar more valuable but also more vulnerable. Why? Because we didn't really have a true booming economy underlying the growth; we had a multibubble economy. The value of a currency in a multibubble economy is linked not to real, underlying, fundamental drivers of sustainable economic growth (like true productivity gains), but to the rising and falling bubbles. For many years our dollars rose in value because of rising demand for dollars to make investments in our bubbles. Now the falling bubbles will eventually lead to falling-value dollars, despite all kinds of government efforts to stop it. (Don't believe us? You will by the end of the next chapter.)

The Government Debt Bubble

Weighing in at more than $8.5 trillion when our 2006 book came out, and topped $17 trillion at the end of 2013, as shown in Figure 3.5, the whopping U.S. government debt bubble is currently the biggest, baddest, scariest bubble of all, relative to the other bubbles in our economy. Much of this debt has been funded by foreign investors, primarily from Asia and Europe. But as our multibubble economy continues to fall and the dollar starts to sink, who in the world will be willing, or even able, to lend us more? (Much more on the fall of the impossibly huge government debt bubble in Chapter 6.)

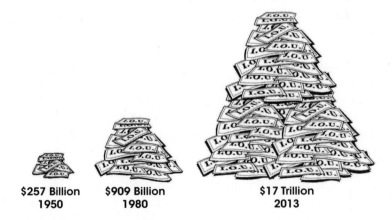

| $257 Billion | $909 Billion | $17 Trillion |
| 1950 | 1980 | 2013 |

Figure 3.5   Growth of the U.S. Government's Debt
The U.S. government's debt is massive and growing rapidly. With no plan and little ability to pay it off, the debt is quickly becoming the world's largest toxic asset.
Source: Federal Reserve.

From Boom to Bust: The Virtuous Upward Spiral Becomes a Vicious Downward Spiral

On the way up, these six linked economic bubbles helped co-create America's booming bubble economy. In a seemingly virtuous upward spiral, the inflating bubbles helped the United States maintain its status as the biggest economy the world has ever known, even in the past few decades, when declines in real productivity growth could have slowed our expanding economic growth. Instead, these bubbles helped us ignore slowing productivity growth, boost our prosperity, disregard some fundamental problems, and keep the party going.

Not only did the U.S. economy continue to grow and remain strong, but the rest of the world benefited as well. Money we paid for rapidly increasing imports poured like Miracle-Gro into developing countries like China and India, quickly expanding their burgeoning economies. The developed nations benefited as well. Because America's bubble economy was booming along with the developing nations, Japan and Europe were able to sell lots of their cars and other high-end exports, which helped their home economies prosper. The growing world economy created a rising demand for energy, pushing up oil prices, which made some Russian billionaires, among others, very happy. Growing demand for minerals, like iron, oil, and copper, pumped money into every resource-producing country. China and India's expanding appetite for steel boosted iron exports from the Australian economy. And on and on. All combined, America's rising bubble economy helped boom the world's rising bubble economy.

Now, as our intermingled global party bubbles are beginning to deflate and fall, the virtuous upward spiral has become a vicious downward spiral. They are linked together and pushing hard against each other. Each time any one bubble sags and pops, it puts tremendous downward pressure on the rest. First, we had the fall of the U.S. housing bubble and its downward impact on the stock market bubble, the private debt bubble, and the discretionary spending bubble. Next, in the Aftershock, the dollar bubble and the U.S. government debt bubbles will be pumped up even more to offset the other popping bubbles. But, when those final bubbles in America's bubble economy begin to burst, so will the world's bubble economy.

It is important to understand that the problems we faced in 2008 and after were due to much more than merely a popped real estate bubble. If all we had was a burst housing bubble, it would not have created so much financial pain here and around the globe. In addition to the housing bubble, the private debt bubble and the stock market bubble also fell. And these problems are not going to be resolved anytime soon. Rather than the housing bubble, private debt bubble, and stock market bubble magically reinflating, they will instead continue to fall. This will continue to put downward pressure on the already vulnerable dollar bubble and bulging U.S. government debt bubble, eventually forcing both to burst, creating a worldwide mega-depression. Unless you know what to look for, the coming Aftershock will be hard to see until it's too late to protect yourself. (Please see Chapters 8 through 10 in this book and *The Aftershock Investor*, Second Edition, for details about asset protection and profits.)

Once all six of our economy-supporting bubbles are fully popped, life in the post-dollar-bubble world will be quite different from the relatively quick recovery most analysts are now predicting. The vicious downward spiral of multiple popping bubbles will move the economy into the coming Aftershock faster than the onset of the troubles we've already seen. And indeed the Aftershock will move quickly to the post-dollar-bubble world. So although there is much more economic change ahead, it will happen in increasingly shorter and shorter periods of time.

While it may seem chaotic and unpredictable, not all this change will be entirely random but will happen as part of a much bigger movement of ongoing economic evolution that will be the subject of a later book. That evolution will eventually involve some very effective solutions for the economy's problems that would be politically impossible to implement today.

If you've read the past few pages, you now know more than nearly everyone else about how we got ourselves into this mess. Now the big question is how bad will this get? How low will U.S. real estate, private credit, and stocks go? The rest of the chapter focuses on these three bursting bubbles.

Pop Goes the Real Estate Bubble

The most important thing to understand about the falling real estate bubble is that it did not begin with a subprime mortgage problem whose contagion spread to other mortgages; it was a *housing price collapse,* a falling real estate bubble. If home prices had not declined there would never have been a subprime mortgage problem at all. If home prices had continued rising as they had been rising in the past, the low introductory, adjustable-rate subprime loans would have simply been refinanced into new low introductory, adjustable-rate subprime loans based on the higher equity in the home, and everything would have been just fine.

But with a housing price collapse, the low introductory, adjustable-rate subprime loans were doomed. These subprime mortgages were not the cause of the problem; they were merely the first to get hit. Because it was a housing price collapse and not just a subprime mortgage problem, as housing prices continued to collapse, the Alternative A-paper (Alt-A, no documented income) "liar loans" started to fail. Loans made on investment properties also got hit. Fancy mortgages to people with good credit that allow the payer the option of paying less than the current interest owed and no principal at all (so called option adjustable-rate mortgages) took a hit, too. Home equity loans got pinched. Eventually, as the housing price collapse continued, perfectly good prime mortgages got hit as well. It was not a "spreading contagion" from the subprime problem, as the press so often tried to tell us. It was just the fallout from a declining housing price bubble that impacted more and more people.

The *falling equity value* (not subprime mortgages) was the single most important factor leading to mortgage default and foreclosure. Falling equity values make refinancing any adjustable loan very difficult. Home equity fell dramatically. In the second quarter of 2007 it passed a milestone, with the percentage of equity Americans have in their homes falling below 50 percent for the first time since 1945, according to the Federal Reserve.

Because of the housing price collapse and the damage it caused to home equity, the number of mortgages that were *underwater*, meaning they have no equity or negative equity, increased very rapidly. Disappearing equity put as many as 25 percent of U.S. mortgages underwater, and not just in California, Nevada, and Florida. The problem has been very widespread.

Now in early 2014, many years after the real estate bubble first began to fall, we are still not out of the woods. As of the first quarter of 2013, in 25 of the top 30 metropolitan areas, more than 25 percent of home mortgages were underwater, according to Zillow. com. That's more than one out of every five mortgages in the

United States. It's an improvement from last year, when the number was closer to one in every four mortgages. But in spite of some improvements, 13 million U.S. mortgages are still underwater.

Coauthor Bob Wiedemer likes to demonstrate the impact of falling home values on the economy by pushing a pencil into a balloon. The pencil represents declining home values. The balloon represents the economy. The more home prices fall, the deeper the pencil pushes into the balloon. As the pencil goes farther and farther into the balloon, more mortgages of higher grade are taken down at an increasing rate, taking the economy down with them. Ultimately, the balloon pops, because house prices can only go down so far before they trigger a major collapse in the mortgage market and the economy as a whole, a process we will describe in more detail later.

Of course, government intervention—in the form of massive money printing and massive purchases of mortgage bonds by the Federal Reserve—can slow things down temporarily. But in the long run, not only will this not save us from a big housing bubble pop, it will actually make the fall even worse, as we will show you in later chapters.

No One Thought Home Prices Would Decline

It was always assumed that subprime loans were risky loans, so they carried a higher interest rate than non-subprime. What was not factored into anyone's calculations was the possibility (to us, the probability) that home prices would eventually fall. The models used by the bond-rating firms and investment banking firms that rated and sold the complex mortgage-backed securities (that included subprime loans) never anticipated home prices falling, at least not to any significant degree. As their analysts now readily admit, they anticipated various levels of home price increases—some low, some medium—but certainly not much of a home price decrease. Were these people crazy? Not a bit. After all, home prices have almost never declined in recent history. You would have to go back to the post–World War I recession to find any serious inflation-adjusted home price decline, and even then only for a short period of time. From 1916 to 1921 home values fell about 30 percent, according to data from the Case-Shiller Home Price Index.

Virtually no one in the investment world, or even outside the investment world, thought home prices in the United States would ever decline significantly, and certainly not for any extended length of time. There was no historical precedent for it to happen.

But, just as we predicted, happen it did. How come? Because home prices were in a *bubble*. As mentioned earlier, home prices were up 100 percent and income was up only 2 percent from 2000 to 2006. If that isn't a textbook example of an asset bubble, we don't know what is. That kind of price growth without comparable income growth to support it is just not sustainable for very long. It had to be a bubble; therefore, it had to pop.

People will give you a thousand reasons to justify the growing real estate bubble: "People love San Francisco," "There is limited land in Boston (or Manhattan, or LA)," "Washington, D.C., has a very stable job base," or "People enjoy living close to the city."

None of these reasons ever explained why prices were increasing so much in a fairly flat economy. And the economic growth that did occur in 2003 and 2004 was due in large part to rising home equity spending and rising home construction.

"Innovations" in the Mortgage Industry Made the Housing Bubble Possible

An important ingredient for growing such a large real estate bubble so quickly was the highly "innovative" mortgage industry. The industry developed new products and enhanced previous ones, such as the adjustable-rate mortgage (ARM), which had been around for a while but now was taken to a whole new level. Innovations included a low introductory interest rate—the same idea credit card companies used to hook consumers. Start with a low rate of 1 or 2 percent for the first two or three years and then jump to a normal adjustable-rate mortgage. Another "innovation" was the willingness to give these mortgages to people who could afford them only at the low introductory rate, not at the rate that was coming later. This made more expensive homes much easier for people to buy, often with the idea of selling them later for a big profit when home prices continued to climb.

The mortgage industry also innovated with no-documentation loans, called Alt-A loans or "liar loans." These loans had been around before but they were pushed much harder during the housing boom. Also, low credit scores were increasingly acceptable, and with the housing bubble on the rise, more people lied about their incomes in order to get their hands on the keys to a piece of the housing boom.

Option ARMs were another incredible innovation. Every month, you had the choice of making a full payment of interest and principal, or an interest-only payment, or—get this—a smaller payment that didn't even cover the interest due! The interest you didn't pay would be added to the principal of the loan until the loan value reached 110 percent or 125 percent of the original amount, at which point you would have to jump to full payment of interest and the payment on the new, much larger principal. No wonder they called them "suicide loans." More than 80 percent of folks who took these deadly loans paid the lowest payment option possible (who takes these loans if you want to pay more than the least possible?). Not surprisingly, the default rates on these loans will, by some estimates, soon reach 90 percent.

Mortgage brokers became much more prevalent during the housing boom, and they became much more aggressive in selling as many mortgages as possible. Bad loans were not their problem. The underwriter judged the quality of the loan. As long as the broker could place the loan with an underwriter, that's all that was necessary for the broker to get paid. What happened to the loan after that was not their worry.

Amazingly, in many cases, it was not the worry of the underwriter either. Many underwriters just wanted to repackage these loans into mortgage-backed securities and sell them in big multi-million-dollar bundles to large investors, often in other countries. The underwriter collected the underwriting fees and never had to worry if the poor suckers who took out the mortgages could ever make payments to the poor suckers who bought the mortgage-backed securities. The foreign and other investors who bought these mortgage-backed securities considered them as secure as government bonds, but with a higher interest rate. *The bond-rating agencies, like Moody's and Standard & Poor's, encouraged these sentiments by giving most of the bond packages their highest AAA rating—which was the same as the U.S. government.* The high rating was often required for many investment funds to buy the bonds.

All of these and even more "innovations" by the mortgage industry were key to making the housing bubble possible. Now that these "innovations" are gone, lending has decreased substantially. In 2003, lending for single-family homes was $3.9 trillion. In 2008 it dropped to about half that amount, according to the Mortgage Bankers Association. And in the years that followed, lending for home purchases has dropped even further. This huge decrease in lending has put enormous downward pressure on the housing bubble.

Had Home Prices Kept Going Up Rapidly, the Mortgage Industry Would Still Be Fine

In fairness to the mortgage industry, if home prices had kept going up and up, none of this would have been a problem. People could have easily refinanced their way out of all their fancy mortgages into other newer fancy mortgages based on the huge rise in home equity. Had home prices continued going up in value, there would have been little risk in making these higher-risk innovative mortgages—that is, little risk that was not offset by higher fees and higher interest rates.

Had Home Prices Kept Going Up Rapidly, Home Buyers Would Still Be Fine

In all fairness to home buyers, if home prices had kept going up, it would have made tons of sense to buy the most expensive house you could possibly get away with. As long as you could make the monthly payments for at least a year (low introductory rate payments really helped with that) and as long as your home's price was going up 10 or 20 percent a year, you would be practically minting money.

For example, for a $500,000 house, a 10 to 20 percent rise in home prices annually created an increase of $50,000 to $100,000 in home equity every year. All you had to do was convert that growing equity into cash via a refinancing or a home equity loan, and you would have had plenty of money to make your house payments and buy lots of toys along the way. When the housing bubble was rising, you were actually getting paid to buy a home—paid a *lot* of money. What could be better? So please do not blame home buyers; they were making excellent investment decisions—*as long as home prices kept rising rapidly.*

Had Home Prices Kept Going Up Rapidly, Wall Street Would Still Be Fine

No one thought housing prices would stop rising rapidly and actually go down. Even the best minds on Wall Street seemed blind to the bubble that they were helping to create. Remember, bubbles are a lot easier to see *after* they pop. And remember, too, that not noticing the housing bubble was making a lot of people very, very rich. So no one complained or criticized. Quite the opposite; they sang the praises of the brilliant new Wall Street mega-millionaires. Bear Stearns's profits were enormous, and many Wall Street insiders made out like bandits. And if the housing bubble had just kept rising, Wall Street would have been just fine.

But, as it turned out for Bear Stearns and the rest of Wall Street, making money by making bad investments and then selling those bad investments to others is a very bad long-term strategy. Even if the federal government comes along and partially bails you out, it's very painful when the boom busts.

"Tell me the fairytale about the economy."

And bust it did because even the most "innovative" mortgages and creative new investment instruments could not get around one fundamental fact: Home prices cannot rise dramatically faster than incomes rise over any significant amount of time. It flies in the face of basic economic principles and has never happened before and never will again. Real estate bubbles don't last.

That is the kind of excellent and honest analysis that Wall Street could really have used before the housing bubble popped, but it would have been laughed at and ignored. Their lack of interest in such analysis has cost them very heavily indeed.

Pop Goes the Stock Market Bubble

The fall of the housing bubble caused many mortgages to default, particularly the riskier subprime mortgages given to people who often could not afford them in the longer term. Some of these subprime mortgages probably would have gone into default even if the housing price bubble were still afloat because they were risky loans. But once the housing bubble started to fall, and lots of people had mortgages greater than the value of their homes, mortgage defaults began to rise dramatically. This caused unexpectedly large losses in the massive mortgage-backed securities market, felt by both the investors who bought mortgage-backed securities and the investment banks that held mortgage-backed securities. Because the mortgage-backed securities market was so big, these losses roiled the entire credit market.

The credit markets began to freeze up partly driven by fear of not knowing which financial institutions were holding what losses (the financial institutions themselves didn't even know, so it was hard for anyone else to know). More important, credit froze because investors who thought they were buying highly secure AAA bonds lost confidence. If AAA bonds could go bad, what was next?

The collapse in credit market confidence and in the value of banks helped start the popping of the stock market bubble. Had the stock market not been in a bubble, it would not have fallen so far so quickly. Not only were stock prices in a bubble, but about two-thirds of the increase in the value of the stock market from 2005 to 2007 was due to increases in financial and energy stocks. With these financial institutions losing the value of many of their assets, their stock prices began to fall. This spread to the rest of the stock market as investors began worrying about a major market correction. Rising financial stocks had been the key driver of the rising stock market, so now that financial stocks were collapsing, the fears of investors were quite valid.

The Collapse of the Mortgage-Backed Securities Market Popped the Private Equity Buyout Bubble and Created a Credit Crunch

In addition to harming the value of financial stocks and overall investor confidence in the stock market, toxic mortgage-backed securities helped punch a hole in the private equity buyout bubble. On its way up, private equity buyouts helped boost the stock market in 2006 and 2007. Back then, private equity firms were able to take on massive amounts of debt on incredibly favorable terms to buy increasingly larger companies. New records for the sheer size of these transactions were being made monthly. At its peak in 2006, 11,750 deals valued at $1.48 trillion were completed, according to Mergerstat. It seemed as if every few days another large public company was bought, and always at a big premium to the market price. The name of the game wasn't to pay a low price; instead, the private equity Masters of the Universe competed to pay the highest price possible for a company.

It was all very exciting, and the stock market loved it. The market didn't need many reasons to go up. The economy was good, and the market players were in a good mood. The private equity buyout bubble was just the tonic needed to push the Dow from the 11,000 range in 2006 to a peak of 14,164 in late 2007. Even after the private equity buyout bubble began to slow, the momentum it had created in the market continued.

Like all bubbles, it eventually popped. Ultimately bondholders, frightened by the credit crunch, began to worry about the incredibly favorable terms being offered to sellers by buyout firms. Many of the loans for the deals required little equity and were called "covenant lite," meaning the borrowers had few benchmarks to meet in order to maintain their loans in good standing. Even riskier, many loans did not even require that interest be paid in cash. Instead, the interest could be paid in more debt, or payment-in-kind (PIK).

But as the mortgage-backed securities debacle continued, investors became increasingly afraid. All of a sudden, there was a greater perception and awareness of risk, which, amazingly, investors did not have during the peak of the private equity buyout bubble. Lenders started asking for better terms. They quit agreeing to covenant lite loans and, most important, they wanted more equity. They wanted the buyout firms to share more of what they now saw as a growing perceived risk. This, of course, put the kibosh on the private equity buyout bubble. Many deals in negotiation fell apart. Even some already-agreed-to deals were called off.

An even bigger problem was that many investment and commercial banks were on the hook for transactions that had recently taken place. They had lent out the money to complete the transactions, fully expecting to be able to sell that debt to other investors. When the money musical chairs came to a halt, a lot of that debt became unsellable, except at a loss—and sometimes at a very big loss.

For the stock market, the party had been ruined. The private equity buyout boom had ended, and so had the glorious tonic that had driven up the market to record highs. The decline of the mortgage-backed securities market and the popping of the private equity bubble caused the Bear Stearns implosion in spring 2008, and then the fall of Lehman Brothers in fall 2008.

It Isn't a Liquidity Problem, It's a Bad Loan Problem!

The mantra during the credit crunch following the collapse of Bear Stearns, and the even worse global credit crunch after the collapse of Lehman Brothers, was that we had a "liquidity" problem, and all the U.S. Federal Reserve and other central banks had to do was inject liquidity into the markets. However, it wasn't a liquidity problem at all—it was a bad loan problem.

A liquidity problem occurs when a bank has sound financial assets (meaning their loans are good loans that will eventually be paid back), but for some reason people want to pull money out of the bank. This used to be called a "run on the bank" and happened frequently before the Fed was created to help prevent such a problem. By loaning the bank money (a.k.a., "injecting liquidity"), the Fed made it possible for the bank to pay off the people who wanted their money. But that assumed that the bank's underlying assets were sound and the loans were good loans and would eventually get paid back. The banks were sound; however, the people who wanted their money back were unsound in their fears.

In the case of the credit crunch during and after the 2008 financial crisis, quite the opposite was true. The bank's assets were unsound (because the loans are not good loans and many or most would not get paid back), while the people who wanted their money back were very sound, indeed. Therefore, the problem was not fundamentally a liquidity crisis but a *bad loan crisis*. Investment and commercial banks made a lot of bad loans and, hence, they had a lot of bad assets. It was not a crisis of confidence; but a crisis of bad investments that was scaring people. Interestingly, bankers are *still* making a lot of bad loans on the false assumption that the economy will turn around and asset values will not fall much more. The loans the Fed and other central banks, primarily the European Central Bank (ECB), made to these banks were essentially to cover losses. How much of a loss is still unknown, but one thing we do know: These losses will continue to increase as the value of the assets declines further later in the Aftershock. As the bubbles pop and asset values decline, these loans and other loans the central banks will make in the future, will also decline in value, and the Fed and the ECB will face horrendous, mounting losses. Rather than being repaid, central banks will take write-offs—which means they will let the money they have created to make these loans to the banks simply remain in the money supply, eventually causing significant future inflation (as you will see in Chapter 5).

So when you hear the experts talking about the "credit crunch" in relation to the stock market or the banks during and after the 2008 financial crisis, simply insert these words, instead: "Bad loans going south." These bad investments ultimately impacted the stock market—most directly and initially on the most vulnerable part of the stock market—the private equity buyout bubble.

The Key Forces Driving the Stock Market Bubble

The private equity buyout bubble was the first part of the stock market bubble to get hit, because it was the *most vulnerable* part of the market. However, there are other stock market drivers creating downward pressure, such as the dramatic decline in large, high-priced merger-and-acquisition activity by corporations and the massive decline in corporate stock buy-backs.

As with the real estate market, most stock market analysts don't like to look at these fundamental drivers of price but, instead, assume the stock market will always eventually rebound, because it has gone up before and it "inevitably" will continue to go up again. While the stock market has so far been responding well to the government stimulus of massive money printing, reaching new highs in recent months, these gains have been almost entirely due to a mix of massive money printing (currently $75 billion per month) and positive "animal spirits" in which positive investor psychology continues to run high. Beyond that, there are no real fundamental drivers that would justify the current market or sustained it far into the future.

Pop Goes the Private Debt Bubble

The full credit crisis hasn't kicked in yet. That will happen only in the Aftershock, when the dollar bubble and the government debt bubble pop. When consumers can still get low-interest-rate financing on a new car, you don't have a credit crisis. When you can get a 5 percent, 30-year fixed-rate mortgage, you don't have a credit crisis. In spring 2009, Toll Brothers was even offering a 3.99 percent 30-year fixed-rate mortgage on the homes they built. Of course, these loans were only to qualified buyers. From 2002 to 2006 mortgage and auto loans often went to unqualified buyers, so that is a bit of a change. We got so used to credit flowing to anyone willing to take it that now we actually think if an *unqualified buyer* cannot get a loan or cannot get the best interest rate possible, then we have a credit crisis.

We also do not have a credit crisis for business loans. Companies like Walmart do not have to pay 20 percent interest on their inventory loans, and they aren't being turned down for loans entirely. It's true that construction loans for buildings that won't make money are being turned down, as are loans for buying commercial real estate at prices that are way too high. But we can't exactly call that a credit crisis. It's more of a return to credit rationality, which apparently is very foreign to many of us.

However, when the dollar bubble pops, we will most definitely have a massive credit crunch. Very few businesses or individuals will be able to get loans at that point. More important, not long after the dollar bubble pops, the massive government debt bubble will burst and the U.S. government will no longer be able to get credit either.

The Private Debt Bubble Will Pop Twice: In Phase 1, Bad Loans Go Bad; in Phase 2, Good Loans Go Bad

In Phase 1 (the start of the multibubble pop in 2008 and 2009), the private debt bubble started to pop, with some bad loans going into default. However, in Phase 2 (the Aftershock—when the dollar bubble pops and *good* loans go bad), the private debt bubble will more fully collapse. This is because even good loans (those with reasonable leverage ratios that normally could withstand a modest economic downturn) will not be able to survive the kind of high interest rates and inflation that will follow the popping of the dollar bubble (explained in Chapter 6). In this chapter, we are focusing only on the first stage of the private debt bubble pop in Phase 1.

The Basis for Many Bad Loans Was the Good Times— And Thinking They Would Go on Forever

Optimism was the basis for the colossal bad loan collapse in mortgages. As we have mentioned many times before, *everyone, including bankers,* thought home prices would just keep rising no matter how much they had already risen beyond people's incomes. This same mentality affected commercial real estate loans as well. Plus, many of those loans were short term because it was a "sure bet" they could always be refinanced, thus keeping rates very, very low.

Huge corporate buyout loans with very high leverage ratios were fine, too, because who thought the value of these companies would ever go down? Why not loan 90 percent or more of the value of the company—it never goes down, right? And history was on their side. Coauthor Bob Wiedemer recalls talking to a friend at one of the largest banks in the United States in 2006. He was in the workout group that handles bad commercial loans. When Bob spoke with him, he joked that he wasn't in the workout business anymore. He said there was no more need for workouts. If they had the rare bad loan, they could just repackage it and sell it off to another lender. Same for the Federal Deposit Insurance Corporation (FDIC)—no banks were going under. Workout departments and the FDIC were like the Maytag repairman. Loans and banks almost never went bad. All they had in 2006 were good loans on their books.

Of course, the good times did end, which should not have been a surprise to anyone. Yet it was a 10,000-volt electric shock to the people in the financial community who made the loans. Now the FDIC couldn't be busier, and yes, Bob's friend at the large bank is hiring like crazy to expand his workout group.

A Nation on the Edge of Default

Consumer credit card balances and other loans were looked at the same way. Americans never thought they would have trouble finding a job or getting more credit. Why would the good times ever go bad? So no one saved much for a rainy day. A June 2013 survey by Bankrate showed that three out of four Americans do not have enough to cover their expenses for even six months if a breadwinner loses a job. And it's not just your average Joe or Jane having problems. A survey by Metropolitan Life Insurance showed that over 27 percent of those making over $100,000 a year in household income don't have enough savings to make their monthly expenses for more than two months.

It doesn't take a Certified Financial Planner to tell you that a lot of people are in for the shock of their lives when they find that rainy days can, in fact, happen. And that's one reason that the economy can turn down so quickly. Not only are a lot of our expenses discretionary, which means they are very vulnerable to deep cutbacks in a recession, but we are terribly vulnerable to job loss because we have no rainy-day savings (let's not even discuss retirement savings!). If job loss hits someone, expenses, even non-discretionary expenses, will get cut fast. This will also create a huge increase in riches-to-rags stories of people going from six-figure incomes to low-wage jobs in just a few months.

One Laid Off, Three More Worried

In a high-spending consumer society like ours, layoffs of small numbers of people can have a big impact on the economy because the large number of people still employed get frightened that they, too, might get laid off. They then cut back on their discretionary and capital goods spending. In reality, it may be too late to start saving for a rainy day, but people cut back on their spending anyway. And it makes sense even if it is too late. But that very fast, very deep drop in discretionary spending also means a very fast, very deep drop in economic activity, and more job losses are a result.

The Feedback Can Really Be Annoying

This feedback loop of job loss creating more job loss is ultimately what really puts the economy in a tailspin. It's not the credit crunch so much as the big downturn in people's spending. Credit is available, but there is a lack of interest in taking on more debt, combined with a lack of interest by the banks in making more bad loans to unqualified borrowers.

If banks were more willing to make the kind of reckless loans they made in 2004 and 2005, the economy would be better off—for a while. But with so many banks being burned by bad loans, they are losing their appetite for and ability to make bad loans. And, of course, making more bad loans would only be a short-term cure that would ultimately harm the banks even more. And, in any case, people who fear losing their jobs are simply less willing to take on new debt for discretionary items even if their credit is good.

Key Drivers of the Private Debt Bubble Collapse

The current thinking in financial and government circles is that we need to clear the *toxic assets* (their term for bad loans going south) out of the banking system. They are wrongly assuming that this group of toxic assets isn't growing much and can simply be flushed away. Of course, nothing could be further from the truth. As we have discussed, the number of toxic assets is growing, not staying the same. But wait, it gets worse. Not only is the number of bad loans growing, these bad loans are becoming increasingly toxic because they are *losing value every day*. As commercial real estate prices continue to go down, and housing prices continue to go down, the value of the assets behind these loans is decreasing constantly. Government intervention that allows banks not to write down assets or allows them to keep bad assets on their books without foreclosing on them can make the situation look better on the surface. But, underneath, the value is declining and, more important, will decline much more significantly, even devastatingly, when the dollar and government debt bubbles pop.

Government regulators and financial analysts desperately want the situation for bank assets to look better than it really is. Otherwise, if toxic assets are instead growing rapidly, how can they be flushed away, and if they can't be flushed away, what will happen to the banking system? That sort of fear is impeding rational analysis and, hence, supporting the mistaken view that the toxic assets are limited mostly to subprime mortgages and the real estate bubble in states like Florida and California.

All of These Problems Happen in a Relatively Good Economy, but Phase 2 (the Aftershock) Will Be Far Less Gentle on the Banking System

Let's not forget that Bear Stearns went bankrupt when the economy had low unemployment, low interest rates, and low inflation. None of those were much higher when Fannie Mae and Freddie

Mac had to be bailed out. Again, they weren't much higher when Citibank, Bank of America, and other big banks had to be bailed out. The same was true when Lehman Brothers, Merrill Lynch, and AIG were bailed out. The economy really wasn't all that bad in October 2008.

But, as we said before, the good times won't last forever. The economy grew worse in 2009 but recovered somewhat from 2010 to 2013. However, unemployment has not significantly dropped and the number of discouraged unemployed and underemployed remain high (see Chapter 1). Hence, bad loans will continue to default. And all that will still be far better than when the dollar bubble pops in Phase 2 (the Aftershock). At that point, high inflation and rising interest rates will put the banks under tremendous pressure. After the dollar bubble pops, even very good loans will go bad.

Pop Goes the Discretionary Spending Bubble

A disproportionately large share of the U.S. economy is "discretionary spending," meaning a good deal of what people have been buying in this country has been optional. Easy money from a rising multibubble economy made big-time discretionary spending possible and fun. Abundant high-limit credit cards and plenty of home equity loans fed the buying party at every income level, from luxury jet-set buyers to everyday Walmart consumers.

But when the housing bubble popped and unemployment rose, easy credit became hard to come by. In fact, home equity withdrawals declined rapidly from their peak of $144 billion in the second quarter of 2006 to just $7.2 billion in the fourth quarter of 2008 according to the Federal Reserve. That's a big drop!

As an incredible example of just how much money home equity withdrawal gave consumers, a study by Alan Greenspan and James Kennedy found that between 2001 and 2005 homeowners gained an average of *$1 trillion* per year in extra spending money! Now that's a little extra in your pocket.

However, with home equity down and easy credit less available, Americans at every level were less likely to rush out to buy things they didn't really need at the same level they did before. Who's going to buy new granite countertops for their kitchen, for example, when they've lost their job or house? And even if you still have income and a home, the old kitchen will probably do just fine for a while longer. Food, basic utilities, and other essentials, yes. New granite countertops, not so much.

Plus, consumers' credit cards also came under increasing pressure. With more people delinquent in their payments, banks became more careful about who they gave credit cards to and how much credit they offered. Consumers lost the ability to borrow money from home equity and credit cards, so even if they wanted to spend, it got a lot harder to do so.

And it will likely get much worse in the future. Much of the credit card debt held by credit card companies is subprime. In 2009, almost 31 percent of Bank of America's credit card loans were subprime, 30 percent of Capital One's credit card loans were subprime, and 27 percent of Citibank's credit card loans were subprime, according to Keefe, Bruyette & Woods, Inc., a financial firm that specializes in the financial services industry. While it is true that credit card losses began to stabilize in 2010 and beyond, and credit card purchases have increased from their rapid drop after the financial crisis of 2008 and 2009, it is also true that credit card spending is no longer fueling as much of the economy as it used to, and that will continue to be the case for quite some time.

More important, there will be no easy home equity loan bailouts for credit card holders. In the past, a lot of home equity loans were used to retire high-interest credit card debt. So home equity loans were a shadow support to the credit card boom that is no longer there, which puts more downward pressure on discretionary spending.

If the other bubbles were not popping, or if discretionary spending were a much smaller slice of the U.S. economy, a decline in discretionary spending would not pose so much of a problem. But our economy is so deeply dependent on discretionary spending that there is simply no way we can return to business as usual when businesses just don't have the buyers at the same levels they had in the past. How can we easily go back to the level of spending we once enjoyed when we no longer have the other big bubbles (housing, stock, credit) to push us back up? And how can the other falling bubbles possibly turn around and go back up unless we have lots of discretionary spending? They can't.

The stock market increases of 2010 to 2013 have helped encourage consumer spending by the top 20 percent of income earners in our country, who make almost 40 percent of the consumer purchases. This has been a key part of the stabilization we have seen in consumer spending, but with high unemployment, lower home values, and minimal increases in credit card debt, discretionary spending remains challenged, especially among the middle- and lower-income groups.

In a multibubble economy, co-linked bubbles rise and fall together. With the huge pink cloud of good-times discretionary spending being replaced by pink slips, our other falling bubbles have no viable way to independently reinflate themselves. And without the other bubbles, especially the private debt bubble and the real estate bubble, discretionary spending has no "bubble fuel" to keep it going at previous levels. While there has been some lukewarm upturn in consumer spending, the American consumer—that Energizer Bunny of bubble maintenance here and around the globe—is beginning to run out of bubble steam.

What can turn all these falling bubbles around and force them back up again? The economic cheerleaders, who are pinning their hopes on "market cycles," just say, "wait a while and everything will get better soon." But they never tell us *how* that is supposed to happen. With the housing bubble, the stock market bubble, the private debt bubble, and the discretionary spending bubble all popping and dragging each other down, what will reinflate our economy? Certainly not a rebound in big discretionary spending by the American consumer.

The only thing that is temporarily delaying the coming multibubble crash is a mix of massive money printing by the Federal Reserve (see next chapter) and continued positive investor psychology, and even that cannot save us forever. Eventually, massive money printing will cause increasingly negative investor psychology, rising inflation and rising interest rates (probably in two to five years) that will only make our multibubble crash all the worse. Even before that occurs, a change in investor psychology could kick things off sooner.

Massive federal government money printing and borrowing, coupled with good investor psychology, certainly made 2010 to 2013 better than it might have been. It has certainly helped the stock market significantly, which has helped boost the housing market recently and may continue to in 2014. But no amount of government intervention or wishful thinking is going to keep these bubbles up forever. And therein lies the rub: falling bubbles—even when temporarily supported—are destined to fall.

The Biggest, Baddest, Bad Loan of Them All

As bad as the financial judgment of private sector bankers and investment bankers is, even worse is the incredible irresponsibility and bad judgment of the public sector—the U.S. government. The government has been involved in the biggest bad loan of them all: the monstrous government debt bubble. We can't possibly pay it off. Our tax base in a good year is only $2.5 to $3 trillion. In a bad year, it's more like $2 trillion. The total government debt bubble is more than $17 trillion and rising rapidly. If you look at the loan from the perspective of any rational loan officer at a bank, you would see a debt-to-income ratio of over 6 to 1. That's pretty steep. Most loan officers would not approve such a loan. And that's assuming interest rates stay at their current incredibly low level. What if interest rates rose to 10 percent? We would have a hard time just paying the interest!

Our track record of repayment is not too good, either. Except for some token payments in the best years of the last couple of decades, we have *never* made any payments to reduce the debt. It's clearly a bad loan, the biggest bad loan in world history. A technical default on our huge government debt will have history-making consequences. Just when most people think things will improve, the next shoe will drop and the Aftershock will begin.

The economic cheerleaders continue to insist we are in a real recovery and all we have to do is sit back and be patient and eventually GDP growth and employment will jump up. Of course, they never explain exactly *what* is supposed to bring about this magical up cycle of greater economic growth. And even more telling, they never, *ever* said anything about a future *down cycle* back when the economy was doing well. Oh, no. As long as the economy was booming, no one said a word about a possible down cycle ahead. They only pull out the "market cycles" theory when they want people to think everything is going to be okay.

We say this is a bubble pop, not a cycle or a normal recession. However, big gains in real productivity could pull us out. But we haven't made big improvements in real productivity in more than three decades, and there isn't much hope of suddenly pulling a quick, economy-saving productivity rabbit out of the hat now. Very large real productivity improvements, such as moving from a nation of 90 percent farmers to less than 3 percent is, by its very nature, a slow process. Equally unlikely is a big jump in demand right now. The recovery of strong demand and the possibility of creating real productivity gains in the future are going to take some time, considerable resources, and, of course, the political will to make tough decisions. So we can't count on productivity improvements or strong demand to help us right now.

How about more rising bubbles? Would that help us? Sure, they would, at least for a while. The trouble is that four of our six bubbles have already begun to burst. So it is hard for a new bubble to be created, since the growth of bubbles is nicely supported by the simultaneous growth of other bubbles. We may be able to pump up a small bubble here or there, but not the huge bubbles we were able to get from combining forces with the massive stock, housing, and credit bubbles. Man, those were the days!

What about big government spending on stimulus packages and bailouts? Won't that save us? At another time, they might have, but not now that we have a multibubble economy on the way down. No amount of stimulus spending can possibly reinflate all these big falling bubbles. And even if it could, how long would that last? Bubbles, by nature, do eventually fall. Big stimulus spending will not be able to bring us back to a strong nonbubble economy. Stimulus spending isn't how a strong nonbubble economy is created in the first place. It's just a bit of medicine that works only if the patient is basically healthy. If the underlying economic health is just not there, simply pouring in more and more medicine is not enough. And, worse, the medicine itself becomes a poison.

Even if you believe in the "market cycles" idea, you still need *something* to get a new up cycle going. We may throw all kinds of spending and bailouts at the economy, and we may even have periods in which people swear a recovery is just around the corner but, in truth, without rising bubbles, or real productivity gains, or a rebound in strong demand, or a previously strong nonbubble economy to revive, we are going to run out of ammo.

Without something to turn this falling multibubble economy around, what do you suppose will happen next? Follow us now to the next chapter, where we will take a trip to and over the coming Market Cliff.

Got Macro?

We did not write our series of books in order to get you to buy something from us. All our current products and services grew out of reader demand over many years. For those who want to prepare for, not just read about, the coming Aftershock, we offer the following:

You are welcome to visit our web site, www.aftershockpublishing .com, for more information as we approach the Aftershock. While you are there, you may sign up for a two-month free trial of our popular **Aftershock Investor's Resource Package** (IRP), which includes our monthly newsletter, live conference calls, and more. Or you may reach us at **703-787-0139** or info@aftershockpublishing.com.

We also offer **private consulting** for individuals, businesses, and groups. Please contact coauthor Cindy Spitzer at **443-980-7367** or visit www.aftershockconsultants.com for more information.

Through our investment management firm, **Absolute Investment Management**, we provide hands-on, Aftershock-focused asset management services on an individually managed account basis. For details, please call **703-774-3520** or e-mail absolute@aftershock publishing.com.

4

The Market Cliff

NOT YOUR FATHER'S DOWN CYCLE

Remember the "Fiscal Cliff"? At the end of 2012, the media was all abuzz about an artificial deadline previously set by Congress after which a slew of budget cuts and tax hikes would go into effect unless lawmakers could reach a budget agreement. Congress had the power to create the artificial Fiscal Cliff dead-line, and Congress had the power—although not necessarily the immediate internal agreement—to avoid this artificial cliff, which eventually they did.

The kind of cliff that we want to introduce you to now is not a cliff that can be avoided by an act of Congress, the Federal Reserve, or by any part of the U.S. government. In fact, this new kind of cliff cannot be avoided at all because it will be the natural and unavoidable result of the end of a falling bubble economy. Once it starts, no amount of massive government stimulus will be able to stop it. In fact, the stimulus will just make it worse.

The combination of slow gross domestic product (GDP) growth and continued lack of growth of high-quality jobs will eventually worry some stock and bond investors. At first, only a few will want to exit some of their bonds and stocks. But over time, the number of investors seeking safety will climb. And eventually, it will hit a critical mass, pushing these assets over the Market Cliff and kicking off the beginning of the multibub-ble pop.

The Market Cliff Won't Be Just a "Down Cycle"

The mantra we often hear in a down market—but rarely during a boom—is that markets are cyclical. Every valley, say the cheerleaders, is just a precursor to the next peak, and every new peak will be even higher than the last. There is some historical truth to this. In a healthy, growing economy, market up cycles do tend to follow market down cycles. And during the rising bubble economy that began in the 1980s and 1990s, every market down cycle was reliably followed by an up cycle sooner or later because the overall movement of a rising bubble is up.

Even now that the rising bubble economy has been replaced with a sagging bubble economy being held up by massive money printing and borrowing, we can continue to expect more up and down swings in the stock and bond markets. But over time, as the artificial stimulus supporting the economy and the markets becomes increasingly ineffective, we'll likely see these up and down swings happening more frequently. With each downswing, the cheerleaders will surely declare that it's just a temporary dip triggered by irrational panic, and, of course, they will claim vindication when the markets temporarily rebound.

But there will be no immediate rebound once we hit the Market Cliff. This downturn won't be soon followed by an upturn because it won't be based on irrational panic but on legitimate fear of a falling multibubble economy and a stock market that simply isn't worth what investors used to think. This time the downturn won't be cyclical. Going over the Market Cliff will be the end of the stock market bubble and that will put increasing downward pressure on the rest of the multibubble economy.

Currently, the stock market has largely ignored slow economic growth and instead has been maintaining the stock bubble and even pushing it higher as the Fed prints more and more money. But with any bubble, the biggest enemy is the *passage of time*. When it takes increasing amounts of new money just to keep the bubble economy from falling, sooner or later people begin to notice and lose faith.

Exactly when investor psychology will turn negative enough to push us over the Market Cliff, popping the stock bubble, is hard to predict. Even after a bubble pops, people still don't know for sure that it has popped for some time. Prior to a bubble bursting, there are always people who recognize the problem early, but they tend to have little effect. (The fact that we have so many concerned readers is testament to that.)

But at some point, enough people get scared and pull out, and that sets the dominoes in motion, spreading fear throughout the markets and collapsing asset values. Sometimes this happens due to irrational fears—or at least it *begins* as irrational fears—for example, back when irrational fear used to drive occasional runs on a bank, followed by rational fear that the bank could go under. Or sometimes the initial fear can be very rational, as it will be in this case when people begin to wake up to the fact that the current bubble-based economy is no longer sustainable.

Why Hasn't the Market Cliff Happened Yet?

The Market Cliff hasn't happened yet because there is so much at stake. The coming multibubble pop will be bigger than any previous bubble pops and therefore far more devastating to the U.S. and world economies when it bursts. Because the stakes are so high, the current bubble economy is being heavily supported by the government. By contrast, the popping of the Internet bubble in 2000 was significant, especially if you were invested in dot-com stocks, but that bubble was only a small part of the economy and we could afford that inevitable correction, even if a bit painful. And it was not as powerfully supported by government intervention.

However, the price of losing a whole series of conjoined bubbles that now support our entire economy will be *much, much more* costly. This is something that everyone wants to avoid, and thus governments, institutions, and investors all around the world are highly motivated to keep the U.S. multibubble economy going. Because of that, we can be sure that the Market Cliff will not occur until all their firepower is fully spent.

The unfortunate reality is that the only way the government will be willing to change the fundamental problems with our economy is to hit and go over the cliff. That will end the worldwide delaying tactics and eventually move us into a period of actually trying to improve the basic drivers of real economic growth.

"What should you do? Here's what you should do: invent a time machine, go back sixteen months, and convert everything to cash."

Bubble Blind: The Powerful Psychology of Denial Is Keeping the Markets Going—For Now

The stock, bond, real estate, and other bubbles have brought us the greatest flow of easy money in our history. There is nothing more seductive than easy money—it is *much* more fun than hard money; it's absolutely intoxicating.

The Internet bubble was a great example of how people can deny reality when there is so much easy money to be had. Even the most sophisticated investors—venture capitalists and investment bankers—fell victim to the seductive siren song of *easy money*. Even more recently, how good is it when you can sell a firm, only a few years after starting it, and with no revenues and no profits, for $1 billion, as was the case when Instagram was sold to Facebook in March 2012. That's pretty darn good. John D. Rockefeller may have made a lot of money, but he never made so much money so fast as did Instagram.

Real estate has had similar tales. Seaside cottages purchased for $10,000 a few decades ago are now worth over $1 million. San Francisco, Boston, and New York have probably benefited the most from the combined real estate and stock bubbles. But there are lots of incredible tales of fast, big wealth in Los Angeles, Las Vegas, Phoenix, and Florida. The bubbles have been very, very good to us. Even if you weren't lucky enough to get a huge windfall and become a millionaire or billionaire from stocks or real estate, many people also benefited from the businesses that prospered along with this enormous explosion of fast, enormous wealth.

Many of those people worked hard for their money, but they made a whole lot more money because of the bubbles than they would have made otherwise. There was a lot of easy-money icing on top of the hard-money cake.

And, finally, many, many more participated in the general increase of easy money in the form of a dartboard stock market that increased more than 1,000 percent no matter where you threw the darts at the stock page, or housing that doubled or tripled in value with little or no improvements. We all gain to some extent from the overall rising bubble economy. And we liked it. Admit it—*easy money is a lot of fun.*

And, we might add, since it is a world bubble economy, there are lots of easy-money millionaires and billionaires around the world, and that has a big impact on Wall Street's thinking as well. They don't want to lose any easy money, whether it comes from the United States or some other country. Fast, big money from China, Russia, or the Middle East will do just fine to keep them happy. Right now in London, the best homes are selling for over $100 million, which is up from just a few million dollars several decades ago. Many are being bought by foreigners, not the Brits, with fast, big money, from Russia, the Middle East, and elsewhere. It is truly a world bubble economy at this point.

Conventional wisdom does not want to officially face any of this—although people who are fooling themselves often know more than they are willing to let on. Instead, most people here and around the world are drawing comfort from the pervasive "groupthink bubble," a term coined by savvy *Aftershock* reader David Mulder in Canada, where, by the way, they are deep in denial as well. (Heavily dependent on their exports to the United States, the Canadian economy will be hit especially hard when our bubbles pop and the U.S. dollar declines.)

Interestingly, when the U.S. and world bubbles do begin to burst, most investors will instantly change their minds about believing that any of this bubble growth is sustainable. Instead, they will instantly and completely understand that they need to get out of the popping bubbles as fast as they possibly can. There will be a stampede to sell, not buy, when these bubbles fall.

Surely, if anyone *really* believed what they say they believe, wouldn't they want to stay in and buy up the so-called "bargains" as prices dropped suddenly? Some will do that, but by far, most will not. At that point, most investors will be *sellers*, not buyers.

Unfortunately, at that point, a whole lot of their money will have gone to Money Heaven. Until then, most investors and "experts" cannot let themselves see the falling bubble economy and the dangerous Aftershock ahead.

Slow Learning

Key to the timing of the Market Cliff is *slow learning*. Most people, although highly adaptable, are naturally resistant to change. This has always been the case, from adjusting to new technologies to accepting that the earth is round. Eventually, most of us come around, but not without some resistance.

When adjusting to new information, particularly new information that requires changing one's behavior, people want to see substantial proof. In the case of the falling bubble economy, it's not enough for us to say we have bubbles or even to show logical proof that these assets are overpriced. Most people need to *see* the bubbles falling before they become motivated enough to try to sell and get out. Investors generally tend to move as a group.

A big reason for this herd behavior is that people want acceptance by others. As long as others around them seem to accept the idea that the economy is fundamentally stable and not a vulnerable bubble, most people won't go against the larger group—especially when the rewards of maintaining the bubble economy are so good.

Of course, not all investors stick so close to the pack. There are always a few independent thinkers who pay attention to actual conditions, not just to current group behavior. When they see opportunities on the horizon that others are missing, they move ahead of the pack and profit on their early bets. And when they see potential trouble on the horizon, they move to safety ahead of the pack, too.

That's what will happen with stocks and bonds approaching the Market Cliff. In the beginning, only a few alert investors will become increasingly worried about slow GDP and quality job growth, especially after so many years of massive government stimulus. They will naturally pull out of some of their stocks and bonds in an early flight to safety. In time, more will join them, but still no mass stampede. A gradual exit will push asset prices down to some extent, but not dramatically.

However, as more time passes and more investors become more worried about the lack of strong economic recovery, general group investor psychology will begin to turn. When enough people finally catch on, it won't take long before nearly all investors will want to run for the exit all at once in a group panic. With so many sellers and so few buyers, asset values will dramatically fall.

It would be nice if people could see the need for change before it's too late and move a little sooner, but that's not how the herd moves. While not so great for any one individual, from an evolutionary point of view, slow learning is actually good (efficient) for the group. It's the way many important changes in human history have occurred, sparing the group from endless false starts. Slow learning may mean we have to hit the wall first before the group changes, but when everyone finally does catch on, change can happen very fast.

After we hit the Market Cliff and Aftershock, there will be much resistance again to making the kind of changes needed to boost productivity and create real economic growth. But in time, the pain of the Aftershock will push us along toward the fundamental changes needed.

This is why we don't think of ourselves as doom-and-gloomers. The short-term future may look bleak, but in the longer term, the future will be very exciting. We will see many changes for creating a stronger economy in the years ahead. And if you're reading this book, you can avoid much of the suffering along the way.

Hitting the Market Cliff

The events leading up to the Market Cliff won't necessarily lend themselves to a perfectly organized timeline, but we are going to do our best to give you our current predictions of how it will happen—something few books would dare to do because the likelihood of getting the future wrong is so high. We are willing to do it anyway because our macroeconomic view has been so reliable for so many years (our first book came out in 2006).

In the following timeline, many events will overlap, and some may occur simultaneously. The general idea is that what begins very slowly can snowball very quickly. As an investor, the odds of your timing any market perfectly are near zero. With the stakes so high, we always say it is better to get out too early than too late.

Stage 1: 2006 to 2009

Stage 1 has already happened, much in line with what we predicted in our first book, *America's Bubble Economy*, back in 2006.

> **Stage 1, Step 1.** *The real estate bubble pops.* After reaching historic levels in 2006, home prices in the United States saw their biggest year-to-year drop on record in 2008, according to the Case-Shiller Home Price Index.
>
> **Stage 1, Step 2.** *The stock market bubble pops.* In *America's Bubble Economy*, we predicted the stock market would fall significantly over a period of a couple years. In fact, it fell below 7,000 in early 2009, less than half what it was at its high in 2007.

Stage 2: You Are Here

The government responds with massive money printing and borrowing. The Fed buys bonds to pump up the stock and real estate markets. Putting money into bonds keeps interest rates low, encouraging more mortgage lending. It also frees up money that investors had been keeping in bonds and encourages them to buy stocks in search of higher yields. A huge increase in government borrowing stabilizes the economy, keeping the GDP from shrinking precipitously. Government intervention stabilizes the economy, but it's a Band-Aid—not a real solution.

Stage 2 can last a long time—years, even. We have been in Stage 2 since shortly after the financial crisis of 2008, and are still here today.

Currently, inflation is still relatively low. Because people and businesses have little incentive toward wage and price increases, inflation can remain low for some time in spite of massive money printing.

Low inflation allows the Fed to continue printing money while the public takes little notice.

Some key indicators to pay attention to that indicate we are leaving Stage 2 and entering early Stage 3:

- The stock market doesn't rise as consistently.
- People become increasingly concerned about massive stimulation, misleading statistics, and financial market intervention by the government.
- People become increasingly concerned about continued slow or no GDP growth and continued slow growth of quality jobs.
- People become increasingly concerned about potential inflationary effects of money printing.
- People take notice of economic malaise worldwide and the extensive government stimulus (especially more money printing here and in other countries) needed to keep global economy stable.

These indicators can be gauged by a close reading of the financial press. More media coverage points to a shift in market sentiment.

Stage 3: Increasing Instability

In early Stage 3, which we are about to enter, we will move toward an oscillating stock market and continued money printing that will at first keep the market from falling significantly.

As Stage 3 advances, investors become increasingly worried about an economy that is taking too long to recover, and people begin to lose faith. The premise that the economy will recover if we can just keep up the stimulation for a few more months or years is losing traction, and that moves us closer to the rapid multibubble pop in Stage 4.

Stage 3 starts slowly and then moves quickly. Therefore, some steps may overlap or happen simultaneously.

Stage 3, Step 1. *The stock market falls gradually in spite of intervention.* We see an oscillating trend, within an overall downward trend.

Stage 3, Step 2. *Interest rates rise in spite of actions by the Fed.* Bondholders are getting more worried about risk. Government intervention begins to lose its effectiveness, as even the Fed can't keep interest rates down. Remember that their primary tool for keeping interest rates low is printing money. Some people expect the bond market to fall before the stock market, but it's unlikely because bonds are easier to manipulate and support than stocks. Currently, bonds are slowly falling, while stocks are doing better. Later, stocks will sharply fall, followed by bonds falling sharply.

Stage 3, Step 3. *More government stimulus by foreign countries, as well as interventions in foreign currencies and foreign economies.* As the situation in other countries—China, for example—becomes increasingly problematic, more drastic measures of stimulus and intervention will be taken by their governments, possibly with U.S. support, to keep their economies afloat and their governments in good standing.

Stage 3, Step 4. *Gold prices increase significantly.* This is a very strong indicator that the Market Cliff is near.

Stage 3, Step 5. *People increasingly begin to see the connection between money printing and inflation, which radically decreases the positive impacts of money printing.* As the public increasingly sees money printing as a negative rather than a positive for the economy, monetary stimulus rapidly loses effectiveness in boosting the markets, and stocks, bonds, and real estate begin to fall.

Stage 3, Step 6. *Foreign capital outflow.* U.S. assets are not performing well, and the lack of good investment opportunities here, coupled with increasing risk awareness, motivate foreign investors to slow the inflow of foreign capital to the United States. After that, they start to move out of some their U.S. assets to greater safety in their own countries. Initially, the outflow won't be too bad and can be offset by additional money printing. However, it will contribute to U.S. stocks and bonds falling, and will also put downward pressure on the dollar in the foreign exchange markets and help some foreign currencies that will be seen as relatively safe compared to the falling dollar.

Please note that the foreign exchange rate is different from inflation. When investors around the world want fewer U.S. dollars, the foreign exchange value of the dollar will fall.

Stage 4: Rapid Collapse

Stage 4 will occur very rapidly. Poor economic growth and anticipation of rising future inflation and rising interest rates (due to rising inflation) alarms investors. Much of the following could take place in just a matter of weeks, days, or even hours, with most people getting caught on the wrong side and going over the Market Cliff.

Stage 4, Step 1. *Gold prices soar.* The U.S. government may increase taxes on gold in an effort to keep some money in stocks, bonds, and real estate in the United States, but gold prices will surge around the world.

Stage 4, Step 2. *Intervention in the stock market fails.* The oscillating market becomes a falling market. Discomfort with the stock market leads to many more sellers than buyers. Stock prices fall deeply on a daily basis, leading to the government's declaring short stock market holidays—at first, for a couple of hours, and later, for much longer. **This is the Market Cliff**.

Stage 4, Step 3. *The bond market falls.* Rising interest rates cause big drops in bond prices. With few investors wanting to sell at a huge discount and even fewer investors willing to buy, the bond market essentially shuts itself down. The government may also choose to shut it down, just as with the stock market, in an attempt to soothe the markets with a little "time out."

Stage 4, Step 4. *The real estate market falls.* High interest rates and scarce mortgage money means nearly no home purchases. Real estate prices are devastated.

Stage 4, Step 5. *The dollar falls.* Collapsing asset values lead to a massive exodus of foreign money. No one wants to hold dollar-based assets. By now, most foreign investors can't find sellers and are stuck with their losses. The pullback further erodes the value of the dollar, spreading a deep mega-recession around the world. **The Aftershock begins**.

The Last Resort: A Stock Market Holiday

As we approach and go over the Market Cliff, the Fed will be entirely unprepared. Instead, officials at the Fed will make decisions moment by moment. And when faced with a free-falling market, officials will need to take fast action. The old way of doing things—massaging numbers and flooding the market with printed money—will be powerless to stop the stock plunge. The last resort will be to temporarily shut down the stock market entirely.

At first, the plan would be to shut down the market for only a few hours and address whatever immediate issue is causing the plunge in prices. Of course, the problem in this case is a falling stock bubble and a bursting bubble economy. That's not something that can be fixed overnight. So when the stock market reopens, the plunge will continue, and the government will need multiple additional shutdowns to try to stop the massive selloff, eventually having to shut down the markets for longer and longer periods.

In 1933, Franklin D. Roosevelt declared a national bank holiday in order to solve the problems that had been leading to runs on banks throughout the country. During that time, the Emergency Banking Act was passed, and when the banks reopened the following week, depositors came rushing back with renewed confidence. Likewise, when the stock market has to be shut down, the government will be frantically looking for whatever reform it can implement that could send investors rushing back to stocks.

But that will not be easy to do.

Officials will try every pep talk they can think of to calm investors and encourage buying rather than selling. What we will *not* hear from the Fed, or from most of the financial industry, is that stocks and other assets have been in a bubble all this time, and that going over the cliff was inevitable. Instead, we'll hear all kinds of excuses, perhaps blaming the crash on activities such as high-speed trading, which may have irresponsibly flooded the market with sellers. Then, of course, there are the short sellers, among the favorite scapegoats from 2008, and fear mongers. We'll almost certainly hear that it's a temporary irrational panic, and that everything will be fine once people come to their senses and renew their confidence in the U.S. markets again. Anything to convince the public—and themselves—that the Market Cliff is just an anomaly.

A big problem with selling this narrative is that, even with the U.S. stock market shut down, the Fed can't stop the trading of U.S. stocks overseas. So even while officials in the government and financial industry try to sell the idea that real stock values are strong, people will be able to log on to the Internet and see the falling prices of U.S. stocks overseas.

Try as it might, the Federal Reserve won't be able to reverse this negative downturn in investor psychology. And eventually it will have no option left but to shut down the stock market for a longer period of time. Investors who weren't able to sell their stocks before the Market Cliff will have little left in their portfolios. When the market finally does reopen, those basement prices will be the new normal.

Will the financial industry ever admit what the problem really was? We're not optimistic. They will continue to blame the wrong things, like irrational fear and political missteps, not a popping bubble. They will continue to insist that the earlier much higher prices that were the correct ones, if only everyone would realize it. Expect that drumbeat to continue for a long time.

But sooner or later, people will understand what happened: we had a bubble economy, it popped, the bubble is not coming back, and the road to recovery is a long and difficult one. This time it will not be fueled by low interest rates and overextended debt, but by slow and steady real growth.

When Is the Best Time to Get Out of the Stock Market?

You won't like our answer: 1999.

Had you exited the stock market at its peak in 1999 and bought gold instead at that time, you'd be very happy today. The S&P 500 rose about 20 percent from 2000 to 2013, while gold is up about 300 percent during this same time period, even with its recent drop in gold in 2013.

It's not possible to go back in time and buy gold in 2000, but there is still plenty of time to profit from the big future run up in gold in the Aftershock. Before then, there is something very important to focus on: don't go over the Market Cliff!

With stocks on the rise and the Market Cliff still a ways off, it's perfectly understandable that some readers will want to maximize their profits before pulling entirely out of traditional assets.

The problem comes from not knowing how long you can safely push your luck. Our best advice is to just get out now and don't play chicken with the approaching crash, even though it may mean missing out on some additional upside.

If you stay in the stock market, be realistic. You are unlikely to see the kind of big rise we saw in the last couple of years continue through the next couple of years. You are not going to get 20 percent or more per year, year after year.

Whenever you do get out of stocks, bonds, and real estate, keep in mind that if you want to do that before you go over the Market Cliff, you will be going against the vast majority of investors, and that is not easy to do. Some people will give you a hard time and maybe even make you question your sanity. Remember, back in 1999 when the markets were booming and the Internet bubble was at its peak, few people thought they should pull out of stocks and get into gold. In 1999, most people would have told you it was crazy to do that. And yet, if you had, you'd be in outstanding shape today.

Most importantly, no matter when you get out, at the peak or no peak, getting out *before* the Market Cliff is absolutely essential—far more important than when you time your move. At this point, timing your exit is trivial compared to simply exiting. For example, even if you had exited the stock and real estate markets at what appeared to be the very worst time—during the depths of the global financial crisis in 2009—you would *still* be far better off in the long term than you will be if you stay with the majority of investors as they go over the Market Cliff. In fact, if you invest wisely before and during the Aftershock, you won't just be better off, you will be quite prosperous.

Even if we can't convince you to get out now, please do not get caught holding on to traditional assets when we hit the Market Cliff. The last thing you want at that point is to be a seller when everyone else wants to be a seller, too. You want to be a seller much sooner than that, when there are still plenty of buyers (even if some people think you are crazy to sell).

If you want to push your luck a little further and stay in stocks, bonds, and real estate a bit longer, the rest of this book can be your guide. But keep in mind that the road to the Aftershock will be a bumpy one. The stock market will not keep going up dramatically every year until one day it suddenly crashes. It's not like we will have perfectly smooth sailing and then abruptly go over Niagara Falls. There will be plenty of potential for losses even before the final crash.

So when is the best time to get out of the markets? Probably 14 years ago.

When is the second best time to exit? Any time *before* we go over the Market Cliff.

CHAPTER 5

Massive Money Printing Will Eventually Cause Dangerous Inflation—So Why Hasn't It Happened Yet?

"Inflation is always and everywhere a monetary phenomenon."
—Milton Friedman, Nobel Prize–winning
expert on monetary theory

W e know what you're thinking. We've been warning for years that massive money printing will cause rising inflation that will push interest rates up and bring the multibubble economy down.

So, *where's the inflation?*

Even though the Fed has expanded the money supply by more than 400 percent since 2008, inflation remains quite low. If money printing really is so dangerous, shouldn't we have more inflation by now?

We agree; it's weird. But there are real reasons behind the current lack of significant inflation. This chapter gives you our latest thinking on why more inflation hasn't happened yet. It also explains how the Fed's money printing medicine will later become a poison, bringing on high inflation and high interest rates that will bring on the Aftershock.

But before we explain where inflation is hiding and why future inflation cannot be avoided, please allow us to provide a little clarity about what inflation actually is. We know that reading about inflation, interest rates, lag factors, and the like can be a bit dry. However, give us a chance to tell you what you need to know about inflation, and we promise by the end of this chapter, you'll understand more about the real dangers ahead than most economists!

What Is Inflation?

There is considerable confusion (even denial) about what inflation is and is not. Most people know that inflation involves increases in the prices of goods and services over time. But not all increases in prices are the result of inflation. Prices can also increase for other reasons that have nothing to do with inflation.

For example, even when there is no inflation, changes in either the supply or the demand for a product or service can lead to rising prices. That's because whenever demand is greater than supply, sellers have the opportunity to raise their prices and still find willing buyers—which explains why a kid with a lemonade stand can charge more on a hot summer day than when it's cold and rainy. Demand matters.

Supply is equally important. If a hurricane destroys half the orange groves in Florida, the unexpected drop in supply (without an equal dip in demand) means the price of orange juice will likely go up that year. But in neither case (lemonade or OJ) has inflation occurred. Instead, prices simply changed due to changes in supply and demand.

The forces of supply and demand also drive up the value of your investments. A change in the perceived value of an asset pushes up buyer demand and therefore sellers can raise their price. Sometimes the reason for the increase in demand is rational, such as when real estate prices increase due to population growth. Sometimes it is irrational, such as in a rising real estate bubble. But in either case, bubble or no bubble, it's not inflation. Prices are simply rising with increasing demand.

In order for price increases to be caused by inflation, they have to be initiated by something the average consumer has little control over: *money printing*. As Milton Friedman, Nobel Prize–winning expert on monetary theory said: "Inflation is always and everywhere a monetary phenomenon." All other price increases are not inflation; they are simply price increases due to increasing demand relative to supply.

What Exactly Is Money Printing?

The process of money printing is a mystery to most people. Because it's been in the news so much lately, many people know it's happening, but they may wonder where the Fed gets all that new money. Are extra dollars actually being "printed" on a press? Where does the new money go? And once printed, can they take it back?

The answers may surprise you.

The process begins when the Federal Reserve's 12-member Federal Open Market Committee (FOMC) comes to a consensus about whether or not to increase the money supply, and if so by how much. A directive is then sent to the Federal Reserve Bank of New York to begin to "print."

The word *print* is a bit misleading because at this stage no new dollar bills are physically created. Instead, the New York Fed decides to buy U.S. Treasury bonds or mortgage-backed bonds on the open market through a handful of primary dealers, such as JPMorgan Chase or Goldman Sachs. These big dealers then make bids to sell bonds to the Fed on behalf of their clients who want to sell the bonds.

After the traders at the Fed pick the best bids from the sellers and make their bond purchases, the transactions are entered on the Fed's balance sheet, sort of like a big checking account register. Today, this is all done electronically, with the funds to buy the bonds being credited to the bank's Federal Reserve account and then transferred to the bond sellers' bank accounts.

Now here is where the surprise of money printing comes in. Before these big bond purchases take place, the money that will be used to buy the bonds *did not exist.* The new money comes into existence at the time the Fed's balance sheet is changed to show these transactions. That's right, they just change the numbers on their balance sheet!

To get a clearer picture of this, imagine that you want to buy a car for $30,000 but you only have $20,000 in your checking account. If you could legally "print" new money like the Fed, you could go into your online bank account and modify your account balance by simply changing the number 20,000 to the number 30,000. Now you can buy the car because you have effectively "printed" an extra $10,000 that didn't exist before, increasing your own money supply by 50 percent!

If increasing one's personal money supply by 50 percent by simply tweaking some electronic numbers seems like an impossible fantasy, consider that the Federal Reserve's bond-buying program (called quantitative easing or QE) has increased the U.S. money supply by *more than 400 percent* since 2008—and they are not even close to stopping.

To provide a certain level of accountability, every new money-printing transaction requires a real government bond to be purchased and held by the Federal Reserve, and every introduction of new money into the system must be recorded on the Fed's balance sheet. Unlike the debt ceiling, there is no legal limit to how much money the Fed can print.

Some people don't even call it money printing, but how else could they buy all these bonds? The Fed cannot tax, so money printing is all they can do.

This process does not involve the physical printing of any actual currency. That task belongs to the Treasury Department, as needed. But all funds entered into the Fed's electronic balance sheet and then transferred to other bank accounts are fully redeemable at any time for paper and printed currency.

It's real money.

How Does Money Printing Cause Inflation?

Money printing adds real money to the monetary base, and over time that additional money causes inflation. To see how, let's now look at where the newly printed money goes next.

The new money (born on the Fed's balance sheet simply by changing some numbers) is transferred from the Fed's bank account to the bank accounts of the people who sold the bonds to the Fed. Now the Fed has the bonds and the bond sellers have the new money. The new money may sit in the bond sellers' bank accounts for a while, but *all of this new money now belongs to the bond sellers*. It's their money and they can do with it as they please, any time they please.

This is an important point that many experts seem to miss. The newly printed money does not belong to the Fed or to the banks; it belongs to whoever sold the bonds to the Fed. And like most people, the people who now have the money are not that interested in letting 100 percent of it just sit in their bank accounts for all of eternity. Over time, they will spend some of it.

They often use some of the money to buy stocks, which works directly to boost the stock market and indirectly stimulates the overall economy when rising stock prices generally encourage consumers to spend more. They may also use their new funds to pay bills, expand businesses, or buy a new yacht or sports car. Whatever they chose to spend it on, the point is that the money does not just sit idly in banks, locked up forever. The new money eventually gets spent.

Half of the bonds that the Fed is currently purchasing are mortgage bonds and therefore the money goes to new home purchases and refinancing. That puts money in people's pockets and they do eventually spend it.

Even if they choose to leave all their money in the bank forever, in time, the bank eventually lends most of it out. After all, that's how banks make a profit. So the idea that some people have that the money from QE is not really in the economy is ridiculous.

This is key to understanding the link between money printing and inflation. By creating money that did not exist before and using it to buy bonds from a handful of big investors, the new money is now in the hands of people who will spend or invest it. Therefore, when the Fed prints money, it goes into the economy. Every bit of that money is available to be spent at any time. And, over time, it does get spent, so it is clearly a part of our money supply.

Okay, so it's real money and it's part of the real money supply. So how will we get inflation?

When there is a massive increase in the money supply, the people who received the new money inevitably go shopping (for stocks, real estate, etc.), *pushing up demand* for whatever they are buying. This increase in demand is what makes money printing a shot in the arm for the falling bubbles (stocks, real estate, etc.), which is why the Fed is doing the money printing in the first place.

But here's the catch. The increase in demand created by the money printing is what eventually causes the price of goods and services to rise, a.k.a. *inflation.* For a variety of reasons, inflation does not happen as soon as the new money is printed, but in time inflation does occur. Prices do eventually rise because demand for goods and services goes up before producers can increase supply.

Currently, inflation is not rising much because sellers have not started to raise their prices yet. Later in this chapter, we will tell you more about why inflation hasn't yet occurred, when it will likely happen, and how it will impact the economy. For now, our point is this: *money printing puts new money into the economy, new money in the hands of buyers pushes up demand, and rising demand eventually causes inflation.*

The money that went to the people who sold the bonds to the Fed will eventually get spent. In fact, some of it has already been spent. Where do you think most of the big stock rally came from?

It is almost silly to think that we can print massive amounts of new money to be spent on stocks and other purchases to boost the economy, and to also believe that the additional spending won't eventually push up demand and cause future inflation. It will. Significant inflation hasn't started yet, for reasons we will explain shortly, but don't confuse the lack of inflation now with proof that we won't have inflation later.

Not only will we have significant inflation later, so will many other countries that are also printing money to boost their own vulnerable bubble economies.

Inflation Means Your Dollar Buys Less

Based on the law of supply and demand, when the supply of a commodity goes up without an equal rise in demand, the value of that commodity goes down. In this case, the commodity is the dollar. The supply has gone up due to massive money printing; therefore, eventually the value of the dollar will go down, meaning the dollar will buy less than it used to. This is inflation.

Inflation erodes the buying power of your money. For example, if inflation is 10 percent, then a box of cereal that cost you $4 last year would sell for $4.40 this year, up 10 percent from the year before. The demand for cereal has not gone up and the supply of cereal has not gone down; the cereal just costs more because your dollar buys less.

As someone once said, "In inflation, everything gets more valuable—except money."

Actually, nothing gets more valuable, everything just costs more because *the buying power of the dollar goes down*.

Central Banks Gone Wild: The World Is Printing Money

To keep interest rates low, boost investor confidence, support stock and bond markets, and stimulate their economies, governments around the world have opened the floodgates of money printing.

In addition to the $75 billion per month the United States now prints (as of late 2013), which has increased our monetary base by more than 400 percent since 2008, Europe has increased its money supply by more than 200 percent to support its economy and financial systems. This has also taken pressure off the U.S. financial markets as well and helped pave the way for the U.S. stock market rally in 2013.

Not to be left out of the party, England has also continued to print, increasing its money supply by 343 percent since the global financial crisis of 2008.

Meanwhile, China's massive government-controlled banking machine also continues to stimulate its economy with a whopping 500 percent increase in its money supply (see Figure 5.1).

And Japan, with an economy only about a third the size of the United States, is now printing an astonishing $75 billion per month. To put that into perspective, it would be the equivalent of the United States printing $200 billion per month—more than twice our current rate, which is already huge.

All this adds up to a truly enormous amount of worldwide money printing.

Interestingly, the earlier discussions about an "exit strategy" for the Fed to pull back some of the new money out of the system, which was quite in vogue a few years ago, have been *completely* forgotten. In fact, the only talk now is about maybe decreasing the rate at which we increase the money supply, much like the discussion about the national debt is only about slowing the rate of increasing it, with no talk of paying it off.

All of this money printing here and around the world has helped boost economies and especially financial markets. It may not appear like much of a boost because world economic growth has been so slow. But it is working, especially on stock markets. Bond markets, too, are being supported by massive money printing that in the shorter term keeps interest rates very low. Without this massive money printing and low interest rates, financial markets could melt down.

In the case of Europe, it is easy to see that bond yields on Spanish and Italian debt would have quickly spiraled out of control without massive intervention by the European Central Bank to keep them lower. Out-of-control interest rates in such large countries as Spain and Italy would rattle financial markets around the

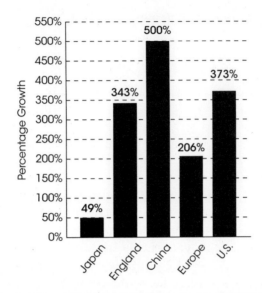

Figure 5.1   Around the World, Central Banks Are Printing Money

In response to the 2008 financial crisis, central banks around the world, not just the U.S. Federal Reserve, have responded by printing money as shown by central banks' balance sheet growth from 2008 to 2013. Continued massive money printing is supporting the world's bubble economy. *Source:* Bloomberg.

world, taking the European, U.S., and Japanese financial markets down with them. So the money printing madness may not look like it's helping because European, U.S., and Japanese economic growth is so slow, but it is most certainly helping keep the financial markets from deteriorating dramatically, which would have a severe negative impact on all of those economies.

But, of course, massive money printing, while supportive in the short term, is simply another bubble, not a solution. Again, if we didn't have a U.S. bubble economy and a world bubble economy, so much massive stimulus could potentially get us back on track. In our current economic situation, however, the only thing gained from all this money printing around the world is a short-term delay in the fall of the bubbles. Money printing is *pure bubble maintenance*; it is not creating real and sustainable economic growth.

Not only is it failing to bring us the real solutions we need, massive money printing will eventually help pop the very bubbles it is now working to maintain.

Even the Fed's Own Research Shows that Money Printing Causes Inflation

Many otherwise smart people seem to be aware that there is a *direct causal relationship* between money printing and future inflation— so direct that future inflation occurs at about the same rate as the money supply is increased. So, if we increase the money supply by X percent, we will eventually get about X percent inflation.

Don't believe it? Even the Federal Reserve's own research shows a strong correlation between money printing and inflation. In a detailed article published in the Federal Reserve Bank of Minneapolis *Quarterly Review* titled "Some Monetary Facts," economists George T. McCandless Jr., and Warren E. Weber analyzed inflation in 21 countries over three decades. Drawing on data provided by the International Monetary Fund, the Fed researchers found that inflation consistently follows the expansion of the money supply. And it does so in almost a one-to-one correlation, regardless of what measure of the money supply was used (see Table 5.1).

In case you are thinking that one single study doesn't prove a link between money printing and inflation, this same Fed paper also cites many other studies showing similar results in more than 100 countries over more than 40 years (see Table 5.2). Such extensive research over nearly half a century confirms that money printing does indeed lead to inflation. The idea that we can increase the money supply by more than 400 percent and somehow magically avoid future inflation is pure fantasy.

Table 5.1   Correlation Coefficients for Money Supply Growth and Inflation

21 OECD countries, including the United States, Japan, Israel, Canada, Australia, and many Europe countries (from 1960 to 1990)	M0	M1	M2
	0.894	0.940	0.958

Inflation is defined as changes in a measure of consumer prices.
M0 is defined as currency plus bank reserves.
Source of basic data: International Monetary Fund.

In an extensive review of monetary expansion and inflation in 21 countries from 1960 to 1990, Fed researchers George McCandless and Warren Weber found that, every measure of the money supply, including M0, M1, and M2, shows a near 1.0 correlation between money printing and future inflation.

Source: Federal Reserve Bank of Minneapolis Quarterly Review, 1995.

Table 5.2 Many Studies Confirm the High Correlation between Money Growth and Inflation

Author (and year published)	Study Characteristics			Time Series	
	Money	Inflation	Countries	Time Period	Finding
Vogel (1974)	Currency + demand deposits	Consumer prices	16 Latin American countries	1950–1969	Proportionate changes in inflation rate within two years of changes in money growth
Lucas (1980)	M1	Consumer prices	United States	1955–1975	Strong positive correlation: Coefficient closer to one the more filter stresses low frequencies
Dwyer and Hafer (1988)	NA	GDP deflator	62 countries	1979–1984	Strong positive correlation
Barro (1990)	Hand-to-hand currency	Consumer prices	83 countries	1950–1987	Strong positive association
Pakko (1994)	Currency + bank deposits	Consumer prices	13 former Soviet republics	1992 and 1993	Positive relationship
Poole (1994)	Broad money	NA	All countries in World Bank tables	1970–1980 and 1980–1991	Strong positive correlation
Rolnick and Weber	Various	Various	9 countries	Various	Strong positive correlation for fiat money regimes

NA = not available.

In the same study that provided the previous table, the researchers also cite seven additional studies analyzing data from more than 100 countries from 1950 to 1991 confirm the Fed's assertion that there is a strong correlation between money printing and inflation.

Source: Federal Reserve of Minneapolis.

Where Is Inflation Hiding?

Okay, now that you have some background on inflation and what causes it, let's get back to that important question we know you must be asking: *If massive money printing causes high inflation, why is U.S. inflation still so low?*

Could it be that the Fed has discovered the economic version of the Fountain of Youth—an endless flow of bubble support with no negative side effects? Has the Fed found a magical way around the law of supply and demand, ending the direct relationship between money printing and future inflation, even though their own research says otherwise?

A lot of people want to believe that fantasy, and one of the key justifications they rely on is the fact that inflation is still very low. Despite more money printing in the past five years than in all of U.S. history, there just isn't much inflation.

What's going on? Where is inflation hiding?

There are three key reasons why the government's inflation numbers are still low—at least, for now:

1. "Lag factors" delay the onset of inflation.
2. Government statistics underreport true inflation.
3. Strong motivation to maintain the bubble economy will delay most inflation until after the Market Cliff.

1. "Lag Factors" Delay the Onset of Inflation

Inflation doesn't immediately occur after an increase in the money supply, not even after very large increases in the money supply, because of what economists call *lag factors*. Typically, lag factors create a delay of about 18 to 24 months between money printing and inflation. In fact, Ben Bernanke, along with several other authors (Laubach, Mishkin, and Posen), wrote a paper in 1999 that examined past periods of inflation and determined that about a two-year lag was the most common estimate among the research they examined.

But the lag time between money printing and the onset of inflation can be much greater than two years, depending on the circumstances.

In Argentina, for example, which has a long history of irresponsibly devaluing its currency, the lag factor is essentially nonexistent. Worse than that, at times it has been negative. That is, not only does money printing lead to immediate price increases, but businesses will often raise prices even *before* the government prints more money in order to gain a competitive edge. In communities where inflation is common and accepted, this kind of practice isn't difficult to get away with.

In a stronger, more developed economy, inflation will have a longer delay due to lag factors. The economy is solid and the government has a better reputation, so businesses and individuals are less inclined to raise prices. In these situations inflation often takes more than two years to kick in after the government increases the money supply.

In the case of the United States, this is a country that has never seen inflation get out of control. Even the last period of significant inflation was a generation ago, before most of today's working adults had entered the workforce. Inflation in the 1970s and early 1980s was relatively minor.

Simply put, the kind of monetary recklessness we're seeing from the Fed right now is unprecedented and is completely out of character given our history. So it's not surprising that businesses are not raising prices immediately. They aren't that worried about inflation. This is a big reason that it will take longer for inflation to begin in the United States than in a weaker economy. In addition, there is also a strong psychological motivation to maintain the bubble economy as long as possible, which we will explain shortly.

It's a Quick Short-Term Gain for Big, Long Pain.

Whatever the length of the delay between money printing and inflation, the positive impacts of increasing the money supply occur much more quickly than the negative impact of inflation.

For example, during and after World War I, when Germany wanted to raise money without raising taxes, the government decided to print more money. Lots of it. Some people may remember the German Weimar Republic for its pictures of wheelbarrows of paper money. What few people remember is that when Germany began to rapidly expand its money supply, it experienced very rapid economic growth and unemployment of less than 1 percent.

Of course, the positive impacts of printing lots of money also came at a heavy future price: the worst hyperinflation the industrial world had ever seen. By late 1923, it took 42 billion German marks to buy just one U.S. cent. And it took 726 billion marks to buy something that once cost just one mark four years before.

So the joys of printing money come quickly, while the pain comes later. There is much short-term gain, but also lots and lots and lots of long-term pain. And, needless to say, it is very hard to control inflation once it gets going because getting rid of inflation causes even more economic pain.

"The Fool in the Shower"

Ignoring the lag factors and assuming there will never be any inflation is dangerous. The easiest way to understand this is the "fool in the shower" analogy first used by Nobel Prize–winning economist Milton Friedman.

The fool in the shower turns on the hot water and, at first, all he gets is very cold water. So he turns the knob higher to get some hot water, and still nothing. So he keeps turning it up more and more, rather than waiting for the hot water to arrive. Then, all of a sudden, the hot water hits and scalds him.

That's what will happen with future inflation and the current lag factors. We don't get inflation immediately, so we see no harm in "turning up the hot water" with massive money printing that increases the money supply. All we see are the short-term benefits and we want more of those, so we keep turning up the money printing without getting burnt.

In fact, as we have said before, the reason inflation could be very high in the future is not because of the money we have already printed, but, more important, because of the even more massive money printing we will do in the future.

Money printing will go from being somewhat discretionary to being mandatory due to the need for increasing support of financial markets here and abroad. Since we are simply trying to support falling bubbles in housing, stocks, private credit, and consumer spending, there will be a continuing need to keep printing more money; otherwise, the bubbles will again fall. Not that the money we have already printed won't create inflation—it will. But the greatest contributor to future inflation will be *future* money printing.

Like the fool in the shower, we will keep cranking up the hot water until we suddenly get burned. As soon as inflation starts to kick in more and more inflation will occur (because more and more sellers will want to raise prices, too).

So far, the water in our shower is still not hot (meaning inflation is still low), but the shower water may already be warmer than we realize because government statistics are not entirely reliable.

2. Government Statistics Underreport Inflation

The Consumer Price Index (CPI), the government's official measure of inflation, put inflation around 2 percent for most of 2013. But it's worth noting that the methods for calculating CPI have not always been the same, and the adjustments made over the past 30 years or so have uniformly pushed the official inflation figure down.

We are not the only ones who think this way. A popular web site called www.shadowstats.com attempts to calculate inflation as it was years ago. If the CPI were calculated by 1990 standards, the figure would be around 5 percent today. If it were calculated the way it was calculated in 1980s, it would be around 9 percent.

It's not clear why the methodology for calculating inflation should have changed from its earlier standard—that is, unless you understand that it is very much in the government's interest to keep reported inflation low. That's true in any environment, but it's especially true in a bubble economy and even more so in a bubble economy supported by massive money printing.

Whatever the government may report, many Americans are feeling the effects of rising expenses, even if their incomes remain flat. A June 2013 report from Quicken showed that Americans saw a big increase in utility expenses, day care expenses, school tuition, and health care costs—increases that were certainly greater than the official 2 percent CPI. Maybe the full extent of these rising expenses aren't showing up in the official basket of goods and services used to calculate CPI, but they are certainly showing up in the lives of Americans, taking their toll on checking account balances throughout the country.

3. Strong Motivation to Maintain the Bubble Economy Will Delay Most Inflation Until after the Market Cliff

In order for money printing to cause inflation, the extra printed money has to push up demand, and then sellers have to *decide* to raise their prices.

Think about it: the government can print all the money they want, and if no one chooses to raise prices, then we will never have inflation, right? No one *forces* sellers to do this, and if they don't want to do it right away, they won't, so inflation won't occur immediately.

Why would sellers of goods and services hold back on raising prices when demand rises? They would hold back on raising prices if they thought it might hurt their business by scaring away potential customers or drive them to buy from the competition. No seller wants to chase off buyers and will raise prices only when they think they can get away with it without losing customers. So under normal conditions, sellers don't always immediately raise prices as soon as demand rises.

However, in a bubble economy that has stopped rising and is threatening to fall, sellers—like everyone else—want to maintain the bubble economy for as long as possible. We all benefit from the bubble economy, and we are all hurt when it begins to fall. Remember 2008? Some people are still out of work, and many are still hurting financially.

There is a general unspoken agreement among not only sellers but just about all of us to not do anything to rock the boat and blow up the bubble economy that we all benefit from. That means sellers have a deep and mostly unconscious motivation to not raise prices because they want to the bubble economy to last.

If this were a strong and rising bubble economy, no seller would worry at all about the effects of price increases. Rising demand would be immediately met with price increases because that is what the market could easily handle.

But in a falling bubble economy that has not fully rebounded since the 2008 financial crisis, no one is feeling as secure as they did in the rising bubble economy of years ago. Therefore, as a group, the whole culture is behaving somewhat differently than before. And this includes sellers of goods and services: they want to play it safe so we can keep the bubbles going. Everyone has a lot to lose.

However, once we go over the Market Cliff (see Chapter 4), sellers—like everyone else—will be in a much different frame of mind. When stocks and bonds have crashed and real estate is falling, sellers are going to be more than willing to start pushing up their prices because the goal of maintaining the bubbles will be replaced by the goal of not losing your own shirt. Once a few sellers raise their prices, others will follow, and soon prices will go up across the board.

The bad economy will not save us from inflation. In the late 1970s and early 1980s in the United States, even in a bad economy, inflation did rise to 14 percent.

The Arguments against Future Inflation Simply Don't Hold Up

None of the three delaying factors (explained in the preceding section) that are keeping inflation low for now will stop future inflation from rising. Like the law of gravity, there is no escaping the law of supply and demand. A massive increase in the supply of any commodity eventually creates lower value, even when that commodity is U.S. dollars. Because of the strength and reputation of the U.S. government and because everyone wants to keep the bubbles going, the dollar can defy this law for a while, but not forever. Money printing eventually does cause future inflation, just as the Fed's own research shows.

But many people don't (can't let themselves) believe that the mighty U.S. dollar could ever significantly lose value. People who believe that we can magically escape the law of supply and demand, and permanently avoid inflation despite continued massive money printing, are relying on arguments that simply do not hold up.

They challenge the idea that big money printing cause big inflation by posing one or more of the following inflation-denying questions:

- Aren't banks locking the printed money in excess reserves?
- Won't falling asset prices prevent inflation?
- Won't future debt write-offs and bankruptcies prevent inflation?
- What if the Fed does "just the right amount" of money printing to boost the economy but avoid future inflation?

Aren't Banks "Locking Up" the Printed Money in Excess Reserves?

Some people argue that the Fed's money printing won't lead to inflation because banks have the money "locked up" in excess reserves. This is simply false. When the Fed buys bonds, the newly created money goes directly into the sellers' bank accounts. The money is theirs to do with as they please: to buy stocks, a new house, a long vacation, or a private island. The money belongs to the bond sellers, not to the banks! So the idea that the bank can stop this money from being spent over time is completely wrong.

But aren't banks keeping increasing amounts of excess reserves?

Yes, but excess reserves are just reserves banks hold beyond what is legally required. For every dollar on deposit at a bank, the bank must keep a certain percentage—not more than 10 percent, and sometimes as low as *zero* percent—in reserve rather than lend it out. When the bank holds more than is legally required in reserve, it is called *excess reserves.*

It's true that banks today are holding more excess reserves than ever before in history due to massive money printing, but that doesn't mean the money isn't in circulation. Look at it this way: Has a bank ever told you that you couldn't withdraw money from your checking account because they had to keep it in reserves or excess reserves? Of course not! All that money is available to be spent at any time, so the amount that a bank keeps in excess reserves does not impact potential spending of the money.

The idea behind the argument is that as long as money is kept in excess reserves, rather than being lent out, we won't see a big expansion in the broader measures of the money supply and therefore won't see inflation. But, in fact, even when banks hold excess reserves, the money is in circulation. Holding excess reserves means that the multiplier effect from lending the money out is less, which can postpone the onset of inflation (i.e., increase the lag factor). But it still doesn't prevent inflation.

We can easily see that the expansion of the money supply has already goes beyond just the monetary base and into the economy.

Economists define the country's money supply in different ways. One definition, called M1, focuses on money's role as an exchange medium for trade. Buyers use coins, paper currency, checks, or debit cards to pay for goods and services. All of these forms of payment are counted as part of M1. However, M1 does not include financial assets such as savings accounts. Economists use M1 to quantify the amount of money in circulation.

As Figure 5.2 shows, M1 has roughly doubled since 2008. So, clearly, the money that the Fed has printed since 2008 is in use in the economy, not just locked up in banks.

The printed money is being spent, but it is not being lent out by banks. That limits the multiplier effect, but it does not stop inflation. *Bank lending does not cause inflation*—otherwise, we would have had high inflation in the mid-2000s when lending was high. Bank lending may speed up inflation once it begins, but it does not cause inflation. *Inflation is caused by money printing.*

Won't Falling Asset Prices Prevent Inflation?

No. Even with inflation, some asset values can fall. Falling prices, now and in the future, do not prove that we don't have or can't eventually have inflation. Many asset values can fall in real dollars (adjusted for inflation) due to changes in supply and demand, even if inflation rises.

This will certainly be true when the bubbles pop. For example, real estate values will fall even though inflation will rise. When the real estate bubble pops, there will be fewer buyers (falling demand) and more sellers (rising supply). That will push real estate values down.

In nominal dollars, prices may rise, but in real dollars they will fall. If the rise in the nominal price is less than the rise of the inflation rate, then real value is falling.

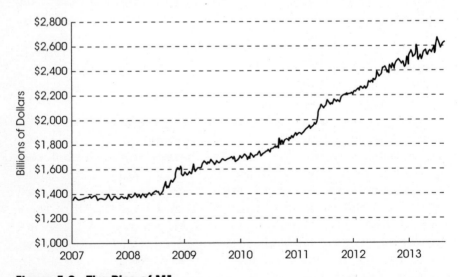

Figure 5.2   The Rise of M1
The Fed's money printing has not just affected the monetary base. M1 has risen dramatically since 2008, which means that money is in use in the economy
Source: St. Louis Federal Reserve.

The fact that we now see or will in the future see some falling asset prices does not at all mean that there is not or will not be inflation. We never call rising home and stock prices "inflation," we call it a good investment. Likewise, falling home and stock prices are not deflation, they are falling asset values due to falling demand.

Won't Future Debt Write-Offs and Bankruptcies Prevent Inflation?

No. The fact that debts cannot be repaid does not mean that the resulting write-offs and bankruptcies will effectively decrease the money supply and therefore prevent inflation.

The idea that money is created as debt, and when debt is destroyed so is the money, is simply wrong. If you lend me $20 for lunch and I never repay you, that $20 is still out there in the money supply, moving from you to me to the restaurant to the wholesale food distributor, and so on. It is still in circulation. Destroying my debt to you does not destroy the money itself.

If destroying the debt really did lower inflation, then the increase in debt in the housing boom would have increased inflation. Didn't happen.

"I told you the Fed should have tightened."

What If the Fed Does "Just the Right Amount" of Money Printing to Boost the Economy but Avoid Future Inflation?

We call this the Goldilocks argument. If the Fed can do "just the right amount" of money printing—not too much and not too little, just the *perfect* amount—then maybe they can boost growth and avoid inflation. Unfortunately, like Goldilocks, this argument is pure fiction.

The Fed knows full well from its own research (shown earlier in Tables 5.1 and 5.2) that money printing causes future inflation, but they hope that won't happen this time.

The Fed hopes that all the money printing will bring us enough economic growth so that they can begin to cut back on future money printing before inflation begins. Then, if economic growth will accelerate even more, the federal government can also reduce its borrowing and the Fed can end the money printing altogether.

Their "hopes" don't end there. If economic growth accelerates even more, the Fed hopes that the booming economy would make it possible for the Fed to, not just stop, but to actually *undo* the past money printing—what they call their "exit plan." If we had a booming economy, the Fed could take the bonds it bought with the previous printed money and put those bonds up for sale. When the buyers give their money to the Fed for the bonds, the Fed could then remove this money from its balance sheet, effectively "unprinting" the money.

If we had a booming economy, the Fed could sell off the bonds it bought in QE 1–3 and eventually eliminate that money from the money supply before significant inflation begins.

This is the ultimate Fed fantasy: do "just the right amount" of money printing to boom the economy and then be able to undo the past money printing before significant future inflation begins.

So far, it's not working and there is no evidence that it will ever work. On the contrary, we do not have a booming economy and the current lukewarm "recovery" is entirely fake (see Chapter 1), so these hopes are nothing more than pipe dreams. There are no buyers for the Fed's bonds at super low interest rates, and without a booming economy there will never be buyers in the future. Without future buyers, the money printing cannot be reversed. And without a strong economic recovery, the Fed's bubble-maintaining money printing must continue.

The Fed's Tiny "Tapering" at the End of 2013 Was Just for Show

In December 2013, the Federal Reserve cut their money printing operations from $85 billion to $75 billion per month. We believe the Fed did this for two reasons.

First, the Fed needed to show that they are being "responsible" with money printing and not going too wild for too long. By tapering their money printing a bit, they hope to show off their prudent restraint. However, this is largely just for show because cutting back from $85 billion to $75 billion per month is no more than a tiny trim.

To put this in perspective, instead of printing $1.02 trillion per year, this puts money printing at a staggering *$900 billion per year.* By comparison, the entire U.S. money supply was only $800 billion in 2007, and now we are printing more than that *every year.* So this isn't much of a cut. It's sort of like bragging that instead of consuming 100 gallons of gas per hour, your speedboat now burns through "only" 90 gallons of gas per hour. It's hardly much of a reduction.

The second reason the Fed cut its money printing slightly was to indicate that they believe the economy is beginning to improve. Again, this is mostly for show. If they really thought the economy was improving, they would have been willing to cut much more.

The bottom line, in our view, is that the Fed's December 2013 taper was too tiny to amount to much. It certainly will not save us from high future inflation, and it does not at all indicate that the economy is doing better.

They could taper again or even stop temporarily, but long term they will have to bring it back in order to keep the bubble economy going. Any tapering or temporary pause will only be done to make the insane seem sane.

Why Can't the Fed Just Undo All the Past Money Printing Now, before Big Inflation Begins?

Theoretically, they could. But in practice, they can't and they won't.

The problem is that this recovery is 100 percent fake and the economy is hardly booming now and has little chance of booming anytime soon because the fundamental drivers of real economic growth are not there; instead, all we have is massive temporary stimulus.

The fake recovery means that the Fed has two big roadblocks to being able to "unprint" or do reverse QE. The first problem is pretty straightforward: in the current economy, there are few buyers for these bonds at super-low interest rates.

Second, and even more important, the Fed printed this money for a reason—to stimulate the economy and the stock market. To whatever extent the Fed may be able to pull some of the money back out of the economy (either by selling some bonds or letting them expire), it can only do so at the risk of losing the beneficial short-term effects that the money printing created.

That is where the real danger lies. Once the Fed opens the money printing spigot, it is very difficult to turn it off. Here are some of the highlights of what would happen if the Fed shut off the bubble-supporting flow of massive money printing today:

- *Interest rates would jump.* Massive money printing keeps interest rates low. Stop the money printing and interest rates would rise and bond prices would fall dramatically. That would scare away bond buyers. Fewer bond buyers would mean the federal government could not sell its debt or rollover past debt at low interest rates.
- *Stocks would fall.* Massive money printing boosts the stock market. Take it away and in time the stock market will cool off. High interest rates would also be a big negative for stocks. The stock bubble would pop.
- *Consumer spending would decline.* Massive money printing boosts the stock market and that boosts general consumption. The top 20 percent of consumers account for 40 percent of spending, so keeping them excited about spending money with a hot stock market helps the economy. A falling stock market would have the opposite effect. Consumer spending would dry up and the bubble economy would pop.
- *Real estate would fall.* Half of the Fed's money printing goes to purchase mortgage bonds. That encourages home buying and lots of economic activity and job growth related to it. Some of that is also used to refinance existing mortgage at lower interest rates, which gives consumers more money to spend. Stop the money printing and not only will these benefits end but mortgage interest rates will spike and the real estate bubble would pop.

If the Fed were to stop the money printing, we would suddenly be left without the bubble-supporting stimulus that is keeping the current economy going. If we have high unemployment now, just imagine where we would be without the economic benefits of money printing. With rising unemployment and rising interest rates, all the bubbles (stocks, real estate, consumer spending, private debt, government debt, and the dollar) would pop, and the economy would decline even further.

So, clearly, they cannot stop printing money, although they may taper or even stop temporarily. The negative consequences would just be too great. Not only will the Fed not be able to entirely stop anytime soon, they will surely have to print *even more* in the future. Ongoing bubble maintenance is going to take ongoing money printing, and that will only cause even more inflation in the future.

There is really no such thing as doing "just the right amount" of money printing, although the reason why is very hard to face:

Without real productivity growth, we cannot stimulate our way out of the falling multibubble economy.

Without a booming economy, money printing cannot be reversed and it cannot even be stopped; therefore, just like the Fed's own research has told us, big money printing will bring us big inflation.

Size Matters

If the Fed had increased the money supply by, say, 10, 20, or even 30 percent, there would be little reason for concern. But as you can see in Figure 5.3, the money supply has quintrupled since late 2008, and as of this writing in January 2014 it is still growing.

This is a stunningly large increase, and its eventual consequences will be equally enormous. Nothing like this has ever been attempted before in the United States, and certainly not in our recent history. Although many people recognize we are printing more money, few people talk about the sheer magnitude of this increase.

Again, *size matters*. A small increase in the money supply that roughly tracks or slightly exceeds the growth rate of the economy would not increase inflation that much. But massive increases in the money supply that dramatically outstrip the growth of GDP most definitely will bring equally high inflation.

This Is Not a Plan, It's a Panic!

If the Fed knows that money printing will cause future inflation proportional to the amount of money printing, why do they do it?

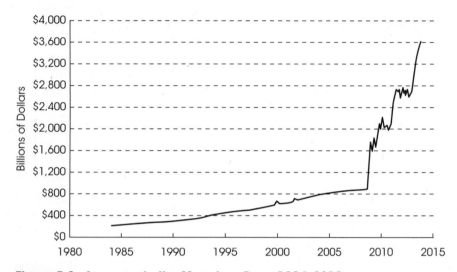

Figure 5.3   Increase in the Monetary Base 1984–2013
Our money supply has increased massively with the Fed's recent money-printing operations—the fuel for the fires of inflation.
Source: St. Louis Federal Reserve.

Because they were in a panic. The Fed initially started money printing after the 2008 financial crisis because if they didn't, the financial crisis would have melted down the economy and financial system within weeks, maybe even days. They had to do something! In early 2009, the Fed had to do whatever it could to keep the bubble economy from collapsing. Massive money printing kept interest rates low. Without low interest rates, the financial crisis would have completely popped the then-falling stock and real estate bubbles, and eventually would have popped the rest of the bubble economy as well.

Now that the Fed has started massive money printing, they are finding it very hard to stop. That's because bubble maintenance takes endless stimulus. Remove the stimulus and the bubbles will start to fall again.

Few people, including the Fed, are willing to see the bubble burst. Instead, they think—hope, really, more than think—that money printing will save us. In the short term, it's sort of working. The economy may not be booming, but neither are we in a deep recession. Because of money printing, stock prices are certainly back up, and that supports more home buying and consumer spending in general. Because of money printing, money is not as scarce; therefore, interest rates are still quite low. That's good for the general economy, too. Low interest rates are also good for lots of government borrowing, which helps us pay our bills without having to tighten our belts.

So, overall, while not successful in creating a booming economic recovery, money printing has done its primary job of maintaining the bubbles, which feels a whole lot better (at least in the short term) than not maintaining the bubbles.

But in the longer term, money printing will cause rising inflation and rising interest rates and that will do just the opposite. At that point, all the short-term benefits will evaporate and our long-term troubles will begin when the bubbles pop.

The Real Problem with Rising Future Inflation: High Interest Rates

At first look, inflation might not seem so bad. After all, if the cost of everything goes up and if your income goes up, too (because it is also part of the cost of everything going up), then there really is no net change to your bottom line. You just get paid more dollars and you spend more dollars. As long as these increases are more or less consistent across the board, nothing has really changed, right?

That would be true if it weren't for two big problems:

1. The first problem is that your income will very likely not rise as fast as inflation. Everything will cost more, but your income may not go up at the same rate. As one of our publishing friends said, "I know that there is inflation, it's just not in my salary!" That will be an increasing problem for consumers going forward.
2. The second problem will be even worse than the first problem: *Rising inflation eventually causes rising interest rates.*

But Doesn't the Fed Control Interest Rates?

Yes, but only to a point. The Fed controls the Fed money-lending rate, and they also affect interest rates through their open market operations. Specifically, money printing lowers interest rates by making money more available.

But the Fed does not have complete control over interest rates, especially in an inflationary environment. When inflation goes up, interest rates eventually have to rise *even higher* than the inflation rate—otherwise, lenders would lose money on every loan. Interest rates always have to climb higher than the inflation rate to compensate for the declining buying power of the dollar. If not, no one would be willing to lend money. Lenders have to be compensated for the future loss to inflation, plus a bit more so they can make a profit on the loan.

For example, if the inflation rate is, say, 5 percent, a lender would have to charge 6 percent annual interest just to earn 1 percent profit on the loan. In time, interest rates always rise higher than the inflation rate.

High Interest Rates Will Pop the Bubbles

Rising interest rates tend to have an overall chilling effect on any economy, even a nonbubble economy, because it slows lending and that slows business expansion, including buying inventory, hiring employees, etc. Rising interest rates are also not good for the stock market, as company earnings are negatively affected. Rising interest rates mean rising mortgage interest rates, which tend to push down demand for real estate as a greater percentage of one's monthly payment must go toward interest. And, of course, the bond market is especially vulnerable to even small interest rate increases. We saw an early preview of this in 2013 when bond prices declined due to a small uptick in interest rates.

If rising interest rates can have a chilling effect on a nonbubble economy, they are pure poison to a falling multibubble economy. Imagine the bond and stock markets, after the Market Cliff, facing rising interest rates. What kind of recovery can happen under such conditions?

Instead of recovery, rising inflation will drive interest rates higher and higher. High interest rates, in turn, will push asset values even lower, including stocks, bonds, and real estate.

In the past, ultra-low interest rates helped drive up the rising multibubble economy. In the future, as inflation rises and pushes up interest rates, just the opposite will be true: high interest rates will help drive down the economy. High interest rates will pop what is left of the first four partially popped bubbles (stocks, real estate, private debt, and consumer spending) and will help fully burst the last two—the dollar and the government debt bubbles—bringing on the global Aftershock (see Chapter 6 for details).

High Interest Rates Will Pop What's Left of the Real Estate Bubble

As interest rates rise, mortgages will become more expensive, discouraging home buyers. Declining demand will keep home values from rising as everyone would like. Instead, unsold inventory will rise, and home prices will fall further (falling demand plus rising supply equals falling prices).

Even a relatively small rise in interest rates can have dire consequences for real estate values. Figure 5.4 shows just how much home prices have to go down to maintain the same mortgage

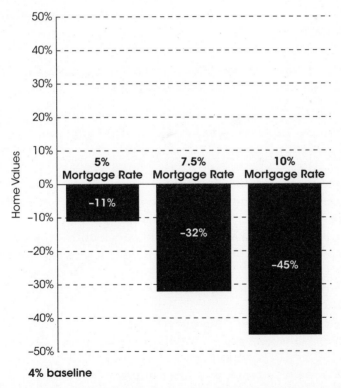

4% baseline

Figure 5.4   Decrease in Home Values When Mortgage Rates Increase
The chart assumes the current mortgage rate is 4 percent. An increase to 5 percent would force home prices down 11 percent to maintain the same monthly payment.
Source: Aftershock Publishing.

payment, if mortgage rates increase even modestly from 4 percent. Remember when mortgage rates were more than 15 percent in the early 1980s? By comparison, a mortgage rate of 7.5 percent is pretty reasonable, but it would mean that home prices would have to decrease by 32 percent.

Even worse, as interest rates continue to rise (in part due to rising inflation), the value of mortgage bonds will fall drastically. That means there won't be much mortgage money to lend, even if home buyers wanted to borrow it at the high rate. So rising inflation and rising interest rates will help further pop the real estate bubble. Increasingly, lenders won't grant mortgages at fixed rates. They will only lend if the interest rate adjusts with inflation. That will make it very difficult for most home buyers to borrow money to buy a house. As mentioned earlier in the book, the falling real estate bubble negatively impacts the wider economy in many, many ways.

High Interest Rates Will Pop What's Left of the Stock Market, Private Debt, and Consumer Spending Bubbles

Rising interest rates are generally bad for businesses expansion, stock prices, nongovernment borrowing, and consumer spending. The higher that interest rates climb, the more negative their impacts.

In this case, by the time inflation gets high enough to create high interest rates, the stock and bond markets will have already fallen over the Market Cliff (see Chapter 4). Investors, businesses, and consumers will all be in a state of shock and certainly not rushing to spend money they either no longer have or they want to try to protect. The sharp drop in spending will create a spike up in unemployment, which will only make spending fall lower, hurting the economy further.

Moderate inflation and interest rates don't cause immediate, significant damage, but as inflation and interest rates continue to rise, the negative consequences accelerate until no one wants to lend money anymore, or they offer impossible terms.

The Fed will respond with more money printing, but that will just bring more inflation and higher interest rates. The higher interest rates go, the deeper stocks, bonds, and other asset values will fall.

High Interest Rates Will Pop What's Left of the Government Debt Bubble

While some inflation is good for the government because it makes debt repayment cheaper than the dollars originally borrowed, inflation is also bad for the government because it pushes up interest rates. Rising interest rates present a huge burden to the country's biggest borrower, the federal government, which has to keep refinancing its debt over and over again because a lot of its debt is short term.

In a rising interest rate environment, each time the government must refinance its debt, the new debt is subject to higher and higher interest rates, which can get very expensive very quickly. Having to keep refinancing massive debt and also running massive budget deficits will make the federal government—and the massive government debt bubble—acutely vulnerable to massive inflation-generated increases in interest rates (see Chapter 6).

The Fed's Big Blind Spot: They Don't Understand Where Growth Comes From (*Hint:* It Doesn't Come from Rising Bubbles or Massive Money Printing)

The Fed and most of today's economists seem to be, not just bubble blind, but completely in the dark about what drives real economic growth. They not only think that maintaining bubbles is a worthy goal, they also believe that massive money printing will put us back on the road to substantial economic growth. It won't.

The Myth of the Natural Growth Rate

Many Americans seem to have a deep faith that the U.S. economy possesses a reliable "natural" growth rate. This is somehow fundamental to our very existence and will never end. Hence, anytime we deviate from that natural growth rate and go into a recession temporarily, we will also, at some point, usually quickly, automatically return to our natural growth rate. That means that we can count on always having a rebound after every recession or, more to the point, after the recent financial crisis.

This belief is also the basis for Americans deep trust in investing in U.S. stocks, bonds, and real estate. If our economy has a natural growth rate, then stocks, bonds, and real estate all have a natural growth rate, too. This explains the rationale behind buy-and-hold investing: just get in and hang on, and eventually that natural growth rate will kick back in.

We have come to believe in this because we were in a rising bubble economy for so long that we started to believe that endless growth was the norm to which we would always return.

But, in truth, there is no "natural" growth rate that we can always count on to return and pull us through. Something has to actually *cause* a recovery; we don't just get one automatically if we wait long enough, like winter turning into spring. The United States does not have a natural growth rate that is in effect at all times and will always save us. In fact, there never has been a natural growth rate—not for any country, not in the past, and not in the future. All economic growth has to be caused by something; it doesn't just happen automatically. That is why not all countries experience economic growth all the time.

China is a great example. What was China's "natural" growth rate in the 1960s? What was its "natural" growth rate in the 1990s? We all know China's growth rate was much higher in the 1990s than in the 1960s. Hence, there is no "natural" growth rate for China (or for any other country). It varies—quite a bit, actually—depending on governmental and business actions. Growth was higher in the 1990s for China because they had made numerous important changes in the way they conducted business and in the way their government worked. Entrepreneurship was encouraged, free markets were encouraged, and more input from foreign investors and businesses was encouraged. Growth happened for some very good reasons, not because it was automatically coming to them.

This may sound like we are saying "there's no free lunch," and that's true. But it has enormous importance for how many economists are looking at the economy. Many economists are assuming that any downturn in our economy is simply a diversion from our "natural" growth rate. In fact, you will even see that term used in many financial and economic articles. Nobody asks the most basic question: where is that growth coming from? Instead, they simply assume it is *always there* and that our economy will naturally bounce back into its natural growth mode.

Curiously, the economists also don't seem too interested in asking: If there is a natural growth rate that we can always count on to eventually return, why doesn't that happen all over the world, in every country? Why do only we get to have this magical natural growth rate?

There is no "natural" or automatic growth rate, not here in the United States and not anywhere in the world. Wherever and whenever it occurs, real economic growth has to be earned.

So if there is no natural growth rate we can count on, where does real growth come from?

The Trouble Behind the Bubbles: Real Economic Growth Comes from Real Productivity Growth, Not Bubbles

Real (nonbubble) economic growth is driven by two forces: population growth and productivity growth. These two are related to some extent because higher agricultural productivity will lead to a larger population. However, our focus should be on productivity since we are primarily interested in becoming wealthier *per person*, not just having a larger economy with lots and lots of poor people. So, *productivity growth* is the source of economic growth. Hence, economies will grow only when productivity grows. An automatic increase in productivity is not natural or automatic. It has to come from changes in the way we produce goods and services. This involves changes in the way we do business, and that often involves changes in government and changes in technology.

Rather than staying the same or accelerating, productivity growth in this country and in the other major industrialized nations in Europe and in Japan has been slowing dramatically. Productivity growth in the last quarter of the twentieth century was much slower than in the first three quarters. These are long periods of time. That's how real productivity improvement works. It is a very long term process.

By the way, you should almost completely ignore the government "productivity" statistics or "output per man-hour." Not that they are biased or wrong, but they don't give you a true idea of *real* productivity growth. For example, productivity by that measure can be improved enormously by simply stopping all research and development. That is a dumb measure of productivity.

So instead of looking at misleading government figures of output per man-hour (although not intentionally misleading as much as just bad information), let's look at *real* productivity growth over a very long period of time. That's the only way to look at it, since significant productivity growth is a relatively slow process. For example, when we look at the productivity growth of food production in the United States over the longer term, we see that two centuries of advancements have made it possible for the number of people required to grow food to drop from 90 percent of the U.S. population to just 3 percent. Now that's real productivity growth!

Across many sectors, we had that kind of robust productivity growth in the United States for many decades. However, beginning in the 1970s, just before the bubbles started to inflate in the 1980s, overall productivity growth began to slow significantly (see Figure 5.5).

Here is another way to look at productivity. Under normal conditions, income generally goes up when productivity goes up. As Figure 5.6 shows, real income growth ("real" because it is adjusted for inflation) has slowed dramatically since 1970. The lack of large increases in real income is another indicator that productivity has not significantly grown since the 1970s.

By focusing on the big picture of productivity—which is the real fundamental driver of economic growth—it is easy to see that we

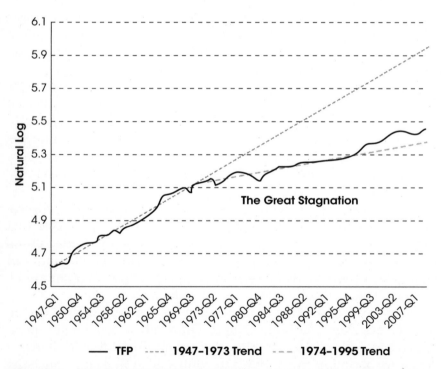

Figure 5.5   Slowing Productivity Growth (Using Total Factor Productivity)
Productivity growth was very rapid until the early 1970s and then grew very slowly afterward.
Source: John Fernald, San Francisco Federal Reserve.

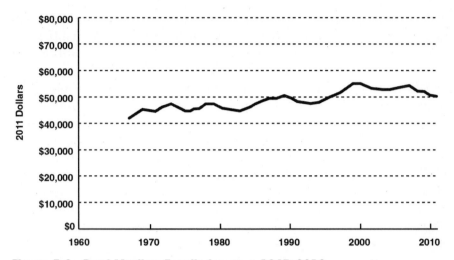

Figure 5.6 Real Median Family Income, 1965–2012
Slowing growth in real (inflation-adjusted) family income after 1970 is another indicator of slowing productivity growth.
Source: U.S. Census Bureau.

are in a long-term productivity slump. We have not taken the steps necessary to improve productivity in many decades, and therefore productivity has not improved much.

Instead, beginning in the early 1980s, rising bubbles have been creating easy bubble wealth in a rising multibubble economy. The bubbles began to fall in 2008 and will fall more fully when inflation and interest rates rise, and the Aftershock begins.

To think we will be able to print our way out of this mess or wait for "natural growth" to save us, without making significant productivity improvements, is pure folly. Until we put our focus on the real economy-boosting power of productivity growth (the subject of future books), we can count on massive money printing to bring us high inflation and high interest rates that will pop our bubble economy and bring on the worldwide Aftershock (described in the next two chapters).

When Will Inflation Begin? When Group Psychology Turns Negative after the Market Cliff

In Chapter 4, we described how continued slow economic growth and lackluster company earnings, despite years of massive stimulus, will turn investor psychology increasingly negative over time, pushing stocks and bonds over what we are calling the Market Cliff.

The reason that massive money printing by the Fed cannot save us from the Market Cliff is because the Fed is buying *bonds*, not stocks. That means the stock-boosting impacts of money printing are not endlessly guaranteed. Eventually, even with massive money printing and relatively low interest rates, the continued slow or no-growth economy will discourage investors and stocks will begin to fall. Bonds, too, will crash over the Market Cliff (see Chapter 4 for details).

On the other side of the Market Cliff, we will have a very different economy than we have today. Certainly, the Fed will desperately try to save the markets and the economy with more money printing. So that won't immediately change. But after the Market Cliff, with stocks and bonds down dramatically, people will feel quite differently than they do today. In fact, people will feel quite negative about the economy.

So when you ask, *When will inflation begin?*, you are really asking *When will the Market Cliff occur?* Inflation may continue to inch up prior to the Market Cliff, but it will only begin with a vengeance after the Market Cliff. So the timing of the Market Cliff is key. It could happen as soon as a year from now or it could be three or four years, and maybe even longer (but not likely). It is hard to precisely predict how long the onset of significant inflation can be delayed because the timing depends so heavily on changing group psychology.

Changing Group Psychology Is Key

In the end, despite all the money printing the world can muster, it will all come down to how people *feel* about the economy and the markets. As long as the positive psychology continues, the bubbles live on. Once psychology shifts and we go over the Market Cliff, inflation will rise, interest rates will climb, the bubbles will pop, and the Aftershock will begin.

The onset of inflation—and therefore the onset of the global Aftershock—ultimately comes down to the behavior of businesses and individuals. The government may increase the money supply, but sooner or later businesses and individuals have to make the decision to raise prices and raise wages. The government cannot *force* people to raise prices and wages (and obviously doesn't want to). Businesses and employees have to do it themselves or there is no inflation.

But in a weak economy, where do businesses get the courage to demand that customers pay higher prices? Where do employees get the courage to demand higher wages? Given that money printing usually occurs in stressful economic conditions, it's a wonder inflation ever occurs at all.

But in a stagnating economy that doesn't have massive asset bubbles driving the economy, such as what India is experiencing now (or Indonesia or Argentina), eventually people don't feel they have anything to lose. It becomes every person for him- or herself. Businesses and individuals *want* to raise prices and wages, even in a slow economy, precisely because of the slow economy. And, that is what is happening in those countries now.

In the 1970s, when the U.S. government was printing a lot of money, we had no huge asset bubbles, so there was not much concern by employees or businesses about fragile asset bubbles being popped by inflation. Inflation climbed to 14 percent by the early 1980s.

Today, the situation is very different. In a bubble economy, people are very cognizant of the fragility of those bubbles (and the economy). After all, we saw what happened in 2008. People have a lot to lose by disturbing the asset bubbles. If those bubbles pop, it's bad for everybody—not only people who own homes or who own stock, but bad for *everybody*. Pushing prices and/or wages up could be disastrous for those asset bubbles. No one wants to be the bull in the china shop that helps to pop them. *Everyone* benefits to some extent from the bubbles. When some of these bubbles (stocks and real estate) began to pop just a small amount in 2008 and 2009, everyone was hurt. Imagine if all the bubbles popped fully.

What this means is that inflation likely won't really take off until after the stock and real estate asset bubbles start to burst. It may rise to significant levels before then, but only when people feel they have nothing to lose (and a lot to gain) by demanding price and wage increases—when the collapsing asset bubbles make them panic—will inflation really get going.

When that happens, inflation will skyrocket. That's not just because of all the money the Fed will have printed by then (likely trillions more than today), but also because the Fed will have no choice at that point but to continue to flood the economy with *even more* money to keep it from completely collapsing. The stock and bond markets will collapse anyway. Money printing won't help them—it will only hurt them at that point. But in an effort to keep the fiancial markets from collapsing too rapidly and fund the government debt as well as replacing foreign money leaving the United States, it will be printing at an awesome rate.

The Fed's Fix for Research Unsupportive of Money Printing: Fire the Researchers

The idea that monetary policy can lower unemployment and boost the economy is part of what's called the "New Keynesian" economic model—and it's a big justification for the Fed's massive money printing. So when a 2008 study by top Fed economists concluded that the New Keynesian model was incapable of predicting employment or economic growth that certainly was not what the Fed wanted to hear.

More than five years later in 2013, with the money supply increased more than fourfold, the Fed found a way to deal with this irritating criticism of the New Keynesian model, not with new rigorous research that would support massive money printing, but the old-fashioned way: they fired the researchers. Patrick Kehoe and Ellen McGrattan, both highly regarded economists at the prestigious Federal Reserve Bank of Minneapolis—considered one of the nation's premier economics research institutions—both got the boot in November 2013.

One of the useful things you might want a new economic model to be able to do is to accurately forecast some aspects of the future economy, such as changes in employment rates. In their paper entitled "New Keynesian Models: Not Yet Useful for Policy Analysis," the fired researchers concluded that the Fed's current model of choice is unable to predict changes in employment and other economic indicators. Therefore, relying on it as the rationale for monetary policy is not justified.

Nonetheless, the Fed continues to print money, and now these two topflight researchers are gone.

The Inflation Deniers Are Liars!

The concept of inflation is very simple: When you have more dollars, they become less valuable. You don't need a PhD in economics to understand this. But we don't think the problem is that people don't understand it. We think, in reality, the inflation deniers are liars.

What if the government announced today that it was cutting all taxes to stimulate the slow economy and that the Fed would finance the entire federal budget through money printing—printing $3.7 trillion per year instead of $1 trillion?

Even the inflation deniers would tell you that this would create inflation on a massive scale.

To keep from alarming people, the Fed is being more subtle. By buying bonds, rather than just printing currency, like Zimbabwe, it's a little easier to fool ourselves into believing that it won't create future inflation. But we are not convinced that the Fed and others really believe that inflation won't happen. They know what's going on. They know inflation is devastating to asset bubbles. They are just trying to come up with every reason it's not going to happen, even though they know that it will. They are desperately trying to convince themselves that inflation won't happen—like a criminal trying to convince a jury, they almost believe their own tall story.

Some of the sneakier inflation deniers will say, yes, of course, printing $3.7 trillion a year would cause inflation, but the nearly $1 trillion a year the Fed is printing now is just the "perfect amount." The people at the Fed who are making these decisions are the smartest people in the world—so smart that they didn't see the 2008 financial crisis coming, so smart that they've never in their 100-year history predicted even one recession before it happened. These smart people know exactly the right amount of money to print without causing inflation. Sure they do.

Of course, if we told any of the inflation deniers 10 years ago that we'd be printing almost $1 trillion a year today, it would stun them. They wouldn't believe it. However, if those same smart people at the Fed decided to print $2 trillion next year to keep the bubbles going, then suddenly that new number would become just the *perfect* amount.

As we said earlier, this is not a plan; it's a panic. When the Fed started printing money in response to the financial crisis, everyone—even the Fed—thought we'd be done with money printing by now. Those smart people at the Fed will continue to do whatever it takes to keep the stock market up but never predicting anything until it all falls apart, just like in 2008. The people who say otherwise are just fooling themselves—and trying to fool you.

Putting the Inflation Deniers to the Test

Here is the ultimate test for the inflation deniers and why we know they are lying when they say they don't think big money printing will bring big inflation.

Just ask them why we can't print a whole lot more money. Starting right now, we could establish several large bonding authorities to stimulate huge economic and job growth. These bonding authorities could sell bonds for specific purposes, such as those listed below. The Fed could buy these bonds to finance these projects with their printed money. The Fed would agree to allow the bonding authorities to sell more bonds to pay the interest and to rollover the old bonds so they never have to be paid off—just as it does with the federal government debt today.

- $500 billion to build new upgraded high schools in the United States.
- $100 billion to rebuild damaged buildings from hurricane Sandy and to erect future flood prevention systems.
- $1 trillion to build new roads throughout the United States.
- $500 billion to rebuild the military after two wars.
- $1 trillion to improved health care, including new hospitals for veterans and the elderly.
- $2 trillion for a program to eliminate all Social Security and income taxes for a year (could be continued for many years).

We picked a range of political interests for the short list above, but certainly there are countless more ways to spend unlimited printed money. Theoretically, if we were willing to print enough money, we could fund hundreds, even thousands of big projects. With enough printing, we could do just about anything we wanted.

Think of the vast number of jobs and huge economic growth that would create. All we need is limitless money printing! The bonds bought by the Fed would never default and would always have low interest rates because the Fed stands ready to buy them.

But we don't do that, do we?

In fact, no one even suggests such a crazy idea. Why? Because if we even discussed such a plan, it would make it much harder to fool ourselves that the current money printing won't cause inflation. And fooling ourselves is absolutely key to keeping the current bubble economy going. We *must* continue to fool ourselves. As soon as we can't do that, the jig is up.

This tells us something very important about the inflation deniers: they know darn well that endless money printing causes dangerous inflation—otherwise, why would they ever want to limit it?

The fact they are willing to do some money printing but not a lot more money printing says it all. These inflation deniers are inflation liars.

CHAPTER 6

Phase 2: The Aftershock

POP GO THE DOLLAR AND
GOVERNMENT DEBT BUBBLES

Most people will be caught completely unprepared for the Market Cliff and rising inflation we described in the previous two chapters. Such conditions are not expected in a typical market "down cycle" or recession. When it occurs, most Americans will naturally assume that the situation cannot possibly get much worse. Unfortunately, it will.

As stocks and bonds fall sharply in the Market Cliff, the rest of America's bubble economy will also begin to pop. The full bursting of the stock market, real estate, private debt, and discretionary spending bubbles will rock the U.S. and global economies, forcing us to pump up even further our two remaining vulnerable bubbles, the dollar bubble and the government debt bubble. When those last two bubbles finally pop, the full Aftershock will begin.

It won't be hard to convince you that we have an enormous government debt bubble, so we'll get back to that in a few pages. Right now, we'd like you to keep an open mind and consider the possibility that we have a vulnerable *dollar bubble*. We know this is hard to believe. All we ask is that you read on a bit more before coming to your own reasonable conclusions. If we are right (and based on our books dating back to 2006, we have an excellent track record), you cannot afford to ignore this. We know it feels fundamentally wrong, but please let icy cold logic be your guide.

The Dollar Bubble: Hard to See without Bubble-Vision Glasses

Remember how hard it was to see the Internet stock bubble *before* it popped in early 2000? Remember when buying overpriced real estate was considered a great investment before the housing bubble began to burst in 2007? Unpopped bubbles really can be very deceiving. Of course, *after* they pop, that's another story. Hindsight is always 20/20. But *before* they pop, you need to be willing to put on bubble-vision glasses in order to see an unburst bubble.

Here are your bubble-vision glasses for the dollar. Once you look at the dollar this way, you'll see for yourself that this bubble has no choice but to pop.

To use your bubble-vision glasses, you must look at the dollar through the two lenses of *supply and demand*—the same two forces that determine the value of any asset.

Whenever there is increasing demand or decreasing supply of any asset, its value rises. Conversely, falling demand or increasing supply tends to decrease value. The combination of both falling demand *and* increasing supply very significantly reduces value.

The laws of supply and demand are especially relevant to a bubble. On the way up, rising demand and/or falling supply drives the bubble higher and higher. On the way down, falling demand and/or rising supply crashes the bubble. But, bubble or no bubble, unless there is significant demand relative to supply, asset values always decline.

While these concepts are logical and straightforward, accepting that the mighty U.S. dollar is actually an asset bubble that will pop due to falling demand and rising supply is pretty hard to swallow. It means that we have to accept that the future value of the U.S. dollar has nothing to do with what a great country we are, or how we have been the greatest economic power the world has ever seen. The future value of the U.S. dollar depends entirely on future *supply and demand.*

We have already devoted most of Chapter 5 to the growing *supply* of the dollar, via massive money printing by the Fed, so let's focus now on falling *demand* for the dollar.

Clearly, past demand has been spectacular. Prior to the bubble economy, demand for U.S. dollars was strong and growing stronger due to our growing economy driven by rising productivity. But our productivity growth began to slow in the 1970s, and instead of real economic growth, we began in the early 1980s to gradually inflate asset bubbles. (You may recall from Chapter 2 that the Dow grew more than 1,000 percent from 1980 to 2000 while gross domestic product [GDP] grew less than 300 percent in that same time period. That was one of many bubbles.)

Rising stocks, bonds, real estate, and other dollar-denominated assets were very, very profitable, which naturally attracted many investors from around the world. In fact, foreign-owned U.S. assets grew from $661 billion in 1981 to more than $25 trillion in 2013, according to the Bureau of Economic Analysis. Foreign investors bought up many U.S. assets over the years, not because they wanted to help us out, but because their investment returns were stellar. The tremendous and growing demand for U.S. assets made the dollar increasingly more valuable. Foreign investors wanted more and more U.S. assets and needed more and more U.S. dollars to buy them—creating lots of demand for dollars.

Sounds great. So what's the problem?

There was no problem with this at all, as long as we were growing our economy with big improvements in productivity, such as laying railroad tracks from coast to coast, or when we developed mass-produced automobiles, or innovated to create other big jumps in output and productivity. All that helped grow a stronger U.S. economy and helped increase demand for U.S. dollars, prior to our bubble economy.

The trouble started when demand for U.S. dollars by foreign investors was driven less by increasing productivity and more and more by something else: rising asset bubbles. In a multibubble economy, the value of a currency can do nothing else but to rise and fall as the bubbles rise and fall.

Why? Because the value of any currency is set by *supply and demand*. When a multibubble economy is on the way up, investment returns go up, and therefore demand from foreign investors for dollars to buy those investments also goes up. And when a multibubble economy is on the way down, investment returns naturally go down, and therefore demand for dollars to buy those investments also goes down.

As hard as it may be to believe, demand for our dollars is not a permanent condition. For many years, our rising bubbles created rising demand from foreign investors for dollars, and therefore the value of the dollar rose. When the real estate and stock bubbles began to pop in 2008, those falling bubbles created a dip in demand for dollars, and therefore the value of the dollar declined modestly.

Since then, demand for dollars has picked up temporarily due to the weakened euro, but the point here is that demand for dollars can and does drop when U.S. asset values fall. It may be hard to believe, but you actually have seen it happen before.

Also hard to believe is the idea that another currency can do better than the dollar. Overall, the euro has done very well. While not a sharp, quick rise, the value of the euro, compared to the dollar, has risen pretty steadily from a low of around 87 cents in 2000 to around $1.50 in late 2009. Although the euro fell in 2010, it has recovered back to the $1.35 to $1.45 range, as of spring 2011. As of this writing in early 2014, the euro has climbed back into that range, but with plenty of volatility on the way. We expect the euro to continue to be volatile due to the ongoing and growing European debt crisis, as well as due to some government manipulation.

But, in the long term, we see the euro and other foreign currencies doing well relative to the dollar because the demand for dollars is driven by demand from foreign investors to purchase U.S. assets, and the demand to purchase U.S. assets will fall. When our bubbles fully burst, demand for U.S. assets—including the dollar—will crash, driving up the value of the euro and other foreign currencies relative to the dollar over the next 5 to 10 years.

It may be hard to imagine the dollar taking such a future beating, but in fact the early start of the beating has already occurred. The dollar will be quite vulnerable to further declines when the U.S. stock market and our other bubbles fall. Again, the underlying problem of the economy—which is declining productivity growth—is ultimately to blame. Instead of productivity improvements, we have had rising bubbles. That gave us lots of easy gains, but they also make us vulnerable to easy losses.

The Hardest Bubble to See Is the One You're In

Back in 2007, everyone we spoke to at presentations about our 2006 book, *America's Bubble Economy*, could see the housing bubble. Housing prices had stopped growing and were heading down substantially in some parts of the country. However, they had a hard time seeing the stock market bubble because the market was still moving steadily upward. And they had a really hard time seeing the dollar bubble because, at that point, the dollar looked fine.

Then, starting in spring 2008 and especially in spring 2009, few people had any trouble seeing the stock market bubble after the Dow had fallen 40 percent from its previous peak. The housing bubble was also easy to see because home prices had fallen substantially in every part of the country and in some parts by 50 percent from their peak. But they still had a hard time seeing the dollar bubble because the dollar still looked fine, like a safe haven in stormy times. If anything, the dollar seemed like an even safer bet due to the European debt crisis. This makes the dollar bubble even harder to see.

But in a few years, the dollar bubble will no longer be so hard to see. As investor psychology turns more negative and stocks and bonds fall off the Market Cliff, inflation will rise. As a result, foreign demand for dollars, which have been heavily in demand to buy U.S. bonds and other assets, will significantly decline as well. At that point, everyone will be able to easily see the popped dollar bubble, just as the real estate bubble and the Internet bubble both became painfully obvious *after* they popped.

What we have seen with a vengeance in the past few years is the fact that *the hardest bubble to see is the bubble you are in*. No matter what the price is, as long as your bubble is moving upward, that is the *right* price. A stock market that slowly moves from 10,000 to 11,000 is thought to be priced properly, and so is a market that very rapidly goes from 11,000 to 16,000. As long as it is moving up, it's priced right.

The dollar is the same. As long as it is relatively stable (or better yet, growing), people assume it is priced *just right*. And the forces that might push it down in the future, like massively increasing the money supply or huge government borrowing with no hope of paying it back, don't really affect people's thinking about the value of the dollar because the government must be printing and borrowing *just the right amount*—certainly not enough to negatively affect the dollar in any significant way! Whether we are borrowing $100 billion a year or $1.5 trillion a year, it's always just the right amount, because the dollar isn't falling *too* much, so it *must* not be in a bubble, just as real estate was not a bubble—until it popped. As Alan Greenspan said, it's hard to see a bubble until it bursts.

What Could Make the Dollar Decline Further?

The answer, as always, is *falling demand*.

Since the 1980s, the rising bubble economy has become increasingly dependent on foreign investment for its capital, and that of flow foreign investment can easily slow down or even pull out when the excellent returns investors used to receive become not so excellent anymore, or worse, they turn into losses.

As we said in *America's Bubble Economy*, foreign investors did not invest in our dollar-denominated assets because they love us; they did it for the fabulous profits. And foreign investors will not slow their purchases of dollar-denominated assets because they hate us; they will simply do it because our investments aren't very good anymore. They'll do it to protect their assets from losses, especially foreign exchange losses.

But what could possibly give foreign investors the idea that they may not be able to make as much profit on their U.S. assets in the future as they did in the past?

How about more declines in our four big already-falling bubbles?

Falling Stocks, Real Estate, Credit, and Spending in the United States Will Create "No Gain, Lots of Pain" for Investors

When U.S. real estate was going up, stocks were going up, easy credit was flowing like joy juice, and everything about investing in the United States was oh so good. There was no reason not to invest here. It was safe, it was easy, and it produced high returns. What more could any investor ask for?

However, when the bubbles pop, falling real estate and stock values, along with declining consumer spending and evaporating credit, will make the United States a far less attractive place to invest. The fall of any one bubble wouldn't be great, but the combined effect of multiple falling bubbles will have a very negative impact the broader U.S. economy, including driving up unemployment and threatening our banking system. That won't help to make the United States too attractive, either, for investors.

But all that will not be enough to drive foreign investors away. After such a wonderful party, it's hard for foreign investors to imagine that the good times could really end, and most will stick around for a while and hope for the best. In the short term, many foreign investors may move from riskier U.S. investments, such as stocks, to less risky U.S. investments, such as government bonds. Also, for a while, U.S. Treasuries may be viewed as a safe haven in a world of turmoil. Many foreign investors, just like domestic investors and economists, believe (or want to believe) that the U.S. economy soon will start growing rapidly, and they naturally want to be ready when their U.S. investments start to pick up.

However, because there is nothing that will magically reinflate these bubbles or quickly bring us huge productivity gains in the next couple of years, we know that the slow economy will have no option other than to continue. But even so, foreign investors will not run away.

Over time, as the big rebound of the economy does not fully happen and instead we have continued anemic GDP and little job growth, investor psychology (both foreign and domestic) will become increasingly negative. That will push us closer to the Market Cliff described in detail in Chapter 4.

Once we fall over the cliff, inflation and interest rates will begin to rise more significantly. Perhaps at first this change will only cause foreign investors to buy slightly fewer U.S. stocks, bonds, and other dollar-denominated assets. Buying a little less is perfectly reasonable. Remember, it takes only a small increase in interest rates to cause a big drop in bond values. With interest rates currently so low, small movements up will have negative consequences. We saw some of this in the spring of 2013 when a small uptick in interest rates pushed bond prices somewhat lower.

At some point, investor psychology will take a more decided turn toward the negative because the long-awaited real recovery is just not happening. When psychology shifts more negatively, demand for U.S. assets, and therefore dollars, will drop further. Instead of risking their money on our stocks, bonds, real estate, and dollars, foreign investors will put more of their investment resources into their own countries, thinking they can always come back and reinvest in the United States when things improve.

But, as we've said, falling bubbles have no viable way to reinflate themselves, and therefore falling bubble economies cannot possibly recover very fast. Instead, they keep falling until there are some real economic reasons for solid economic stability and sustainable growth. Until then, foreign investors will continue to adopt a very reasonable "wait-and-see" approach.

Unfortunately, there's nothing like a very reasonable wait-and-see investment approach to really kill a falling bubble economy that is so deeply dependent on foreign investors. How can things possibly turn around when not enough of the people responsible for our past growth are willing to buy more or at least not sell?

If you think we are perhaps exaggerating the risk of a big drop in future demand, consider this. According to the U.S. Treasury, net inflows of long-term capital from foreign investors into the United States (mostly into stocks and bonds) fell almost in half when the financial crisis hit—dropping from about $540 billion in 2007 to about $290 billion in 2008.

This large drop in late 2008 and early 2009 was one of the key reasons that the Federal Reserve had to step in and buy over a trillion dollars' worth of bonds—foreign buyers were disappearing at a rapid rate. In November 2008, gross foreign purchases of U.S. Treasury bonds fell almost 40 percent before recovering to more normal levels in June 2009 when the Fed's bond purchases gave people confidence to buy bonds again.

With massive U.S. money printing and the rebound in U.S. stocks, the inflow of foreign capital into the United States rose back up to nearly $560 billion in 2010.

But it didn't last.

More recently, foreign investors' inflow of capital in U.S. investment has been negative, with a net *outflow* of $195 billion from October 2012 to September 2013. This may be a key reason the Fed has given itself no limits in its latest round of quantitative easing (QE3). The unprecedented open-ended printing is designed to boost both the stock and the bond markets. While it has worked to raise these asset prices, it has not yet worked to bring back the previous flow of foreign capital as before.

When employment and GDP growth continues to remain slow or declines further, investor psychology (both domestic and foreign) will change. Dropping demand for stocks and bonds as we approach the Market Cliff will put increasing downward pressure on the value of the dollar, creating a negative feedback loop of falling demand, leading to falling prices, leading to falling demand.

At first, just a few foreign investors will decide to end their wait-and-see approach and will want to sell some of their U.S. holdings. Some of that early selling may be by sophisticated investors, as well as by foreign pension funds and life insurance companies that have to be somewhat risk averse in their investments because of the nature of their fiduciary responsibility to protect the assets of their retirees and beneficiaries. This early selling will lower demand even further, and prices will drop even more, motivating more foreign investors to flee. Fairly quickly, the number of foreign investors selling their U.S. assets will hit a critical mass, and a perfectly rational panic will kick in, further bringing down the already bursting asset bubbles. It's all about falling demand.

Once U.S. stocks and bonds fall over the Market Cliff, the massive government intervention of printing and borrowing that helped support the dollar so much in the short term will begin to have terribly negative consequences on the dollar due to inflation (see Chapter 5) and increased fear of more inflation due to the size of the U.S. debt. Inflation and fear of more inflation in the future will drive investors away from the dollar and pop the dollar bubble.

One way to look at this is to think of the United States as a big mutual fund. When our performance is good, foreign investors throw their money at us, but when performance is not so good, they throw less money at us. And when performance becomes bad enough, they are going to want to take their money and go home. The future inflation that will result from the Fed's massive money printing to stimulate the economy will only reinforce this desire to go home.

Needless to say, not too many U.S. investors will want to stick around at that point, either. And some of them will move their money out of the United States early along with foreign investors, making enormous profits in the process. Fear and greed will drive the process of pushing the dollar down: foreign investors' fear of losing money, and U.S. investors' greed to make money by moving money into rapidly rising foreign currencies (relative to the dollar) and gold.

The U.S. Dollar Will Remain a Reserve Currency after the Aftershock, but Confidence Will Be Gone

This might surprise people because if the dollar collapses, many people think that means it won't be a reserve currency. Currently, about 62 percent of foreign exchange reserves around the world are held in dollars and about 24 percent in euros, according to the International Monetary Fund. Clearly, the dollar and the euro completely dominate the reserve currency market. What makes a currency good as a reserve currency is scale and liquidity. These characteristics make a currency excellent for world trade. Hence, it will be easy for a nation, such as South Africa, to trade with Brazil using the dollar.

(Continued)

Also, huge reserves of dollars are being held by China and to a lesser degree Japan, not for trade, but to manipulate the price of the dollar in favor of their exports to the United States. In the Aftershock, those manipulations will fail and their reserves of dollars will decline precipitously, making the euro an increasingly important reserve currency by default. But simply due to the size and scale of our economy and its worldwide trade, the dollar will remain a reserve currency for future trading, even if it falls to being the second most important reserve currency in the Aftershock.

So the dollar's reserve currency status is fairly secure. But the real issue goes beyond those technical points. The larger truth is that, because of our falling bubbles and rising inflation, the once-mighty U.S. dollar and U.S. economy will have lost some respect, regardless of whether dollars continue to be held in reserve in other countries.

The Biggest Myth about the Dollar Is That Investors Have "No Place Else to Go"

Before we move on to the next big bubble pop (U.S. government debt), we need to answer a question that is probably on your mind right now: *If the United States is no longer a good investment, where in the world will foreign investors go?* Won't the United States still be the best place to invest, relative to other countries whose economies will be in even worse shape than ours?

Lots of people we talk to find it difficult to believe that foreign investors will ever significantly pull out of their U.S. investments because many Americans believe that most foreign investors have no other profitable place to go.

Coauthor Bob Wiedemer has found in his presentations to financial analysts and asset managers that most people have a hard time accepting the idea that foreign investors have profitable non-U.S. choices for investment. The most common question we get about a potential fall in the value of the dollar is: "Where else would foreign investors put their money except in the United States?" We've heard this from individual investors, highly respected economists, senior Wall Street asset managers, and even senior Federal Reserve officials.

Apparently, many otherwise intelligent Americans simply don't realize that foreign investors *already* put most of their money someplace else: *in their own home countries!*

It's a bit arrogant on our part to think that foreign investors have to invest *all* of their money in the United States. In fact, they often keep most of their investment capital in their own local or regional investments. Think about it. If foreign investors actually did put all of their money in the United States, how would other countries get any capital at all? This idea is really very silly. *Most foreign money is already in their home countries, not in the United States.*

As the U.S. bubbles continue to fall, foreign investors will simply decide to reduce their dollar-based investment exposure so they can keep a little more money at home. Wouldn't you? There is always some foreign exchange risk in any investment outside your own country. Certainly, U.S. investors think about this when considering investments outside the United States, and, of course, foreign investors do the same when they weigh the costs and benefits of investing in the United States. This is perfectly reasonable. Even if the asset growth is the same in both countries, fluctuating foreign exchange rates can make foreign investments in another country less attractive.

This is especially true over the long term with low-yield investments, such as government bonds. For example, a German bond may yield 3 percent, and a U.S. bond may give a more attractive 3.5 percent, but if the exchange rates move even 1 percent, the advantage of owning the more profitable U.S. bond instead of the German bond is entirely wiped out. When exchange rates become volatile, this risk increases. This is an important consideration for foreign investors when deciding whether to buy U.S. bonds and other U.S. assets.

It is important to recognize that any move out of U.S. investment will be part of an overall flight to safety by foreign investors. Not only will investors reduce their foreign exchange exposure, they will also reduce their exposure to riskier assets in their own countries, especially stocks. So when they bring their money back home, they won't be putting it into stocks, but instead will be putting much of it in short-term debt instruments and precious metals.

Maybe the United States Is Too Big to Fail?

Some people think that because the dollar and U.S. government bonds are so important to the world economy, the rest of the world won't let the dollar or government debt bubbles burst. This is often used as a reason why China will want to maintain the dollar's value—because it is so heavily invested in dollars. The reality is that China does not control the market. In fact, no one group comes anywhere close to controlling the market. Because of that, it is in everyone's individual best interest to get out of dollars, even if it is not in the group's best interest—just as people fled the falling Internet stock bubble and the real estate bubble, even though it hurt us as a group to do so. As we have said many times before, last one out is a rotten egg. And no one will want to be the rotten egg.

Most Foreign-Held Investments in Dollars Won't Flow Out of the United States—They Will Go to "Money Heaven"

Remember Bear Stearns? In early 2008, the value of its stock went from about $28 billion to just $2 billion, practically overnight, but not because $26 billion was actually moved out of Bear Stearns stock. In fact, only a small portion of stock was sold before the stock price collapsed. Where did that $26 billion in wealth go? We like to say it went to "Money Heaven," meaning it simply disappeared.

When the dollar bubble falls, most foreign-held investments in dollar-denominated assets will not have a chance to run out of the United States. Instead, that capital will go to the same place your home equity went when the housing bubble popped. It will go to the same place your 401(k) and other retirement account funds went when the stock bubble dropped to half its peak value. It will go to the same place that all bubble money goes when a bubble pops: it's all going to Money Heaven.

Still Can't Believe the Dollar Bubble Will Pop? It Takes Only a Small Change in Demand to Create a Big Change in Value

You need only a relatively small change in demand to significantly impact value. For example, if the last person at the end of the day buys GE stock for $100 per share, then all GE stock is worth $100 a share even though almost none of the people holding that stock paid $100 a share. Conversely, if the last share of GE stock sells for $50 at the end of the day, all GE stock is worth $50 a share, regardless of what price you paid before. Asset values can go up and down very quickly because they are priced at the margin.

The same thing will happen to the dollar. Like stocks, dollars are priced at the margin. It won't take the sale of a lot of dollars to make the value of the dollar drop significantly. Once it starts to seriously decline, the value of the dollar can and will fall very rapidly—so rapidly that most foreign investors won't have time to sell (just as you may not have had time to sell a given stock before the price went way down). Only those who sell early will escape seeing their money go to Money Heaven, which is a big motivating factor in the sell-off as the dollar starts to fall—no one will want to be stuck holding dollars or dollar-denominated assets after the dollar collapses. Again, last one out is a rotten egg. So this early selling will only accelerate the fall.

Keep in mind that it doesn't take a lot of sellers to create a problem. All that is necessary is a drop in buyers. When you lose buyers, any asset will lose value very quickly. So it is a decline in demand (buyers), not a sudden increase in supply (sellers), that will make all the difference for the future of the dollar and dollar-denominated assets.

All Dogs Go to Heaven, and So Will a Whole Lot of Money!

People often ask where the massive amount of investment capital in stocks, bonds, and real estate will go in the future. The answer is Money Heaven. Most investment money will go to Money Heaven in the future because most people won't pull their money out of falling stocks, real estate, and bonds soon enough. Anyone who doesn't move money out early won't be able to move it out at all. That's because other people will have moved their money out of those investments earlier. Most important, there will be little demand for those investments afterward. Hence, the value of most people's investments will decline dramatically.

At that point, most people will realize they should have moved their money out, but it will be too late. Their portfolios will have been automatically rebalanced for them, heavily weighted toward Money Heaven. For the money managers and financial advisers who will preside over this reweighting of investors' portfolios into Money Heaven, it's going to feel a lot less like Money Heaven and a lot more like Money Hell.

We believe that during this period there will be a fierce fight to save the dollar by central banks around the world and by the U.S. government, including a variety of federal interventions to attempt to stop or slow the sell-off. Such interventions will delay but not prevent the dollar's full fall.

Once the dollar bubble falls significantly, foreign and U.S. investors together will start moving their money out of the United States in hot pursuit of the enormous profits to be made by selling falling dollars and buying rising assets elsewhere, such as foreign currencies and gold (see Chapter 9).

The Second Biggest Dollar Myth: In a Worldwide Recession, the Relatively Good U.S. Economy Will Always Make the Dollar More Valuable than Other Currencies

First of all, the dollar is already worth 30 percent less than it was in 2001, according to the U.S. Dollar Index. More important, the value of the dollar is *not* a function of the relative strength of the U.S. economy compared to economies of other countries. Even if the United States has a stronger economy than other world economies in the Aftershock (and it will), the value of the dollar will still be determined entirely by *supply and demand*. Demand for dollars always depends on how attractive our investments are. So, if U.S. investments do poorly, the dollar will still go down. As we said earlier, foreign investors will simply go back to lower-risk investments in their own countries.

As mentioned before, when the Aftershock begins to hit, foreign investors will make a general flight to safety. They won't sell U.S. stocks and invest in European or Japanese stocks. They will invest in short-term, highly liquid cash securities. Foreign investors will prefer their own countries' cash securities over U.S. bonds because there is no foreign exchange risk involved in buying cash securities in their home countries.

This has nothing to do with the relative strength of economies; it's all about investor safety.

Also, some foreign investors and U.S. investors, will be piling into gold as an alternative to stocks and bonds from any country to greatly improve their returns.

But Hasn't the Dollar Been a Safe Haven Currency?

Yes it has, and it will continue to be seen as a safe haven for a while longer. International investor psychology has to change to catch up with the new reality of the dollar. That new reality now includes more than a threefold increase in the U.S. money supply since 2008 with an annual economic growth rate of less than one-hundredth of that.

In the past, the U.S. dollar has always been the strongest and most reliable currency in the world and many international investors still view it as such. But that view was created before we had a massive government debt of more than $17 trillion, before we had the massive inflow of foreign capital into our country chasing and pushing up our economic bubbles, before we decided to triple our money supply, and before even more money printing in the future. The idea that the dollar is "safe" is still firmly with us, but the evidence to support that idea is being significantly eroded over time.

Although the economic conditions surrounding the dollar have been changing for many years, international investor perceptions have not been as quick to change. They are similar to U.S. investors. They don't really see the fundamental economic bubble until it begins to pop, and then, of course, they see it all too quickly.

Our "Safe Haven" Status Is Not Permanent

The speed with which fundamental economic conditions are changing for the worse has increased rapidly. In fact, the stress can be seen in the need for the Federal Reserve to buy more than $4 trillion worth of government bonds, Freddie Mac bonds, and Fannie Mae bonds since spring 2009. Clearly, the world's appetite for our dollar-denominated debt is limited, or the Fed wouldn't have to buy the bonds.

The Federal Reserve is acting as an enormous buyer of last resort. This has helped boost international investors' confidence in the dollar from 2009 to 2013 and will likely continue to do so in 2014, since it guarantees there will be no confidence-shaking failed Treasury auctions. A failed auction would be highly damaging to investors' confidence in the dollar. But in the long run, the purchase of these bonds via massive money printing will also damage investors' confidence since it runs the high risk of creating dollar-damaging inflation. It's a short-term move that boosts the dollar temporarily with very bad long-term consequences. Sound familiar?

When Japan's Bubble Economy Burst the Yen Didn't Collapse, So Why Will the Dollar Bubble Pop?

That is true, but we wouldn't expect it to collapse. Japan's bubble economy of the 1980s had only two major bubbles—stock and real estate. It didn't have a yen bubble, a private debt bubble, or a public debt bubble that were anything like those of the United States. It didn't have to increase its money supply to handle a massive collapse in the private credit markets. It didn't further massively increase its money supply to buy its own government bonds to help save its stock market, stimulate the economy, and finance a massive public debt bubble. The Japanese stock market fell 75 percent. Hence, there was little threat of inflation. Also, Japan had high internal savings rates, relative to the United States. Also, it did not have a huge inflow of foreign capital over decades chasing its economic bubbles.

Japan had a very different and much milder bubble economy. In fact, it was less of a bubble economy and more like an economy that had experienced very high *real* growth rates due to rapidly increasing productivity. Then, because that high productivity growth declined, Japan's real economic growth also slowed and a small amount of bubble growth occurred. That is certainly not the situation in the United States.

The Real Reason Most People Don't Believe the Dollar Will Fall: The Consequences Are Too Terrible to Think About

The debate over the future of the dollar is not academic. If the dollar falls, it will deeply and negatively affect everyone in the United States and most people around the world. That's pretty scary. Unfortunately, this fear colors the debate about what is ahead, with most people carrying a strong bias against the possibility that the dollar could actually ever fall. This makes open and honest discussion about the future value of the dollar much more difficult, especially for financial journalists, financial analysts, and economists, most of whom would be deeply and negatively affected personally and professionally by a collapse.

Some people avoid the debate entirely because they assume the fall of the dollar will mean the end of the world. It won't! It may be the end of the asset bubbles we have come to know and love, and much of the bubble wealth that came with it, but it won't be the end of the world. The United States will not become a third world country. In fact, we will remain the biggest economy on earth—just not a big bubble economy. Life will surely be different without all that bubble money, but life will go on and eventually we will solve these problems—although it will likely take many years.

All we ask is that you not let fear stop you from absorbing the facts. Based entirely on logic and the evidence at hand, there simply is no other plausible scenario. The dollar can and will fall. Again, if we didn't have a falling *bubble* economy, things would be very different. Unfortunately, falling bubbles are exactly what we do have.

Won't China Bail Us Out?

As you might expect, the United States and other countries will make all sorts of heroic efforts to save the dollar. Keeping the dollar bubble pumped up is now and will continue to be a major focus of central banks around the globe, especially the Chinese central bank, which now has bought over $1.2 trillion of U.S. government bonds to prop up the dollar's price. Japan also has over $1 trillion, but it is no longer accumulating a significant number of dollars.

China's primary motivation in buying dollars is to keep the price of their currency, the yuan, lower relative to the dollar, and thus keep the price of their goods low for their number-one customer, the United States. The more goods they sell to us, the more jobs they create at home, and more jobs mean more political stability. If China stops producing jobs, political instability will rise and Chinese political leaders fear that another Tiananmen Square, or worse, would not be far off.

Of course, China exports to other countries, as well, but no other customer base has been as large as the United States over the years. In large part because of our voracious rising-bubble appetite for their low-labor-cost goods (clothing, furniture, kitchen gadgets, tools, lamps, towels, pens, shoes, and so much more), China's economy was growing at an astounding rate of around 10 percent annually. After the global financial crisis of 2008, China was still growing at a fast, but more modest 9 percent rate—although much of that growth was due to the government's enormous construction stimulus program. That stimulus program was funded with printed money, which will eventually create high inflation, some of which is already showing up in the Chinese economy. The stimulus is also not producing the same growth. China's current growth rate is about 7.5 percent, according to the Chinese government.

Most important for the dollar, at some point, the Chinese central bank will no longer be willing—or for that matter, able—to keep buying our dollars in order to support its price.

In the Fierce Fight to Save the Dollar, Government Interventions Will Ultimately Fail

The U.S. Federal Reserve and the central banks of other governments, such as China, will work hard to hold up the value of the dollar.

There is not much the Fed can do to *directly* affect the value of the dollar. However, it can take *indirect* actions, raising interest rates to attract more foreign investors. Of course, that would also damage the U.S. economy, which is a reason they don't do it. Because the dollar is still considered a "safe haven" currency, this hasn't been a big issue yet.

In the future, there is one thing the Fed could do *directly* to support the dollar that it has never done before. If necessary, the Fed could borrow currencies from other countries and use them to buy dollars. But such actions can have big negative consequences.

Manipulations of other currencies by foreign central banks also make it difficult to predict movements in the dollar's value in the short term. But we must emphasize *short term.* In the long term, market forces, meaning the *supply and demand* for dollars by foreign investors, will ultimately determine the value of the dollar. In the meantime, expect foreign governments to support the value of the dollar.

Why are they helping us? They do it because the value of the U.S. dollar is not only our concern; the whole world is impacted by it. No one wants to see the dollar fall and all major governments will work hard to keep it up because the international losses and global financial instability caused by its fall will hurt everyone. Also, a strong dollar makes foreign exports to the United States less costly. They want and need us to keep buying.

However, wanting a strong and stable dollar is not the same thing as being able to hold up its value. So expect a lot more talk than action.

Ultimately, good investor psychology and active government manipulation will not be able to overcome fundamentally bad investment performance. As the bubbles that were so attractive and profitable for foreign investors fall and pop, no one is going to be very interested in supporting (buying) the dollar, supply will rise, demand will drop, and the dollar bubble will pop.

"It's just a flesh wound. I got it defending the dollar."

The Enormous Government Debt Bubble Is Also Putting Downward Pressure on the Dollar Bubble

Weighing in at more than *$17 trillion* at the end of 2013, the U.S. government debt bubble is certainly the biggest, scariest bubble of all. As we mentioned earlier, debt, even big debt, is not intrinsically bad. But debt makes sense only when it is in reasonable proportion to the debtor's ability to pay it back within a reasonable amount of time.

As Figure 6.1 indicates, our current $17+ trillion debt is *six times* our government's current annual income (taxes) of around $2.8 trillion. That makes it impossible to pay back. How many banks would lend money to a company or an individual with a debt-to-income ratio of 6 to 1, with no plan to pay it off, and projections of further huge increases in their future debt?

But that's comparing our debt to income. It is much more common to compare the government's debt to GDP. Looking at it that way, our debt is about 108 percent of GDP. But we don't pay our

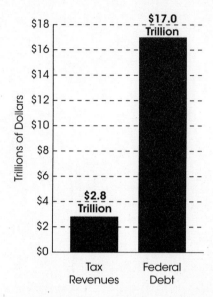

Figure 6.1 Ratio of U.S. Government Debt to Tax Revenues 2011
Our debt-to-income ratio is 6 to 1. Is that a good debt?
Source: Office of Management and Budget.

government debt with GDP; we pay it with taxes, and, again, our debt is *six times* our tax income. People use the comparison to GDP partly as a way of making the debt look smaller and more manageable than it really is.

Although growing a bit slower now than in past years, the total government debt is still expanding. As Figure 6.2 indicates, we added an additional $700 billion in 2013. That's 300 percent greater than we added in 2007, before the financial crisis.

Why so much borrowing? When the federal government's income goes down, it doesn't even consider significant spending cuts as states have to—it just borrows more money to make up the difference! In fact, the federal government spends far more money when its income declines. What a life!

Who is lending us all this money? Much of this debt has been funded by foreign investors, primarily from Europe and Asia. In fact, the percentage of U.S. debt held by foreign investors has almost doubled since 1980, climbing from 15 percent to almost 30 percent in 2009. More recently, in 2013, they hold more than 33 percent of U.S. debt.

Keep in mind that the $17 trillion we have already borrowed is effectively a bad loan. We have almost never paid down the principal of the debt, much less pay it off. All we seem to do is add to it

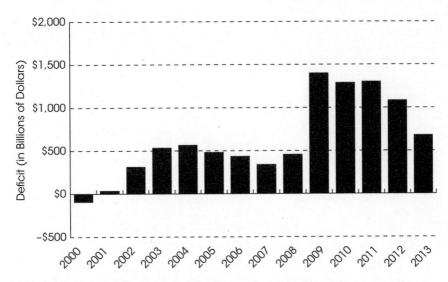

Figure 6.2   The Federal Government Annual Deficit Has Increased Greatly since the Financial Crisis
Even though 2013 saw a decrease, our annual government deficit has grown enormously in the wake of the financial crisis, adding to our huge and growing total government debt (accumulated annual deficits).
Source: Federal Reserve.

enormously. Nobody thinks of it as a bad loan. But that perception can and will change over time.

At this point, our biggest investor is the Federal Reserve, which now buys more than $1 trillion in government or government-backed bonds—even more than our annual deficit. Although the Fed is not buying these bonds directly from the federal government, it still indirectly supports the government bond market and therefore helps loan money flow to the government.

Why Not a 100 Percent Tax Cut to Stimulate the Economy?

Even better than our "triple-zero" plan for reviving the housing market (in that plan the government guarantees mortgages at 0 percent interest, $0 down payment, and zero credit check) is our 100 percent tax cut stimulus package! Now this will really get the old economy going. No more arguing about who pays what taxes; let everybody

(Continued)

get a complete tax cut! It surely will get very broad bipartisan support. Instead of collecting taxes, we can just borrow all the money from foreign investors! If we can borrow $700 billion a year to stimulate the economy and never worry about paying it off, why don't we borrow more and really stimulate the economy?

Of course, no one would ever do this because it uncovers a big unmentionable problem: eventually, we'll have to pay the money back, or inflate our currency, or default on our government debt. Whether it's $17 trillion going up at a rate of a half-billion dollars a year, or $17 trillion going up at a rate of $3.5 trillion a year, it really doesn't matter, but it certainly looks a lot worse if we fund 100 percent of our expenses with borrowed money rather than 20 percent. It also makes it more obvious how irresponsible we really are—whether we borrow $700 billion a year or $3.5 trillion—in an attempt to maintain our bubble economy.

The Hidden Dollar Bubble Won't Fall until the Aftershock; Then It Will Pop Very Quickly

The dollar bubble will remain relatively hidden until the Aftershock, but when it starts to blow up, it will look a lot like the financial crisis of late 2008, meaning it will come on very quickly. Unfortunately, the financial crisis of 2008 and 2009 was relatively small compared to the coming dollar crisis. When it hits, it will be too large for central banks to solve, as just explained. The reason it is stealthy is that prior to the final dollar bubble pop, much effort will have already been made to prop up the dollar, and much is currently being done. So it will take a long time for big problems to appear on the surface, but when they do, it will be like a fire that firefighters can no longer control. It is not uncommon for foreign currency crises to come on quickly and dramatically. What is very uncommon is for it to happen to the United States. In fact, it will be a once-in-history event.

What About the Huge Trade Deficit?

While not directly part of the dollar bubble or the government debt bubble, the big U.S. trade deficit is a glaring symptom of our fundamental problems. If we hadn't had a rising bubble economy for the past few decades, we would not have not seen such a wide gap between our massive imports and our relatively modest exports.

Since the financial crisis, a small drop in the dollar has made U.S. exports slightly cheaper for foreigner buyers, but that has hardly taken even a tiny bite out of the huge trade deficit (see Figure 6.3).

The bubbles, especially the dollar and government debt bubbles, have made it possible for the United State to be not only the world's biggest customer for other countries' products, but also the world's biggest big spender when we really could not afford to be.

Where did we get the money to buy so much from other countries, such as China and India? We've been blowing bubbles. Importing heavily has been part of our multibubble American lifestyle, driven by the rising real estate and rising stock market bubbles, which both directly helped fund much of the shopping.

Without the bubbles, we still may have imported more than we exported, but certainly our trade deficit would never have grown so large.

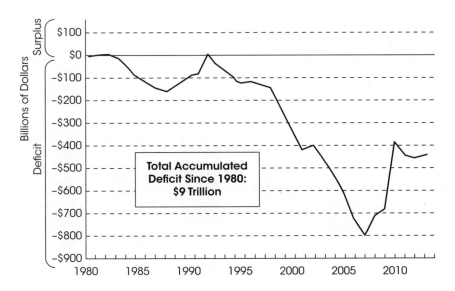

Figure 6.3 U.S. Balance of Trade 1980–Present
Except for a brief period in the early 1990s, the U.S. trade deficit has exploded with the growth of the bubble economy.
Source: Federal Reserve.

The Government Debt Bubble Pops

Of our six big bubbles, the government debt bubble will be the last to burst. Once we go over the Market Cliff (Chapter 4), inflation will rise significantly, and that will eventually bring us high, bubble-popping interest rates (Chapter 5).

As Figure 6.4 shows, our interest costs are low right now. If they rise, our interest costs can quickly consume over half of our tax income. Remember, the White House expects to bring in only about $3 trillion in taxes in 2014. If interest rates go back to where they were in the early 1980s, almost all of our taxes would go just to pay interest costs alone. This is the big difference between the $1 trillion debt that we had over two decades ago and the $17 trillion debt we have today. This current debt is much more dangerous because we are becoming increasingly vulnerable to rising inflation and rising interest rates, just like the homeowner who has an adjustable-rate mortgage.

The risk of rising interest rates fueled by inflation is greatly compounded by the Federal Reserve's recent massive increases in the money supply, which will cause even more future inflation. Rising inflation will cause rising interest rates, and high interest

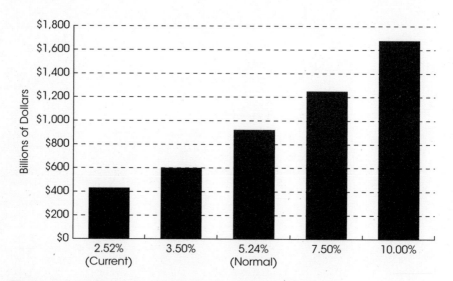

Figure 6.4   Interest Costs of U.S. Government Debt
Even small increases in interest rates can dramatically increase the interest costs on such a massive government debt.
Source: The Foresight Group.

rates will make it increasingly hard and then impossible for the federal government to pay its debt or to borrow more—finally popping the massive government debt bubble.

In the short term, massive money printing by the Fed will likely continue to boost the stock market and help temporarily stimulate the economy. However, in the long term (likely in the 2015–2020 range), a heavy price for this temporary stimulus will have to be paid. Over time, investors will become increasing uncomfortable with low GDP and job growth, coupled with anemic company earnings and a vulnerable bond market.

To calm the markets, boost liquidity, and keep the outflow of investor capital from driving interest rates up even further, the Fed will be forced to print even more money to purchase the bonds that foreign and domestic investors are no longer purchasing.

At this point, the world will start to perceive high risk in U.S. government debt. Even if the government pays much higher interest rates, as it will have to because interest rates and inflation are rising rapidly, there will be an even faster increase in perceived risk for government bonds. U.S. government bonds are supposed to be AAA. But just like AIG or mortgage-backed securities, U.S. government bonds will increasingly be viewed as toxic assets. As we saw in 2008, assets can go from being AAA to XXX in a relatively short period of time. As with AIG and mortgage-backed securities, once these assets go toxic, trading starts to freeze up very quickly, and these assets cannot be sold. It will also become increasingly difficult and eventually impossible to sell fixed-rate bonds in such a high-inflation and high-fear environment.

Once the government can sell only adjustable-rate bonds, such as Treasury inflation-protected securities (TIPS), the Treasury market will effectively die as a means of raising funds for the federal government. Instead, we will turn, once again, to printing even more money, with the Federal Reserve purchasing massive amounts of bonds with printed money, further fueling the fires of inflation.

Increasingly negative investor psychology will reach the tipping point, and stocks and bonds will go over the Market Cliff. The Fed will try to add more stimulus with more money printing. However, at that point, the Fed's medicine will rapidly become poison, as more and more investors fear inflation from the Fed's money-printing operations.

Sharp declines in stocks, bonds, real estate, and the value of the dollar will create a greater sense of perceived risk among lenders, which will further reduce capital availability and further push up interest rates. Real interest rates—the difference between the inflation rate and the interest rate—will eventually soar, with the perceived risks and the real risks of lending increasing rapidly.

In this downward spiral, the Federal Reserve will launch additional bursts of money printing as it has done in the past, but to a much, much greater degree, in an attempt to stimulate the economy. This will, of course, create ever-increasing amounts of inflation. The exact inflation rates will be changing constantly and will not stay at one level for any length of time. Fortunately for the investor, the exact numbers at any given time will not be relevant. What will be relevant will be to understand what is going on and what will happen next.

The combination of high inflation, rapidly rising interest rates, and rapidly rising perceived risk (and real risk) of any lending will quickly put the U.S. government, the world's biggest borrower, in a position it has never been in before. Unlike in the past, when the U.S. government could ride to the rescue of Bear Stearns or AIG when investors, lenders, and counterparties had lost confidence, this time the U.S. government will increasingly find itself needing to be rescued, and, unfortunately, the government cannot rescue itself.

Long term, we will need to solve this high inflation problem in the same way that many governments have successfully fought high inflation: spending cuts and tax increases. These massive spending cuts and tax increases will ultimately help the government bring inflation back into the low double digits. Although that is high by current standards, it will be an improvement.

What about the option of selling all our gold to pay off our government debt? Sounds promising until you run the numbers: Assuming the federal government owns about 8,100 tons of gold, which is what the published figures indicate, and it was willing and able to sell all of it, that would bring us only about $350 billion or so, at current values. Clearly, that is not a solution. We just have way more debt than we have ways to get out of debt. Eventually, our debt party will be over because we will not be able to borrow any more money, and we will not be able to pay any of it back.

Despite concerns about a collapse of the financial system, the U.S. government will definitely be able to maintain enough liquidity to maintain checking accounts. This will allow normal check processing to occur within the United States and outside the United States. But, clearly, the government will not be able to borrow money, since it will have ruined its "credit rating." The old debt will mostly have been inflated away, and the little remaining debt will likely be defaulted on.

The government debt bubble will be no more.

What Is the Repayment Plan for the National Debt? 10 Years? 15 Years? 20 Years?

Well, as everyone knows, there is no repayment plan. Borrow all the money you want, and you don't even need a repayment plan! What a country!

This question is like asking what our credit limit is. It's very useful for understanding our national debt. So, since we don't have a payment plan, let's create one. Let's keep the math simple. Given that we owe $17 trillion, if we begin an annual payment of, let's say, $500 billion, then it would take 34 years to pay it off, assuming we don't do anything sneaky like borrowing more money during that time. Thirty-four years is not a particularly aggressive payment schedule, but let's see how easy that would be to accomplish.

To make that payment, we would also have to eliminate our annual deficit of $700 billion. So we would need $500 billion plus $700 billion, or $1.2 trillion in total, in taxes to start on the 34-year road to paying off the debt. Currently, we are bringing in about $2.8 trillion in taxes—a little less than half of that from individual income taxes and the rest from Social Security and other taxes.

We would need to increase all taxes by 40 percent or income taxes by 100 percent to begin a very, very slow road to paying off the debt. This is not politically or economically feasible. And, again, that is assuming we don't increase our deficit and don't have any interest rate increases above the incredibly low interest rates we are paying today. All this is not going to happen; therefore, by any measure, this is a toxic asset. There is no hope of paying it off.

Of course, right now none of our lenders care if we can't afford to pay back our debt because, for now, we can keep rolling it over and refinancing it—with the help of the Fed's massive money printing.

(Continued)

But any loan you cannot afford to pay off or successfully refinance is likely to default. That will happen when investors, especially foreign investors, see the reality of the situation, and that perception of true reality starts to affect the value of the dollar. In the end, it will be like a giant Ponzi scheme that's destined to fail. As Bernie Madoff so plainly put it when he was arrested, "I knew this day would come eventually." The same will be true for our monstrous national debt with no repayment plan.

What Is the Government's "Credit Limit"?

Anyone with a credit card understands the basic idea of a credit limit. It is the top amount you can borrow before the lender stops lending. Does the U.S. government have a credit limit? Most people, including investment bankers and government leaders, don't even ask such a question. They seem to implicitly assume that there is no credit limit and the government can just keep borrowing forever at record low interest rates. They probably know this can't possibly be true, but like so many other false assumptions underlying the bubble economy, they don't really think about it.

However, this is probably the most important question of all in determining when the bubble economy will finally fully pop. We will reach our credit limit when investors stop or dramatically reduce their lending to the U.S. government because they are concerned about the risk of being repaid with future dollars that are worth far less than the dollars they are lending. This fear will be heavily driven by rising inflation.

To be clear, the credit limit is not the same as the debt ceiling, which can be raised by Congress at any time. The credit limit is the point at which it becomes very difficult for the government to sell bonds due to investor fears of inflation or default. Of course, the Federal Reserve could easily purchase massive numbers of bonds— thus, preventing a failed Treasury auction—but that will fuel the fires of inflation. The end result is the same as not being able to sell bonds because the inflation the Fed creates in the process will drive away investors. It will also become increasingly difficult and eventually impossible to sell fixed-rate bonds in such a high-inflation environment. Once the government can sell only adjustable-rate bonds, such as TIPS, the Treasury market will effectively die as a means of raising funds for the government, and we will have hit our credit limit.

In Reality, We Already Hit Our Credit Limit Back in 2009

What we just described in the preceding section will be the *technical* pop of the government debt bubble, but in reality the government debt bubble is already essentially over right now. It died back in 2009 when we could no longer raise all the money we needed by borrowing at low interest rates and had to turn to massive money printing instead.

The fact that the Fed has to print so much money to keep interest rates low to allow more government borrowing effectively means that without the massive money printing, the government could not borrow so much at such low rates. Without massive money printing, the government could not keep borrowing at current levels.

So the government debt bubble is entirely on life support provided by massive money printing by the Fed. Technically, this bubble is still alive and growing, but in practical terms, this bubble is already dead.

Money from Heaven Is the Path to Hell

We have said before that we think the government will likely have to hit the wall before deciding to cut spending and borrowing, stop money printing, and start repaying our debt.

Instead of dealing with these difficult problems sooner rather than later, when they will be far worse, we are putting it off as long as possible and then dabbling in small changes that are too little, too late.

The United States is behaving a lot like General Motors, which chose not to address its problems of too high expenses, declining revenues, and too much debt. Instead, GM, once the world's greatest company, chose to hit the wall first rather than change their ways before hitting the wall. Whatever changes they did make were small changes, doing too little too late to avoid bankruptcy. We seem to be following the same path.

What will be our wall, and when will we hit it?

For the government debt bubble, the wall has essentially already been reached—otherwise, we would not need to do so much money

(Continued)

printing to make more borrowing possible at low interest rates. The wall will be more officially reached later when the government can borrow no more. Of course, at that point the government will essentially extend its credit limit by printing more money—something General Motors could never do. Printing money will help extend our credit limit by making the market for our bonds more receptive in the short term. So until the money printing ends, the wall keeps getting pushed farther away.

The dollar bubble will hit the wall when rising inflation and high interest rates finally make further money printing unacceptable. Until then, the Fed will surely print and print until they can print no more.

Congress seems to view our ability to borrow and print money as "Money from Heaven." What it and many voters don't realize is that when the government hits its credit limit, it doesn't just mean we cannot borrow more in the future. It also means the government's entire past debt comes due. The entire $20 trillion or $25 trillion—or whatever the number is when we finally can't borrow any more—will be due because we won't be able to refinance our debt any longer. And we are constantly refinancing our debt because we can't pay off even a little bit of it.

When you stop paying and you can't refinance, your loan is 100 percent due and if you can't pay you are in default. Game over.

The Fed can print lots more money to make up for the loss of our lenders, but at that point it creates so much inflation that it not only destroys all dollar-denominated asset values, it could virtually destroy the economy. Eventually, money printing too will have to stop.

Borrowed and printed money may seem like "Money from Heaven," but every bit of it will later be "paid back" almost entirely from a massive loss of value in all our assets—and much of the world's assets—caused by massive inflation and ultimately, a U.S. government debt default.

"Money from Heaven" will eventually lead us down the path to hell.

The Aftershock

The Aftershock will begin when all our bubbles have fully burst. With the dollar and government debt bubbles popped and interest rates and inflation very high, we will see unemployment soar, the U.S. stock market crash further, real estate prices drop, consumer discretionary spending dry up, and the number of banks still in business greatly reduced. The dollar will be worth a fraction of its peak value relative to other currencies, and gold will be a stellar investment for many years to come (see Chapter 9).

Most Americans (who don't follow our protection advice in Chapter 8) will lose most of their money when their asset values fall before they can sell, but they won't starve in the streets. In fact, because we have so much wealth to begin with, the United States will be in better shape than other countries (see Chapter 7), although life in the post-dollar-bubble world will be quite different than it is today.

One of the most striking differences will be the dollar itself, which will still exist but will no longer buy nearly as much in imported goods. Like all the other bubbles, once the dollar bubble pops, it will not reinflate. However, over time, the cheap dollar will make our exports cheap for foreign buyers and that will eventually help even up the difference between the dollar and other currencies. But we won't see a soaring dollar bubble like we use to have in the good old days. Remember Lehman Brothers? Being big and powerful is not enough; you also have to be a good investment.

The Six Psychological Stages of Denial

As the dollar and government debt bubbles pop in the Aftershock, people will naturally be very upset. We believe there will be six distinct psychological stages in which individuals, businesses, and governments will first ignore, then react to, and ultimately solve the economic problems. Each of these psychological stages performs the function of keeping people feeling as comfortable as possible while avoiding making any more changes than are absolutely unavoidable at that point in time. Change is threatening, inaction equals safety, and comfort comes from avoiding any changes that might threaten the benefits of the status quo. But the consequences of inaction also create pain, so eventually some actions are taken.

Over time, as the U.S. and world economies worsen, complete denial and inaction will not be entirely possible. Still, people will strive to ignore what is happening and do the least they can because the many benefits of the old multibubble economy are hard to give up. Our understanding of the underlying *psychology* of coping with and resisting change is one more thing that sets us apart from all the other bearish analysts. We know that at each stage of the falling economy, there will be a deep longing to return to the past and get back to the good times. Actually, the really good times are still ahead, but first we will pass through six psychological stages.

Although these stages are distinctly different, there will be some overlap between them so we may be experiencing multiple stages at the same time.

The six stages are:

1. Denial
2. Market Cycles
3. Fantasized Great Depression
4. Back to Basics
5. Imagined Armageddon
6. Revolutionary Action

Stage 1: Denial

This is the stage in which the United States has been firmly planted for quite some time. This is the "Don't worry, just go shopping" phase of dealing with (or more correctly, not dealing with) the reality of our vulnerable multibubble economy. Regardless of the facts, in the Denial stage, people firmly believe that home prices cannot drop any farther, the stock market has already hit bottom, and the mighty U.S. dollar will always be king.

The big advantage of the Denial stage is that people do not have to take any unpleasant actions at all. We don't have a problem, and therefore we don't have to change. But this stage involves more than simply ignoring the problem. In the Denial stage, we actively keep our multibubble economy pumped up and expanding. Governments, businesses, and individuals continue to borrow their way to prosperity, regardless of the future price tag. And even when things start going bad, the Denial stage just won't let the party quit. We continue to buy homes we can't afford until we can no longer get mortgages, and run up more and more debts we can't easily repay until we can get no more loans. And we continue to entrust our retirements and other investments to Wall Street even when stock prices have far outstripped an economic basis because we want to believe in Tinker Bell.

It can be very comfortable to live in denial—in a big, multibubble economy that has only begun to fall. In the Land of Denial, there's no need to recognize economic bubbles before they grow too large. After all, this is the United States of America, the biggest, most powerful economy in history. *Everything is fine.* And besides, if things really start to look bad, we can always turn to our next stage of dealing with our economic problems, which is to rely on our abiding faith in repeating market cycles.

Stage 2: Market Cycles

In the Market Cycles stage, an increasing number of individuals, businesses, and financial analysts come out of denial and begin to notice that something is wrong. They can see home sales falling or not rising as quickly as they would like, consumer spending slowing, jobs being lost, credit drying up, and stocks on the decline. They may even be able to recognize an individual falling asset bubble, like the declining real estate bubble. But few people at this stage will recognize any yet-unpopped economic bubbles, let alone be able to see an entire multibubble economy. Instead, they will explain the falling stock market, the failing real estate market, and the overall economic downturn in terms of historical up and down market cycles. While not as cozy as the Denial stage, the Market Cycles stage provides some significant comfort, too, because every "down" cycle is guaranteed to be followed by an "up" cycle.

The key comfort advantage of the Market Cycles stage as the multibubble economy begins to fall, is that we don't have to take any scary new actions. We can take actions similar to those we've taken before, even much bolder actions, but nothing fundamentally different that would deeply change the status quo. In fact, the actions are taken to preserve the status quo to the extent possible. Many individuals and businesses will just wait passively and tough it out thinking that, sooner or later, the economy will automatically improve. It always did before, right? Even world-class economists hold tightly to this outdated faith in repeating market cycles. The current recession may be lasting longer than we hoped, but just hang in there—it's bound to turn around soon.

Eventually, when the unrecognized multibubble economy does not turn around soon but continues to fall, people worry that maybe things really are different this time; maybe (can we even say it out loud?) the economy is heading into another, full-fledged Great Depression!

Stage 3: Fantasized Great Depression

During this stage, considerable fear starts setting in. Consumers and businesses significantly cut spending, more jobs are lost, banks further restrict lending, and the federal government ramps up spending money like there's no tomorrow. The words "another Great Depression" increasingly work their way into the national conversation, and the government begins taking unusual steps, like massive government spending to stimulate the economy. The psychological advantage of this stage is the comfort we get from seeing the government run big deficit spending—supposedly it worked in the past, and we can sit back passively and wait for it to work again.

But, in fact, there is no Great Depression on the way. What we have instead is something new, a multibubble economy on its way down, so all the government spending to stimulate the economy does not have the intended positive effects that it would have in an actual depression. Instead, massive federal deficit spending just sets us up for an even bigger fall down the road, when both the dollar bubble and the government debt bubble eventually burst in the Aftershock and no one wants to lend us any more money. At that point, printing dollars will be our only option, creating more future inflation.

Stage 4: Back to Basics

With everything getting significantly worse and worse, the next stage in the ongoing process of dealing with our failing multibubble economy will be the urge to get Back to Basics. The impulse in this stage is to figure out what went wrong in the past and try to set it right in the present. If we can just rectify our previous mistakes, we will be okay, and the way to rectify those mistakes isn't to create a whole new financial and economic structure, but go back to where we were before all this mess happened—go back to basics. In the Back to Basics stage, we will see federal and state governments beginning to enact tough regulations that would have helped protect us *in the past* from some of the problems we now face, such as defaults on subprime mortgages and the dangers of credit default swaps.

But at this late date, these measures will do little, if any, good to undo our current problems. Such attempts will be the equivalent of installing highly sensitive smoke detectors and fancy sprinkler systems, *after* the house has already burned down. Certainly, none of that will help us rebuild. Instead of protecting the current economy in any meaningful way, going Back to Basics with tough backward-looking regulations will do little to reverse the damage that has already been done, and it won't put us on a course toward future recovery. The psychological advantage of this stage is the comfort people get from returning to the past and making as little fundamental change as possible so they can feel safe.

Stage 5: Imagined Armageddon

These backward-looking actions won't help us in a falling multibubble economy. With the dollar bubble popping, more and more people out of work, and the economy continuing to deteriorate, we are likely to next enter the stage of Imagined Armageddon, in which many people may come to think everything is hopelessly going to hell. Feeling angry, helpless, and scared, some people may imagine horrible scenarios of unlikely wars, long breadlines, sharply rising crime, and other calamities that simply will not occur. The invalid analogy to this stage was the earlier rise of fascism and World War II. The psychological advantage of this unpleasant stage is the opportunity to feel like passive victims in order to avoid the discomfort of having to make real decisions that bring about real change. It's hard to know how long this nonproductive stage could last or what short-term consequences it would create. Politically and socially, it's bound to be a difficult time.

Stage 6: Revolutionary Action

Finally, after other actions have been tried and failed, the nation will enter into the final stage of dealing with the collapse of the multibubble economy, in which we will give up the last vestiges of comfort in the past and take major steps toward Revolutionary Action. This will include big changes to improve global financial stabilization, increase economic productivity, prevent asset bubble formation, provide targeted stimulation, and create sustainable capital generation.

The truth is that we could potentially make any and all of these changes at an earlier stage, including right now. But, politically, such radical changes will be impossible to implement until we absolutely have to. Eventually, people and governments will face reality and figure out the changes necessary to get us out of this mess. We'll certainly be there to help. It will be a very exciting time.

Is There Any Scenario for a Soft Landing?

Yes, but it would have had to occur many years ago, back when the government debt bubble was still under $1 trillion, and before the rise of the real estate bubble, the private debt bubble, and the stock market bubble, and before the massive money printing by the Fed to stimulate it all. In other words, we could have created a softer landing for America's multibubble economy back when the mother of all bubbles, the government debt bubble, was still manageable. Even when the bubbles grew larger, we still could have ended the problem, but with a not-so-soft landing. But at this point, now that the bubbles have grown so large and are so interconnected, the fall will be far, and the eventual landing will be anything but soft.

The Hamptons Effect

Rising bubbles created a rising bubble economy and plenty of bubble-money wealth. If you have a big, expensive house in the Hamptons, and a grand lifestyle to go with it, you are keenly aware that a collapse in the stock market, real estate market, and the other asset bubbles would mean an end to the good times you have come to think of as permanent. Naturally, that isn't too appealing. Therefore, you have a powerful incentive not to see the bubbles or the bubble economy, and instead to believe in wishful thinking that assures you everything is, and will continue to be, all right.

We call this the "Hamptons Effect." Wealthy people, stockbrokers, and asset managers have a deep need to keep believing we don't have any bubbles and to keep investing in the stock market. The Hamptons Effect is part of the reason for the stock market rallies over the past couple of years, and it drives plenty of other irrational decision making, as well. It is part of the Denial stage we told you about. The bigger your house, the more denial you need to sleep at night.

Global Mega-Money Meltdown

IT'S NOT JUST AMERICA'S BUBBLE ECONOMY, IT'S THE WORLD'S BUBBLE ECONOMY

A popular fairy tale gained favor in early 2008, proposing that the rest of the world, especially China, had magically "decoupled" from the naughty U.S. economy. The idea was that regardless of whatever foolishness and financial problems we happen to get ourselves into here, China (and to a lesser extent, the other emerging markets) would continue to be a reliable hotspot for investment profits. Even more magical, these burgeoning economies might actually help buffer the rest of the world, and even the United States, from the full impact of the U.S.-led recession.

Unfortunately, by the end of 2008, it became fully evident that this decoupling myth could not be further from the truth. It was just another failed attempt at wishful thinking and economic cheerleading. In fact, when the U.S. housing bubble, stock market bubble, private debt bubble, and discretionary spending bubble all began to burst in late 2008 and 2009, the speed at which the rest of the world fell into deep recession was staggering. In the fourth quarter of 2008, gross domestic product (GDP) in the United States declined by 6.2 percent on an annual basis; in the United Kingdom, it declined by 5.9 percent; in Germany, GDP declined by 8.2 percent; Japan declined by 12.7 percent; and South Korea declined by a staggering 20.8 percent.

Both Germany and Japan had accelerating declines in the first quarter of 2009 with Germany falling at an annual rate of 14.4 percent and Japan falling 15.2 percent. Mexico actually topped the list in the first quarter 2009 with a 22 percent decline. As the U.S. economy reduced its imports of goods from overseas, particularly in the fourth quarter of 2008, the rest of the world's economies, joined at the hip to ours and each other's, simply *fell off a cliff.*

Now that the U.S. economy is no longer declining, those economies are also no longer declining and are growing. With the world economy growing again, the myth of Chinese decoupling is growing again, too. However, China's recent growth is heavily driven by various government stimulus policies (see the sidebar titled "Now That's Stimulus!"). The Chinese government became extremely worried when tens of millions of Chinese were put out of work due to declining exports. After the global financial crisis of 2008, the government panicked over worries of potential political unrest and launched massive stimulus programs, to promote real estate and infrastructure construction funded by massive money printing, which is helping to stimulate their economy in the short term. More recently, China is not growing as quickly as before and inflation has picked up, although getting accurate statistics on the Chinese economy is nearly impossible.

In any case, China's economy is certainly not decoupling from ours. China is deeply dependent on its exports to the United States and to slow-growing Europe. To think otherwise is pure fantasy. In fact, China and so many other economies are so tightly linked to the fate of the U.S. economy that we almost titled our first book *The World's Bubble Economy.* But our book targeted a U.S. audience, so we accepted a less encompassing title.

Nonetheless, just as we predicted in *America's Bubble Economy,* when the U.S. multibubble economy started to fall, the world's multibubble economy had little choice but to fall, too. And as we fall further in the future, the rest of the world will end up in even worse shape. We should add that the world is starting to take notice of what we are saying. *Aftershock* has been published in Chinese, Korean, and Japanese language editions.

The United States Will Suffer the Least

The U.S. economy is by far the most flexible, diverse, and stable economy in the world. We have the biggest, strongest economy, and we are less dependent on exports than most of the rest of the developed world and far less that the emerging markets. Therefore, the United States will naturally suffer the least in the coming Aftershock. This may seem unfair because we started most of these problems by pumping up so many bubbles in the first place. However, many economies around the world benefited handsomely from our seemingly virtuous upward bubble spiral. They also actively supported it by lending us the money and not complaining when the many bubbles began to rise. Plus, many have pumped up their own bubbles. So it's only logical that during our vicious downward bubble spiral, the rest of the world will suffer as well. And, fair or unfair, because other economies were never as strong as our own, even at the height of the global bubble party, the rest of the world will suffer more than we will during each stage of the multibubble bust.

After the United States, western Europe will suffer the second least, followed by Japan, and then eastern Europe and Russia. Developing nations, such as India and Brazil, will suffer more, and the underdeveloped, poor countries of Africa and elsewhere will do quite badly indeed. China will be hit very hard, and much of the country will be pushed back into rural poverty (more details later in this chapter).

Think of the World's Bubble Economy in Two Categories: Manufacturing and Resource Extraction

We can better understand why and how the world economy will suffer so badly if we analyze the economy in terms of two broad categories: manufacturing and resource extraction.

Manufacturing

The manufacturing category includes high-end manufacturers, primarily Germany and Japan, and low-end manufacturers, primarily China and other Asian Tiger nations. India is similar to low-end manufacturers because it provides low-end service exports.

Low-end manufacturers are directly affected by America's multibubble economy, both on the way up and on the way down, for the simple reason that we are the world's largest importer of low-end manufactured goods. So when the U.S. economy goes up, many other countries' economies go up.

There is an additional multiplier effect in terms of job creation. For each job created to produce exports sold to the United States, roughly two more jobs are created in support of those jobs. This is true not only of nations, but of cities and regions, as well. Any job that produces a good or service that is exported from a region also produces secondary jobs to support those people in the export industry, such as jobs in medicine, government, and housing.

These multiplier effects are extremely important to the export-driven economies of China and the other Asian Tigers, like Korea, Taiwan, Hong Kong, and Singapore. Because of these multiplier effects, a large increase in exports can create a massive economic boom in an export-driven economy. Of course, the very same thing is true in reverse: A big export decline can cause a massive decline in an export-driven economy.

The United States also drives the economies of the second subgroup of manufacturers, which produce high-end manufactured goods, especially Germany and Japan. The United States imports both consumer goods, such as electronics and automobiles, and industrial goods, such as machine tools and construction equipment. This provides a big boost to the Japanese and German economies, not only because of the exports themselves, but also because of the same job multiplier effect described previously.

In addition, it is important to realize that the low-end manufacturing countries such as China import enormous amounts of high-end machinery from Germany and Japan to produce their manufactured goods and to build their economies. This demand helped Germany become the world's largest exporter in 2008. Obviously, this helped further boost the German and Japanese economies before the Great Recession.

Resource Extraction

The other big group in the world's bubble economy includes countries that have large resource extraction industries. This group benefits nicely from growth in both the low-end and high-end manufacturing nations and also from America's multibubble economy. Nations within the resource extraction group include both poor and wealthy countries such as Australia, Russia, Canada, and nations in the Middle East, Africa, and South America. Interestingly, this group also includes China, which is heavily involved in both low-end manufacturing and resource extraction.

Naturally, economies that rely on resource extraction are especially impacted by the rising and falling demands for their various minerals, oil, lumber, grains, and other resources by the booming manufacturing economies of the world's bubble economy. The benefits to these resource-producing nations are double-boosted by both greater quantities of exports and much higher prices for their resources as demand rises. These higher prices can propel a normal economic boom into a hyperboom, creating enormous job growth, highly valued companies, and billionaires just about everywhere there is a mining shovel operating.

America's Bursting Bubble Economy Will Bring Down Both Low-End and High-End Exporting Nations

On the way up, America's multibubble economy fueled the expansion of the world's bubble economy. As each economy expanded, it stimulated and expanded other economies, not only because the United States imported many goods and services from around the world, but also because many other nations have been trading back and forth in a positive feedback loop of economic stimulus. Europe and the more developed economies bought from the underdeveloped and developing countries, and those countries, in turn, bought from other countries.

The popping of America's bubble economy will rapidly pull the plug on every exporting nation in this complex web of interdependence. Given that America's bubble economy has a heavy discretionary spending component, and given that we already have quite a lot of big capital goods in place that will keep us going for a while (like cars and refrigerators), it will be relatively easy for American consumers to drastically reduce their purchases of imported goods (now at sky-high prices due to the falling dollar) as the U.S. economy heads deeper into recession. And in any case, after the dollar bubble pops, the costs of imports into the United States will soar astronomically.

Resource extraction economies will suffer greatly when demand drastically declines. The earlier double boost of growing exports at higher and higher prices in the rising world bubble will easily turn into a double downer of falling exports and falling prices in the falling world bubble.

"A TEMPORARY SOLUTION WOULD BE TO WHITE OUT
THIS PART OF THE CHART."

At the same time we will be importing far less, we will begin to export far more than we do today, because the dollar will have fallen and U.S. goods priced in dollars will be relatively cheap. This will also hurt other resource extraction economies, because cheap U.S. goods will compete with their goods for export to other countries.

The United States produces quite a few resources itself. However, the United States has a very diverse economy and will not feel the effects of either the resource boom or bust to the same extent as other countries.

Salt in the Wound: Not Only Will Foreign Investors Suffer as Their Own Economies Fall, They Will Also Lose on Their U.S. Investments

While the U.S. multibubble economy was booming, domestic and foreign investors from around the world made tremendous profits on their U.S. holdings, including their investments in U.S. stocks, bonds, Treasuries, real estate, and other dollar-denominated assets. As the bubbles pop and these assets lose value, the once-rising profit tide will rapidly flow in reverse, leaving foreign investors with tremendous losses. The economic consequences of this worldwide evaporation of wealth cannot be overstated.

More Salt: Other Governments Have Large Debts As Well

In addition to being hit hard by a huge downturn in exports, many of these export-dependent countries, like Germany and Japan, have built up large government debts of their own during the last two decades. Japan's debt-to-GDP ratio is now far higher than the United States', which is also quite high. And, just like the United States, these countries are also rapidly adding to those deficits with big stimulus packages in the hope of saving their economies. Growing government deficits in the exporting countries will only add to their economic problems later.

When their economies hit the Aftershock, their people and economies will be hit harder because their governments are strapped for cash with huge debts, and they will not be able to fund social welfare programs at anywhere near the current, accustomed levels.

It will be a real shock, especially to Europe, but also to Japan, to have governments that move from being perhaps overly lavish in their benefits in the past to being much stingier in the future.

How the Bursting Bubbles Will Impact the World

Although all the economies of the world will suffer as we approach the Aftershock and during the coming Aftershock mega-depression, some regions will do better than others. Similar to reactions to flu, those who are healthier and stronger before trouble hits tend to hold up better under stress. Here's what we see ahead.

Europe and Japan

As mentioned earlier, the U.S. economy will fare best in the Aftershock, followed by the countries of Europe and Japan, which have larger shares of their economies devoted to exports than we do, and so will be hit harder when their exports radically decline.

At the same time, Europe and Japan will have to continue to import some goods from other countries, although far less than before. Much more than the United States, Europe and Japan will have to continue to import food and energy. To keep manufactured imports to a minimum, these countries will enact protectionist tariffs to protect what remains of their manufacturing industries, and higher taxes on food and energy, slowing the flow of imports into their countries. This will naturally decrease other countries' exports to Europe and Japan even further than they will have already fallen, adding to the already negative downward spiral for the overall world economy.

Because their export industries will be so hard hit across the board, Europe and Japan will suffer very high unemployment, again with that multiplier effect mentioned earlier, in which each lost job that is directly related to exports is coupled with several additional jobs lost that are indirectly related. Stocks will do quite badly, and real estate values will crash. But despite this grim picture, some governments in Europe, such as Germany, the Scandinavian countries, and Switzerland, will likely not need to default on their debts. Japan will not need to default either, despite its more massive debt. Ironically, although the U.S. economy will do better than these other economies in the Aftershock, we will be forced into default and they will not. That's because these governments did not depend so heavily on large amounts of foreign capital that will suddenly disappear.

Like the United States, these countries will print money out of necessity and suffer extremely high inflation, just as we will. But the value of the euro and the yen will hold up relative to the dollar, because Europe and Japan won't have the massive outflow of capital that we will experience, as the massive investment inflow into the United States first slows, then stops, and eventually reverses, with capital pulling out of the United States and flowing back to home countries.

Europe and Japan will be further protected from the need to default on their debts, because inflation will help reduce their debts, as it will reduce ours. However, U.S. inflation will be much greater than in other countries, because we printed so much more money. Our dollar will be crashing faster and deeper because foreign capital will be leaving.

Three other factors will keep these countries out of default. First, massive inflows of new capital into those European countries and Japan when U.S. and foreign investors sell their U.S. assets and buy euro-denominated assets will keep more capital available for European governments.

Second, as many governments seek more stimulus money to save their economies, there will be a shrinking money pie, meaning the total money available worldwide will decline just as more and more is needed. The U.S. government will gobble up a big share of this smaller money pie, going into debt further and faster than some countries in Europe. That will help keep those European governments from running up more massive increases in their debt.

Third, investors who buy those European government bonds will encourage those European governments not to go too far into debt because they will be worried about a possible bankruptcy.

Europe Faces a *Debt* Problem, Not a Euro Problem

Europe is facing a massive debt problem. Whether that debt is denominated in euros or drachmas (the previous Greek currency) doesn't matter. It's still debt. If Greece could get rid of their debt by just dropping the euro, they would have done that a long time ago. And if Greece could pay off its debt to French and German banks by converting back to drachmas, the banks would have agreed to that a long time ago. But the currency isn't the problem, the debt is. That is part of the reason that despite a huge increase in the European debt problem since we wrote the first edition of *Aftershock*, the euro has actually risen relative to the dollar. The euro has been volatile and will undoubtedly see more volatility, but the bottom line is that getting rid of the euro will not solve Europe's debt problem. If only their problems were that easy to solve.

China

China has had unbelievable growth in the past two decades, and under other circumstances you might expect China to do fairly well despite a global economic downturn—but not in a global *bubble economy*. Much of China's recent growth has been driven by America's and the world's bubble economies. While the economies of some of the poorest countries, such as in Africa, will be in far worse shape, none will suffer the pain of crushed expectations in the coming Aftershock more than China.

China's Slowdown and Possible Construction Meltdown

China may still be considered one of the strongest and fastest-growing economies, but don't be fooled: China is now a bubble economy. It wasn't earlier, although much of their growth prior to 2008 was dependent on our own rising economy. But more recently, especially since the global financial crisis in 2008, China has been self-inflating its own bubbles.

Just as in the United States, China is pumping up two giant air bags to try to support its bubble economy: massive money printing and massive borrowing. But in China, the story is a little different. Their government doesn't borrow money at the rate we do; instead, they print massively, give the money to the banks, and the banks lend it out to stimulate the economy. This is creating a massive Chinese debt bubble. Debt, both public and private combined, as a percentage of GDP, has grown substantially since 2008, indicating an increasing reliance on greater amounts of debt for economic growth (see Figure 7.1).

As in our own multibubble economy, one bubble pushes up another. In China, their massive debt bubble is fueling a huge and unsustainable real estate construction bubble. In the past decade, China's construction boom is unprecedented in human history. By some estimates, as much as 50 percent of their GDP is now driven by fixed investment, a large part of which is in construction. That is almost an inconceivable amount of new construction.

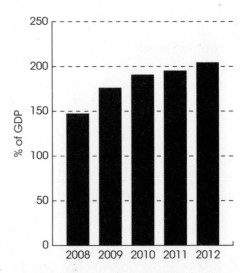

Figure 7.1   China's Increasing Debt-to-GDP Ratio (Combined Public and Private)
For years, China maintained a stable ratio of debt to GDP, despite big rises in both. However, since 2008, lending has exploded relative to GDP.
Sources: People 's Bank of China, State Administration of Foreign Exchange, CEIC, CLSA Asia-Pacific Markets.

By comparison, at the height of the U.S. housing bubble, construction represented only about 17 percent of our economy. During the height of Spain's housing bubble, it was 23 percent. And in Dubai—the world's former poster child for supersized real estate—construction approached about 30 percent of GDP at the peak of its speculative construction boom. China seems to be exceeding them all.

China's massive construction bubble is driven not by real economic demand but heavily by massive bank lending. The government prints money, gives it to Chinese banks, and then forces them to lend it out—often for construction projects that will never see a dime of profit. For example, they built the stunningly huge South China Mall, which is twice the size of the Mall of America (our biggest one), but now sits more than 90 percent vacant. More recently, loaned money was used to build the mammoth New Century Global Center, three times the size of our Pentagon.

All this tremendous lending with little chance of full repayment puts China's banks in a very vulnerable position. China escaped a credit crisis in June 2013 with government intervention and has since recovered. This seems eerily familiar to our own Bear Sterns crisis: we dealt with it quickly and declared all was well, only to later face an even bigger crisis with the loss of Lehman Brothers. The recent Chinese financial crisis, although resolved for now, may very well signal more trouble ahead.

It is hard to see it going any other way, given the huge level of debt and the unlikeliness of repayment. So we think there is a good chance that China will face a bubble pop and economic meltdown due to a collapse in construction and a banking crisis.

For the world's bubble economy, a meltdown by China would have unusually harsh consequences. That is part of the reason so many people are cheerleaders for China's construction bubble, even though they wouldn't normally support such extreme nonmarket intervention in their own country.

China is not only the second biggest economy in the world; it is providing almost *all* of the growth in the world since 2008. So any big slowdown or meltdown in China will have a big impact on the world and on the United States, depressing the exports of many countries. In addition, any major problem in China's banking system will impact many countries and will hurt our banks as well.

Like so much about China and its economy, it is hard to know exactly what is happening or when such a meltdown could occur.

But it is likely we will see a more pronounced slowdown in the next couple of years. Just like our own government, the Chinese government will fight this with even more money printing, but they have been doing this for a while now, and at some point it

Jim Chanos—A Realistic View of China

There are a few voices out there saying that China's problems are far greater than most economists and financial analysts realize, most notably hedge fund manager Jim Chanos of Kynikos Fund, which is why we give him an ABE Award for Intellectual Courage (ABE stands for the name of our first book, *America's Bubble Economy*).

Jim Chanos is the founder and president of Kynikos Associates, a hedge fund with a particular focus on short selling. While the practice of short selling has been somewhat controversial, especially in recent years, one value of companies like Kynikos is that they can point out critical flaws in the market long before most people see them. For example, back in 2000, Kynikos took short positions in a huge energy company, one that *Fortune* had consistently labeled America's most innovative company. Within the next 14 months, the stock had lost 99 percent of its value and the company ended up in bankruptcy. You've probably heard of Enron.

Chanos admits that he's not a "macro guy." His focus is intensive fundamental research and analysis to find stocks that are overvalued. But that hasn't stopped him from seeing some big-picture problems, too, and in recent years he has pinpointed a major bubble in the world economy: the Chinese construction bubble.

Chanos noticed several years ago that property development in China was reaching unsustainable proportions. If the average Chinese couple makes a combined $8,000 or so a year, how can they afford condominiums that can easily cost up to $150,000? It didn't add up. Much of this growth was driven by bad loans pushed by the government. In fact, Chanos found that many new apartment buildings stay empty and are flipped from speculator to speculator on the greater fool theory.

Mr. Chanos's insights aren't especially popular in a financial community that's counting on China to lead the global economic recovery. He has been publicly berated by some, though the attacks against him tend to be very short on data. Jim Chanos deserves big kudos for ignoring the cheerleaders and letting the facts speak for themselves.

simply won't work. China is already a huge economy, and maintaining its high growth rates will become increasingly difficult under any circumstances. And when that growth stops, it won't go gently into the night, but rather will likely go from dream straight to nightmare.

When the United States, Europe, and Japan drastically cut their imports from China, China will experience their great boom in reverse. Unlike in the United States where people will try to maintain their consumption levels as much as possible, Chinese citizens are not so used to prosperity that they can't easily return to lower consumption, like eating less meat, for example. And when Chinese consumers do pull back, their fragile economy will collapse. In fact, after a while, the Chinese stock market and banking system could suffer a semi-shutdown for a period of time. Eventually, there will likely be a massive migration out of the depressed urban centers and back into the countryside, with widespread poverty and even malnutrition because there are no safety nets.

What Happens in China Will Impact Other Economies

China's growth has been one of the few bright spots in the world's bubble economy since the global financial crisis of 2008. It helped drive forward the economies of countries such as Brazil, Australia, and Germany, which are big exporters to China. Everyone wondered how Germany could have had significant growth while the rest of Europe was struggling. The answer is China. Germany is one of the world's biggest exporter, and a lot of those exports go to China. Coauthor Bob Wiedemer will always remember watching a Chinese businessman and a German businessman at a trade show in Guangzhou, China, speaking to each other in English. It emphasized how important exporting to China is to Germany and, as a side note, how important the English language is as a universal common second language.

So China not only spurred a lot of growth for exporters in other countries, including in the United States, it also boosted the hopes of professional stock market investors for a stronger United States and world economy. But more recently, China's growth has started to cool down. And as it cools further in the approach to the Aftershock, it will have a negative impact on the U.S. stock market.

However, we wouldn't expect a wholesale popping of China's economy to happen in 2014 because the government can do a lot to keep it alive for a while longer—but the next few years could be a different matter. Growth of less than 5 percent in China could be a big shock to the stock market. Such a slowdown would also be a big shock to the commodities markets, which have been driven heavily by China. Almost the entire growth in demand for oil since 2005 can be traced to China and to countries that supply China with materials. The same is true for many other commodities as well, such as steel and copper. Even some growth in the price of agricultural commodities, such as corn, can be traced to China and, in particular, growing Chinese demand for more meat in their diets.

China has long been a country of mystery. Exactly when and how the Chinese bubble will pop is also somewhat mysterious. But there is no question that the country is currently on an unsustainable path and that their bubble economy will pop. This dragon is blowing more smoke than fire.

The Middle East and Elsewhere

With the exception of Israel, which will react more like Europe and Japan, the Middle East will look a lot like China in many ways. The big problem for the Middle East is oil. The massive decline in economic activity worldwide in the Aftershock will dramatically decrease the demand for oil. Plus, the world's largest consumer, the United States, will be faced with skyrocketing prices for imported oil because the dollar has fallen. So demand from the United States, which will be declining because of the terrible economy, will take an even bigger hit because of the high price.

Although exploration for oil will dramatically decline in the Aftershock due to falling prices, it will take many years for supply to decrease enough to match up with rapidly falling demand. The collapsing demand will ultimately push oil down to the $10 to $25 (in 2014 dollars) per barrel range.

Such a dramatic decrease in income will devastate the Middle East, especially because some of these countries are already significantly poorer than the United States, Europe, and Japan, even before the world bubble economy bursts. Like China, the Middle East will suffer massive unemployment. And like China, the global mega-depression will likely accelerate political turmoil, especially in the Kingdom of Saudi Arabia. The monarchy there could quite possibly go the way of the monarchy of Iran, since there is already considerable underlying tension in the Kingdom.

Outside of the Middle East, many other countries will also suffer. When the world's bubble economy falls, the already very poor countries of Africa and Asia will be truly devastated. With commodities and mineral exports slowing to a trickle, citizens of the poorest countries will face a real struggle for basic survival. Eventually, the richer, more developed nations, like the United States, will step in and help. We won't have all the money we did before, but we will still likely have some money and political will to help other countries who desperately need survival support.

The Green Economy Won't Produce a Lot of Green

Although there may be some good green technologies in the works, as the world's bubble economy goes down, so will investments in the green economy. In fact, the investment climate for green tech/ clean tech will turn increasingly negative as stocks fall and returns on investment increasingly evaporate. In such a down market, good investments will be taken down along with the bad. Also, demand will fall as the economy falls, as there is less spending on capital goods and construction. A final blow will hit when the government debt bubble pops in the Aftershock because government subsidies will be eliminated. Subsidies are very important for a lot of green technologies. Some of those subsidies may be eliminated before Phase 2, in 2011 and 2012.

Many investors are pumping money into green technologies, and no doubt some will succeed in making money. Some even seem to hope it will be the next financial bubble. We think the clean tech investment boom will be the Bubble that Never Will Be.

Long term, we will need to greatly improve the productivity of our energy sector, just as we will need to improve the productivity of other sectors of our economy. But, like other sectors of our economy, this will involve far more than just new technologies.

If the World's Bubble Economy Is Hit Harder than the U.S. Bubble Economy, Won't That Be Good for the Dollar?

No! This is the most common misconception about the value of the dollar. Even if the rest of the world is devastated economically, and it will be, the value of the dollar will still fall relative to the euro, yen, and other major currencies. That's because the value of a currency is *not* a reflection of whose overall economy is better relative to the others, but a matter of *supply and demand* (see Chapters 5 and 6).

After investor psychology turns decidedly negative and U.S. stocks and bonds go over the Market Cliff (see Chapter 4), U.S. inflation will climb. That will make U.S. dollar–denominated assets far less appealing, greatly reducing the demand for dollars.

The initial concern about the dollar will become a self-fulfilling prophecy. As a small number of investors stop buying dollar-based investments, the already reduced dollar will fall, causing other investors to become more concerned and stop buying dollars. At some point, the market can change quickly from people merely reducing their purchases of dollars to a full-scale panic where they try to sell off whatever dollar-denominated investments they still have, causing a traumatic collapse in the dollar's value. Unfortunately, the majority of investors will not be able to sell their dollars fast enough to get out, and their investment money will go to Money Heaven in the Aftershock (see Chapter 6).

However, the dollar, despite its collapse in value, will still be one of the most widely traded currencies simply because of the size of the U.S. economy and the size of its imports and exports. As such, the dollar will retain its role as a reserve currency. However, the U.S. financial system and the dollar will have lost much of the hard-earned credibility it has had for more than a century. Being a reserve currency is more a function of size. But the credibility of the economy is what is key to foreign investors, and it will be gone.

If the Rest of the World Is Collapsing, Won't That Be Good for Gold?

Yes! Gold will especially benefit from the collapse of economies around the globe because it is a favorite safe haven investment for people in Asia and the Middle East. Those countries buy most of the gold in the world. In fact, the United States accounts for only 10 percent of the world's total gold market. China and India, however, represent almost half of the world's gold demand and will be eager to get their hands on more as insecurity rises. Demand for gold has already been exploding in China partly due to fear of inflation.

So it is important to view gold from a global perspective and not a U.S. perspective. The rest of the world looks at gold as a very viable and particularly safe investment. People at every economic level often own or want to own gold. It is much more favored culturally around the world than it is in the United States and even Europe. Gold will rise sharply in the Aftershock whether U.S. investors participate or not. And they certainly will participate.

Instability in Asian and Middle Eastern economies will motivate investors in those countries to buy a lot more gold, further accelerating the rising gold bubble. Yes, gold is another bubble on the ascent, and eventually it, too, will fall. But in the meantime, you

A $100,000 Toyota Camry? A Weak Dollar Will Make Our Imports Very Expensive

An important side effect of the dollar bubble collapse is that the price of imported goods will soar. This is an exchange rate issue, not a price increase due to inflation.

Imported cars, for example, will be priced so high in dollars that the United States will no longer buy a significant number. This is the market's way of restoring trade balance after so many years of imbalanced trade.

Some goods we will have to import because we no longer have the facilities to make them, such as toys, clothing, and some electronics. They will be expensive, but we will still buy them. Even though expensive, the imported prices will be less costly that the alternative option of creating new factories in the United States with very high cost capital and with relatively high labor costs.

The lower dollar will make our exports much cheaper for other countries to buy, and we will do a booming business in exporting necessities, such as coal and wheat. However, most other goods will be hard to export because the world demand will have collapsed, and other countries will likely use import restrictions to protect the remaining companies in their countries that still produce those goods.

Coal is an especially good export for the United States because many countries don't have it, yet will still need it to produce electricity, even during the depths of the economic downturn. Plus, we have an awful lot of it, and it will be dirt cheap for other countries to import because of the much lower dollar.

might as well learn how to profit from its coming meteoric rise (see Chapters 8 and 9).

International Investment Recommendations

Our general investment suggestions are offered in the next two chapters, and are provided in much more de tail in our recent book, *The Aftershock Investor*, Second Edition (Wiley, 2013). But for those of you who just can't wait, here's your executive summary:

Our Best Advice for U.S. Investors Looking to Invest in Foreign Markets

In general, foreign markets will follow U.S. markets but with higher beta. In the short term, there may be ways to profit, if you are sophisticated about these kinds of investments, and you very actively and correctly manage them. However, in the long term: *stay away!* Both the low-end manufacturing and high-end manufacturing economies and the resource-driven economies we just discussed will not recover until America's economy recovers. And since America's economy won't recover until after the dollar bubble pops, there is no reason to invest overseas for many years.

Obviously, there are always exceptions, but, in general, investments will not do well because overseas economies will be in much worse shape than the U.S. economy. Many are more dependent on exports and not as diverse and flexible as we are. Plus, many invested heavily in the U.S. economy, which is about to cost them dearly.

Our Best Advice for Foreign Investors Looking to Invest in Their Own Markets

If the long-term investments in your countries are not good for U.S. investors, they certainly aren't any better for you. Short term, there are opportunities. But it is a bubble, so you have to be aware of that. Even long term, there are always individual exceptions but, in general, when economies nosedive, normal stock and real estate investments in your home countries will lose you tons of money.

Gold will offer easy gains. Also, depending on your home currency, some foreign currencies, such as Canadian dollars, Swiss francs, Norwegian krone, and even euros, in the form of short-term debt instruments, may offer returns above normal interest rates. Shorting stocks will also be quite profitable for those willing and able to move into that arena, as many non-U.S. stocks will be plummeting just like U.S. stocks, only faster in many cases.

Our Best Advice for Foreign Investors Looking to Invest in the U.S. Markets

In the short term, as long as investor psychology stays positive and the Federal Reserve continues to print massive amounts of new money, the U.S. stock market is basically a safe bet. U.S. bonds, however, have less upside potential than before and have become riskier.

In the longer term, given that the value of the dollar will fall significantly in the Aftershock, low-cost investments in the United States will eventually become quite profitable for foreign investors. In fact, this is where a great deal of money will be made in the next couple of decades and, unlike the bubble money of the past, which will largely disappear, the money made by smart foreign investors in the United States after the dollar bubble pops will last because it's not bubble money.

The biggest challenge, however, is timing. Most foreign investors will think that U.S. investments have hit bottom when, in fact, they still have a long way down to go. By jumping in too soon they will lose an enormous amount of money. A simple rule for anyone interested in purchasing U.S. assets is to refrain from investing until *after* the bubbles pop and stabilize.

PART

II

AFTERSHOCK DANGERS AND PROFITS

Covering Your Assets

HOW NOT TO LOSE MONEY

Most of us find *making* money far more interesting than simply not losing it. But knowing how to protect yourself is absolutely crucial to surviving and thriving in the years ahead, so please don't skip this chapter. Much more detail about investing before and during the Aftershock can be found in our last book, *The Aftershock Investor*, Second Edition (Wiley, November 2013), where we offer separate chapters on each type of investments, including stocks, bonds, real estate, cash, retirement, life insurance, annuities, and gold. In this book, we've condensed our investment advice into two chapters (this one and the next), in order to focus more on our macroeconomic views and predictions.

The Three Rules for Not Losing Money

There are three basic, but uncomfortable, rules for how not to lose money before and during the Aftershock. Please understand that these protection strategies are intended for the *long term*. In the shorter term, because of the massive stimulus that is temporarily supporting the bubbles, these protective steps are not immediately necessary. There is no immediate crisis or need for panic. But there is a real need to know what is coming and how to protect yourself from what is ahead.

For the long term, there are three simple rules for where *not* to invest as the dollar and other bubbles fall:

Rule 1: Exit stocks well before the Market Cliff.

Rule 2: Stay away from real estate as a long-term investment until after all the bubbles fully pop.

Rule 3: Avoid bonds and most fixed-rate investments (including some whole life insurance and annuities, depending on their terms) as interest rates rise.

Again, we are *not* saying you must do all this now, although you could. We are saying these are the three rules you must follow before the bubbles pop and Aftershock. Timing when to follow these rules is not easy and will be addressed in more detail later in the chapter. Right now, we want to talk about the rules themselves.

These Rules Are Simple but Not Easy!

We said three *simple* rules; we did not say *easy*. After years of investing in stocks, real estate, and fixed-rate investments, we know that the idea of pulling out of these bulwarks of wealth building may feel counterintuitive and just plain wrong.

At the risk of repeating ourselves, we feel we need to tell you once again what you are up against, because following these three simple rules is going to be hard to do—especially if you are the only one you know who is doing it.

As we've said many times, we are not in the middle of a down market cycle. The U.S. and world economies are not merely fluctuating back and forth between "up" business cycles and "down" business cycles. The economy is fundamentally *evolving*. We are not going backward to where we once were; we are going forward to where we have never been before. At this moment in history, going forward involves the bursting of a series of interconnected economic bubbles.

On the way up, these expanding bubbles created tremendous wealth both here and around the globe. On the way down, these bursting bubbles will destroy a very impressive amount of wealth as well. How much of *your* wealth will be destroyed in the years ahead is entirely up to you. Ignore the problem, or react as you may have in the past, and things could get away from you rather fast.

Again, we are not saying this is going to happen in a few weeks or months. Unless there is a wildcard event that we are not expecting, there is still time to ease into our recommendations in stages. What we are trying to impress on you is the need to see this coming and to *take action* before it's too late.

As pointed out in earlier chapters, massive stimulus to support the bubbles is working in the short term to keep the multibubble economy going, but it is not producing large gross domestic product (GDP) or quality job growth—certainly not as much as the stock market has recently been growing. Over time, when growth does not improve, investor psychology will turn increasingly worried, pushing stocks and bonds over the Market Cliff. At that point, the negative effects of massive money printing and massive borrowing will begin. Rising inflation and high rates will be counterproductive for supporting the sagging bubbles. As time passes, each falling bubble will put increasing downward pressure on the others, creating a combined, cascading, multibubble fall.

Hence, our key advice for the coming Aftershock is to purge your mind right now of the false idea that if you just wait long enough, economic gravity will somehow disappear and that falling asset values (like stocks, real estate, etc.) will defy gravity and automatically return to an "up cycle." These popping bubbles are not going to float back up just because we want them to!

People who tell you otherwise are simply trying to cheerlead the economy. As you may recall from the discussion in Chapter 6 about the psychology of how people react to changing economic conditions, we are currently in the Market Cycles stage of psychology regarding the evolving economic collapse. In the face of the evidence, people can no longer say that everything is fine, so the next best way to ignore reality is to say we are experiencing a "down" economic cycle. Clearly, given the amount of stimulus we are throwing at it, the economy is growing only modestly. We aren't getting much bang for the (newly printed) buck.

We know beyond any doubt that this is no more than cheerleading because these same experts who are now insisting we will return to an up cycle soon, never once said a word about a coming *down* cycle back when stocks and real estate were soaring high. Yet when the bubbles are falling, these same people will try to convince you that an automatic and reliable up cycle is inevitably on its way. It's all just part of the broader attempt to cheerlead the economy and keep investors relaxed. Just be patient, they say. Everything will get better soon. The economy (and your particular investments) will be just fine.

Helping to support this cheerleading point of view is, of course, the massive government stimulus that is driving and supporting the current fake recovery (see Chapter 1). Because of massive money printing and borrowing, there has been an artificially created boost to stocks and real estate, and the cheerleaders love to point to this as good evidence that we do in fact have a solid and reliable "up cycle" with more "up" to come.

Please don't fall for this! Multiple, linked, collapsing bubbles cannot and will not magically reinflate. The bubbles are not fully falling yet, but the fake recovery is not sustainable and will eventually have to end when investor psychology turns more negative, we go over the Market Cliff, and inflation and interest rates rise.

"I got out of tulips after the market collapsed, but I'm slowly getting back in. Especially pink ones."

Long Term versus Short Term

Before we dive into the details of our three rules for protecting assets, we want to be very clear about the difference between the *long term* (most likely beginning sometime between 2015 and 2018) and the *short term* (prior to 2015).

In the longer term, as GDP and employment don't significantly improve, we believe that investor psychology will significantly change enough to push stocks and bonds over the Market Cliff (see Chapter 4). Inflation due to massive money printing will then rise and interest rates will rise as well (see Chapter 5), popping all the U.S. bubbles (see Chapter 6), which will pop the world's bubble economy, too (see Chapter 7).

Prior to that occurring, in the short and medium term, inflation will be less of a concern, and investor psychology will still be relatively good regarding most U.S. assets.

Therefore, it is important to distinguish the difference between the long term and the short term because these periods will be quite different. In fact, in the short term we are already seeing the exact opposite of what will occur later, depending on how aggressively the federal government continues to stimulate the economy and support the bubbles.

As we have already pointed out, many of the government's actions designed to stimulate the economy in the short term will only make things that much worse in the long term when the bubbles fully pop. But in the short term, all this stimulus has many temporary, short-term benefits that most people will confuse with a real recovery (which we certainly are not having).

One of the most powerful *short-term* benefits of the actions by the federal government include the huge stock rebound from the crash of 2008 and 2009 to 2013, created by the Fed's massive money printing operations. With QE1, the Fed purchased $1.7 trillion worth of Treasury, Freddie Mac, and Fannie Mae bonds.

When the Fed stopped its bond purchases in April 2010, the stock market promptly ran into trouble. Less than two months later, the May flash crash occurred, followed by a negative summer for the stock market. Things were looking down for stocks. But for Federal Reserve Chairman Ben Bernanke, that was no problem. Uncle Ben (Uncle Sam takes your money; Uncle Ben makes your money) had the solution and announced another round of massive money printing. If QE1 worked wonders, maybe QE2 would work even more wonders—and it did!

Almost as soon as QE2 was announced, the stock market headed back up in an almost unbroken line through the end of 2010. The market would have finished *down* 15 percent or more in 2010 (as defined by the S&P 500), but with Uncle Ben's magic money-printing machine, it finished *up* 11 percent. The market continued to go up from 2011 to mid-2012, largely due to QE2. Then, beginning in September 2012, the Fed unleashed QE3 and, as of this writing in January 2014, they are now printing a stunning $75 billion per month *with no end date.* The stock-boosting magic of quantitative easing can be seen in Figure 8.1.

The stock market loves money printing and at this point is addicted to it. Take it away completely or even reduce it, and stocks may fall or may coast for a while and then decline. Either would spur another round of Fed printing. Therefore, there is little reason to think that the Fed will entirely stop massive money printing anytime soon.

That means stocks could rise even further before the stock market bubble pops. So when you read in the sections that follow about our long-term rule for protection in the stock market, keep

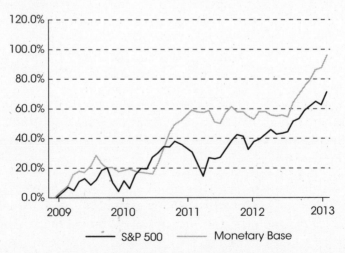

Figure 8.1 Correlation of Quantitative Easing (Fed Money Printing) and S&P 500
When the Fed prints money, investors listen.
Sources: Federal Reserve and Standard and Poor's.

in mind that in the case of stocks, the long term and the short term are definitely not the same thing.

Of course, no one knows exactly what the Fed will do next or exactly how the stock market will react to it in the next several months, so we can't give you a rule for the short term, other than to say anything is possible. You could play it safe and get out *before* investor sentiment changes. Just be aware that if you choose to do so, you may miss out on more of the potential upside before the Fed's medicine (money printing) becomes a poison (causing inflation) that will eventually pop the stock bubble. This can be hard to time, so if you have already gotten out of the market, don't worry; you have protected your assets, which is most important.

In regard to real estate, our long-term rule is the same as our short-term advice regarding real estate: in general, stay away—unless you can get in and out of a real estate deal quickly and profitably, or unless you have some other compelling reasons to buy or hang on to real estate. The section below on real estate will explain why.

Our long-term rule regarding bonds and most other fixed-rate debt is not dramatically different from our short-term rule. In the long term, stay away. In the short term, stay away or proceed with caution. Fixed-rate debt offers only low returns and faces very high risk as interest rates rise. In the spring of 2013, we saw how a small rise in interest rates can push bond prices down. We will surely see much more of that later, as inflation and interest rates rises.

If you want to own fixed-rate assets in the short term, choose those that mature in five years or less because they will fall less sharply than longer-term debt, and be prepared to get out of these quickly when interest rates start to go up. Much more detail on all of this is offered in the sections that follow. We just want to make sure that you understand that the short term and the long term are *not* the same. *This economy is evolving.*

Rule 1: Exit Stocks Well Before the Market Cliff

Just after the financial crisis and stock market crash in late 2008, coauthor Bob Wiedemer had dinner with a friend. After a few drinks, the man revealed that he had recently made one of the biggest financial mistakes of his life. A fan of our first book, Bob's friend admitted he only half believed our 2006 predictions in *America's*

Bubble Economy, and therefore he sold only about half of his stocks prior to the 2008 crash. For sure, this guy saved himself from what could have been twice the loss by selling half his holdings near the market peak. But he felt terrible having not sold the other half, too.

Let Bob's friend spare you his learning curve. Despite the huge stock market rebound from the crash since 2009, stocks are vulnerable to a crash or a series of smaller downturns, and will eventually fall much farther than the crash of late 2008.

As we said before, when it comes to stocks, the long term and the short term are not the same.

In the short term, more massive money printing by the Federal Reserve could continue to support the stock market and could even push it higher, assuming there are no Black Swan events that spook investors.

We made this point clearly in our previous books. In the August 2011 publication of the second edition of *Aftershock* we said:

> *In fact, if the Fed wanted (and if there was enough political support for it), continued massive money printing could potentially push the Dow back to its 2007 all-time high of 14,164 or higher.*

We include this quote here because that is exactly what happened. The Dow topped 16,000 in 2013 and could go even higher in 2014. But that does not mean stocks won't go over the Market Cliff in a few years. They will.

After the Market Cliff inflation and interest rates will climb, and the stock market (and all our asset bubbles) will fall. Again, if we did not already have a multibubble economy on the way down, big economic stimuli, like massive government deficit spending and massive money printing, might do the trick of jump-starting some real economic growth.

But we do have a multibubble economy on the way down, and big stimuli funded by more massive government borrowing and more massive money printing are only going to make things much worse in the *long term*, when the bubbles fully pop.

When to Exit Stocks?

In the *short term*, the answer depends on your particular investment style, goals, and risk appetite. Some people have already exited the stock market completely, and that's fine. If you want to own stocks for a while longer to take advantage of any potential additional upside, in large part driven by massive money printing by the Fed, please be aware that at any time conditions can change very quickly, depending on what the government decides to do. Conditions can also change quickly due to any potential triggering events in the Middle East, Europe, or China, or other bad news.

Even if no wildcard events occur, simply the passage of time will be enough. With continued poor economic and job growth, investors will become increasingly concerned how much stocks have gone up despite slow GDP growth and company earnings. At first, only a few investors will decide to exit early to take some profits and the market will correct downward. Then, in time, more investors will follow and stock prices will dip lower. With fewer buyers, most stock holders will stay in the market and will be wiped out when stocks hit the Market Cliff. There will be some bargain hunters but they will get creamed, as they did in 1928 and 1929. They won't think it is a popping bubble; they think it's a bull in a downturn.

Can you get out at just the right time? Probably not. It will be quite difficult to tell when the market has topped out and is going down long term. As they say on Wall Street, nobody rings a bell when the market peaks.

This new investment environment takes very active, time-consuming, and complex portfolio management. Unless your financial advisers have the correct macroeconomic view of what is going on (very few do), you will essentially be flying solo. Therefore, you will need to watch the news, have the correct macroeconomic view of what is occurring, and know how to apply it to your particular investments.

Even with active management of your stock portfolio, the short term will evolve into the long term, and at some point you will want to exit stocks before they begin to drop significantly. The fall may occur in a few stages, with some stabilization between the drops, or all at once. There is an increasing possibility of a catastrophic collapse that could happen very quickly. Once the market starts to rapidly crash, it will become increasingly difficult to sell your stocks because there will be so few buyers. If everyone is running for the gates at the same time, most people can't get out.

As we explained in the Chapter 4, one action the government might take to try to slow down this financial death spiral is to halt stock market trading. At a certain point, market declines could be very large—like a flash crash that doesn't rebound. Hence, government and market officials may decide that the best option is simply to close the market for a few days or a week to let investors settle down and get their confidence back. They might make changes to limit high-frequency trading as an excuse for closing the market. Blaming the market's decline on high-frequency trading or some other technical issue is certainly a lot better than blaming it on a fundamental lack of confidence. These market stoppages—there may be several—might even work short term, but more likely they won't, and they certainly won't work long term. The downward spiral will simply resume after the stoppages since the fundamentals won't have changed.

Ultimately, automated selling may be completely blocked. In addition, after a market stoppage, selling may be limited when it reopens and there may even be incentives for buying stocks. Shorting stocks may also be limited or stopped completely.

Perfect Timing Is Impossible, Seeking Safety Early is Best

We sometimes hear from readers who decided to exit the stock market early because they thought it would crash sooner rather than later. This put them in a position of maximum safety. However, when the Fed's massive money printing drove up the market and they missed out on some potential gains, they felt frustrated.

Ideally, we would all chose to enter and exit markets at just the right time—when all profits can be maximized and all losses can be avoided. Other than by pure luck, such perfect timing is impossible to achieve. And even if you get lucky, odds are you can't do it again. Instead, people enter and exit markets at various times, based on their overall macroeconomic view, desire for safety, and tolerance for risk. Risk and safety are often at odds with each other. It's rare that you can maximize both at the same time. When you try to maximize profits, potential for risks often rises. When you try to maximize safety, potential for profits often declines.

Given that it is nearly impossible to time your exits perfectly, you will likely either get out of the market a bit too early or get out a bit too late. Which would you prefer?

We cannot tell you in a book exactly what will happen and exactly when it will happen. We can give you excellent and proven advice regarding long-term economic trends. How you translate this into your personal decisions regarding when to exit the stock market is up to you. If you feel confident in our point of view and are ready to act on it now to maximize safety, there is no harm in getting out early.

However, if you need to see more future evidence that our macro view is correct, or if you are willing to sacrifice some safety in exchange for the potential of some more short term profits, then you can hold off on exiting stocks for a while longer. Just stay alert and be ready to get out quickly before too many others do. Don't push your luck too close to the Market Cliff.

Only you can decide what you think is a reasonable time frame for exiting the stock market, depending on your macro view and how close to the edge you are willing to go. In our view, missing out on some potential future upside is far preferable to taking big losses because you waited too long.

This same general advice applies to the stocks in your 401(k) plan or other retirement accounts. Within what you believe is a reasonable time frame, begin to move your money out of stocks and into cash.

How Long to Stay Out of the Stock Market?

As a general rule, once the stock market begins to crash, stay clear of all stocks, until each one of the interconnected asset bubbles has fully popped, especially the dollar bubble. There are a few small exceptions to this rule (see Chapter 9), but in general, *get out* and *stay out* of your stocks until after the dollar and government debt bubbles fully pop.

As the market goes down in stages, resist the temptation to throw money away on what may look like bargains.

Do not get lured back into stocks *until after all the bubbles fully pop*, if you still have any interest in investing in stocks at that point (most people won't). As mentioned earlier, it is very hard to predict exactly when all the bubbles will fully pop because it is so heavily influenced by investor psychology, additional money printing by the Fed, and the willingness and ability of governments, like China, to intervene in the foreign exchange markets. Another factor that makes precision timing difficult is the real possibility that the stock market is occasionally manipulated by certain powerful forces (see the Appendix).

But Don't the Recent Gains of the Last Few Years Mean the Worst Is Now Behind Us?

If we didn't have a stock bubble to begin with, and if the recent gains were due to something other than massive money printing, then, yes, the recent gains in the stock market would be very impressive indeed.

But stock prices have been at bubble levels since the early 1980s. We know the stock market is a bubble because the Dow rose 14-fold from 1982 to 2007, while company earnings and GDP rose only about threefold for the same period. Over the long term, as Nobel Prize–winning economist Milton Friedman and others have shown, earnings rise about as fast as GDP. But neither GDP nor earnings rose 1,400 percent, as the stock market did during that time—a classic picture of a bubble.

There are only two ways to push a fallen stock market bubble back up again:

1. Reinflate the bubble, which is not possible at this point because the previous drivers of the stock bubble are gone.
2. Temporarily stimulate and boost up the stock market with massive money printing by the Federal Reserve.

With option 1 gone, we are heavily pursuing option 2. Not surprisingly, the stock market has returned to previous highs and even risen higher. Of course, the boosted stock market bubble will pop again when a growing number of investors begin to notice that we don't really have much of a broader economic recovery with little GDP growth. That will eventually lead to the Market Cliff, followed by rising inflation, and then rising interest rates. High interest rates will poke a pin in what is left of all the bubbles and the bubble party will be over.

Before the Market Cliff, if you want to participate in this kind of market, you have to be able to differentiate short-term gains from long-term trends and understand the long-term economic fundamentals that ultimately drive those trends. Money can be made by being "long" in this market but only for a relatively short time. The longer-term trend for the stock market, based on economic fundamentals, is definitely negative.

Bubbles are not sustainable indefinitely, not even when we really want them to be. Without real productivity increases to fundamentally drive real economic growth, the only thing temporarily keeping the current stock market bubble going is continued massive money printing by the Fed and continued positive psychology by investors. Lose either one of those in the future and this bubble will be over.

The next chapter offers ideas about what you can do to make money before and during the Aftershock, but right now, you need to wrap your mind around this very difficult to accept idea: *in the long term, stay away from investing in stocks.* This is also true for U.S. investors looking to invest in foreign stocks and for foreign investors looking to invest in the United States or in their own countries. *Stay away!*

While it is true that profits can be made in any market as long as it is moving either up or down, trying to survive and profit in this stock market will take an extraordinary amount of time-consuming, active, and complex management, with precision timing and a good dose of plain luck. Very few people will do it successfully, and even those who do may not be able to do it again, as things keep changing. The only exception to our no-stocks rule is if you are extraordinarily talented and have a whole lot of time on your hands, or if you are working with a very sophisticated money manager who closely follows the macroeconomic analysis of *Aftershock* and can proactively and correctly exit the stock and bond markets at the right times.

Rule 2: Stay Away from Real Estate Until after All the Bubbles Pop

Despite what the cheerleaders want you to believe, real estate prices have not hit bottom, and despite the recent upturn in real estate due the rising stock bubble, the real estate bubble is not making a grand comeback.

It's true that in many cities home prices have risen significantly, but they are still not back up to their prefinancial crisis highs, and there are many forces that will again push home prices down in the mid- to long-term future. So unless you find an exceptional bargain that you can realistically flip fairly quickly to a ready and qualified buyer, long-term investing in real estate is not a good idea until after all the bubbles burst.

What is left of the partially popped real estate bubble is being temporarily supported by massive money printing, which is keeping interest rates, including mortgage rates, low. Home prices are also being supported by the rise in the stock market, which makes home buyers feel more flush. That's great for now, especially if you are trying to sell. But don't feel you must rush in and buy now before home prices go higher. In time, this bubble is going to fully pop and prices will fall.

After investor psychology turns negative and we hit the Market Cliff, inflation will rise significantly, pushing interest rates higher. Rising unemployment will mean fewer home buyers, and high interest rates will shrink the already small pool of able buyers even smaller—further driving down prices.

As much as rising interest rates will harm the stock market, they will be even more toxic to the real estate market because high interest rate mortgages and tough credit requirements will put home buying out of reach for most Americans.

So, in general, stay away from real estate. Do not be tempted by past profits you may have made or wish you had made. Now is not the time. Rest assured there will plenty of *real* real estate bargains in the future.

What to Do with Owned Real Estate

As we have already said, real estate values are not going to significantly recover, even though they are temporarily moving up in some areas of the country in the short term. Over time, with rising mortgage rates and growing unemployment, real estate prices will continue to fall and will certainly crash once the stock market, dollar, and other bubbles pop. So if you own a primary residence, vacation home, investment property, commercial real estate, or farmland, the coming months and years will likely present some challenges. Here's what we recommend and why.

Vacation Homes, Investment Properties, and Commercial Real Estate

Unless you have very compelling attachments to or very strong sentimental interests in any vacation homes, give some serious consideration to selling them while the real estate market is experiencing a temporary upturn. You can always just rent when you go to your favorite vacation spots. Even if selling a vacation home now will result in a financial loss, it will not be as much as you will surely lose later. Ditto for investment property and commercial real estate. *Sell them before the bubbles pop* and prices fall. What we saw in 2008 and 2009 is only a small sampling of the drop we will see later when the whole multibubble economy falls.

It is always better to be a seller when more people want to be buyers. Don't wait until most real estate owners want to be sellers.

Later on (after all the bubbles pop), if you have the means, you will be able to buy vacation homes and other real estate very, very cheaply, but only if you don't lose all your money in the collapse. So be practical and wise, and resist the cheerleaders. Later, you are going to look like a genius.

Your Primary Residence

For your primary home, the situation is trickier. Many people have a sentimental attachment to their homes and may not want to sell them to capture any current equity before home values fall. In addition, it may not be easy to find an equivalent rental. As we said before, for many people, renting would be difficult. None of the authors have sold their primary residences. But we do have realistic expectations about our homes' future values and are willing to keep our homes anyway.

However, if you are planning to move or retire in the near future, by all means, speed up that process and sell your home sooner rather than later. Home prices have risen in many areas due to the massive money printing, rising stock prices, and still-low mortgage rates (although they've started to rise a bit). So now, or in the next year or so, is a good time to sell.

Get Fixed

If you are going to keep your home, make sure you have a *fixed-rate* mortgage, not an adjustable-rate mortgage. If you have an adjustable-rate mortgage, we suggest you try to refinance to a low fixed-rate mortgage. Mortgage rates are still at historic lows and will likely stay low for a while longer due to massive money printing and not much inflation. If you can, move now to lock in a low mortgage interest rate before it's too late.

If you have a fixed-rate mortgage when the dollar bubble pops and inflation rises, your monthly payments on your home will not rise. That means, assuming you have income that rises more or less with inflation, you will be able to repay your mortgage with "cheaper dollars" than the dollars you borrow. That essentially dramatically reduces your mortgage payments.

Of course, the value of your home will also be greatly reduced, but at least you will have a good, cheap place to live for as long as you wish.

Unfortunately, just the opposite will be true for anyone holding an adjustable-rate mortgage. As inflation and interest rates go up, the rapidly increasing monthly payments will quickly make repaying the loan difficult, if not impossible. So refinancing from an adjustable-rate to a fixed-rate loan is absolutely essential.

What about refinancing an already fixed-rate mortgage? That only makes sense if you can lower your current mortgage interest rate by at least 0.75 percent. If your saving will be less than that, it is probably not worth the trouble and expense to refinance.

Pay It Off Faster or Slower?

Once upon a time, accelerated mortgage repayment made good sense because it got you out of debt and out of paying interest that much sooner. But not so going forward in this popping-bubble environment. It may seem counterintuitive, but you do not want to pay off your low-interest, fixed-rate mortgage any faster than is minimally required. That's because you are no longer trying to increase your equity when home values will fall in the future and wipe out the additional equity.

In addition, eventually, high inflation is going to all but wipe out this kind of debt for you in the future because you will be repaying your mortgage with "cheaper" dollars. However, you do have to have enough money at that time to make your mortgage payment each month or you'll risk losing your home.

Pull Out Equity?

Rather than paying off your mortgage faster, some people may choose to pay it off even more slowly by refinancing and pulling out equity. The rationale is that with rising inflation, you will be repaying this loan with cheaper and cheaper dollars. High inflation will essentially make your fixed-rate mortgage payment tiny compared to the number of dollars you will have as the value of the dollar drops and your income goes up more or less with inflation, assuming you still have a job or inflation-protected assets to sell, such as gold.

This is a risky proposition that we are not advocating, but if you do decide to extract some equity from your home, you may want to consider investing in something other than real estate that will rise as the bubbles fall (see next chapter), to the extent that you feel comfortable and agree with our forecasts. This clearly has risks— the big one being difficulty in paying your monthly mortgage payments if you do not save and properly invest the excess proceeds from your home. But as soon as high inflation hits, you will be able to pay your fixed-rate mortgage payments with cheaper and cheaper dollars.

Is a Reverse Mortgage a Good Idea?

It can be in some circumstances, but it is not without risk in the Aftershock.

A reverse mortgage is a special type of home loan that lets you convert the equity in your home into monthly payments to you, while you continue to own and live in your home. Because older people tend to have untapped home equity at the same time that they may have reduced income, a reverse mortgage may make sense for some people *in a normal economy.*

Under normal conditions, the majority of reverse mortgages are insured by the Federal Housing Administration (FHA). If the lender or bank later becomes unable to make your payments, the FHA would continue to pay you monthly.

But here's the problem: Normal conditions will change in the Aftershock. Just like other government funds, such as the Federal Deposit Insurance Corporation (FDIC) insurance fund, this FHA mortgage fund is not infinite. Under normal conditions, there is ample money in the fund to cover occasional losses. Even if the FHA fund were to run out of money, the federal government would step in and cover any additional needs.

However, once all the bubbles fully pop, we don't expect the government to be able to fully meet all of its many obligations. This will not happen overnight. At first, when these various federal insurance funds (FHA, FDIC, etc.) begin to run low due to so many claims, the government will add new money to these funds through more money printing.

But in the later stages, when money printing ends due to too high inflation, the government will not be able to bail out so many funds and institutions. At that point, you would get reduced payments, hardship-only payments, or perhaps no payments.

Right now, it's hard to imagine a time when the government will be unable to borrow or print more money. Even if you don't believe we are headed for the Aftershock, given that the Fed has already increased the U.S. monetary base by *more than 400 percent* since 2008, we will certainly have high future inflation. That means whatever you get for your reverse mortgage monthly payment will buy a lot less in the future than it would today. Even an inflation rider will not compensate for such high inflation.

So a reverse mortgage may make sense for some people in some circumstances, depending on age and many other factors, but in general, we do not give a blanket endorsement to all reverse mortgages. If you get one, please make sure to include both yourself and your spouse's name on the new deed. Otherwise, the company can take your home as soon as the lone person on the deed dies, leaving your spouse homeless and with no more payments.

If you are considering a reverse mortgage, it is important to consider what you will do with the money (live on it or invest it), whether you can get an upfront lump sum, and whether you have the confidence and experience to handle the potential risks if you chose to invest it. If you are hoping to live on the payments for many years, you will also need to consider whether it will be enough when inflation rises significantly in the Aftershock.

What to Do if You Are "Underwater," Facing Foreclosure, or Cannot Make Your Mortgage Payments

As we already mentioned, the best plan is to refinance to a low, fixed-rate mortgage that will lower your monthly payments to an amount you can manage. If you are underwater (owe more than the home is worth) or you are facing foreclosure, be on the lookout for any mortgage bailout programs you may qualify for in the next couple of years. If not, you may decide that it is not a good idea to throw good money after bad and may choose to walk away your mortgage, depending on your situation, especially if your income does not depend on your credit score or you don't have high-value assets that could be jeopardized, based on the laws in your state.

Even if all else fails and you cannot refinance, don't qualify for any bailouts, and simply cannot make your monthly mortgage payments, you do not necessarily have to abandon your property immediately. Even now, it can take one or two years or longer from the time you stop paying your mortgage until you are evicted.

After all the bubbles pop, it will take much longer to be forced out of a property because the courts will be so backed up. When the dollar and government debt bubbles pop, banks will be overwhelmed and foreclosures will become increasingly harder to enforce. You will probably be able to stay in your home as a squatter for longer than you think. But not forever. Eventually, squatters will lose their homes, too. At that point you may also be able to rent your home from the bank or government very cheaply and avoid eviction. We are moving into a very dynamic situation that we have never seen before in the United States, in which many actions will become possible that would not be possible today.

There are also some delaying tactics you can use to put off foreclosure for as long as possible. For example, you can claim that records are not accurate and ask for depositions; both will buy you time. Or try negotiating with whoever owns the mortgage note by offering to make a partial payment each month to bypass or delay foreclosure. Keep in mind that banks do not like to foreclose on a property if they can avoid it because they will most likely have to sell the property at a loss and then show that loss on their books. Also, foreclosing costs the banks money and time they would rather spend elsewhere. So if you get in trouble, don't immediately assume that you cannot cut a deal of some kind, such as a loan modification, refinance, or temporary partial payment. It's worth asking.

Banks won't even talk to you unless you are behind on your payments, so you have to be a few months late before you can make your request. However, if you are underwater, it gets a lot harder to get the bank to modify your mortgage because it is no longer fully collateralized by the home's value.

In general, we recommend doing a short sale (selling the property for less than the balance due on the mortgage) rather than a foreclosure if the bank will allow it. However, in a short sale, the difference between what you owe on the loan and what the home is sold for can be counted by the IRS as a gain to you that may be taxable (check this with your CPA or tax attorney).

The key is to not give up easily. You can fight foreclosure and the government does have programs to help you do that.

Income-Producing Residential Rental Properties

Right now, it may seem like owning rental property is a good idea. In some areas of the country, demand for residential rentals has gone up significantly. More people are renting because they have lost their homes to foreclosure or have put off buying, either because they are waiting to see if real estate is recovering or because they cannot get a loan. In the short term, this higher demand for rentals has led to higher rents in some areas, and will likely continue for a while longer.

However, in the longer term, these higher rents will not last. Future rents will decline because:

- Rents always eventually track real estate values. As real estate falls, rents will eventually fall, too.
- Later, as unemployment climbs, rents will fall because a growing number of renters will lose their jobs and will stop paying rent altogether. Renters are usually the first to get hit in a downturn. In the Aftershock, the courts will be too backed up for a quick eviction and your renters will simply squat in your property without paying anything, perhaps for years.
- When enough people are squatting without paying rent, those who do still pay rent will not be willing to pay too much.

If you are willing to own these properties after they no longer produce significant rental income, then there is no reason to worry about any of this. Maybe you will use it for other purposes by then (perhaps as future rent-free homes for your friends and relatives who didn't read our books).

But if you don't want to hold on to rental properties when they no longer bring you income, then you will at some point want to sell these while you still can.

It is hard to let go of income-producing real estate while the money is still coming in, especially if you count on that income. So it's understandable that you would want to put off selling for as long as possible. However, the longer you wait to sell, the harder it may be to find a buyer who is willing and able to pay your asking price. And if you wait too long to sell, you may not be able to find a buyer at all.

Income-Producing Commercial Real Estate

As the bubbles fall, commercial real estate will decline for the same reasons that residential real estate will decline: rising supply (because more properties will be up for sale) and falling demand (because there will be fewer willing and able buyers). Right now and in the near-term future, commercial real estate values are not dropping significantly, if at all. Some have dropped but have more recently rebounded. When to sell is a tricky decision, but clearly selling while there are still potential buyers who think we are in or on the verge of an economic recovery is a lot better than trying to sell when your potential buyers are less enthusiastic about buying because they see real estate prices falling. As we keep saying, if you wait until there is a lot of proof that there is no recovery, there will be far fewer potential buyers.

In the long term, commercial real estate values will decline substantially in the Aftershock because unemployment will rise, consumer spending will drop, and demand for rental space will fall dramatically. Retail, wholesale, warehouse, and office space will simply not be needed at current levels.

We don't have to be 100 percent right about this for you to be 100 percent out of luck. Even a 20 percent drop in your occupancy rate could kill your profits.

We agree with conventional wisdom that *medical* commercial real estate is different—but not that different. Medical commercial real estate will take longer to fall in value but will not be immune. Some medical practices will be more Aftershock-proof, but many will not, particularly discretionary practices, such as cosmetic surgery and medically supervised weight loss centers, as well as high-end boutique practices in general. Even basic medical and dental practices will sustain a big income loss due to cuts in government and insurance reimbursements, and will seek lower-cost leases in order to stay in business. At first, you may see only a slight decline in medical real estate values, and then as the bubble economy falls further and pops, a faster exit of high-end medical practices and then other medical practices, as they can no longer pay their leases.

We also don't recommend that you count on government programs, such as "Section 8" housing payments, to hold up forever. Even if they continue, they will not keep pace with rising inflation, and in time your costs will outstrip your income on these rentals.

Farmland

Of all real estate, we like farmland the best. But it is still real estate and will still be affected by all the same forces, although with some buffering.

There are two very separate types of farmland: income-producing farms and non-income-producing farms. Our advice depends greatly on which one of these you have.

For farmland that is non-income-producing, the value of the land will fall with the rest of the real estate bubble. Most family farms that are currently being used for residential homes and perhaps family recreation (hunting, fishing, etc.) should be considered as any residential property, rather than a "farm." If the farmland does not have a house or other usable structures, and it is not being used for raising crops or animals, it is essentially raw land that will rapidly fall in value as the bubbles pop.

However, if you have farmland that is producing an income, either from crops or livestock, then you have more than just a piece of real estate—you have a business. In valuing that business, the general trend of falling land values is only one consideration. A larger consideration is the current and future business income, plus the value of the equipment the business may own.

As inflation rises, the price of agricultural commodities in the United States will increase as well, so if you own farmland that produces food, your gross income should rise with inflation—which is much better than most businesses will do as inflation rises. More important, as the dollar falls, exports of agricultural goods will increase and real prices (adjusted for inflation) will rise. However, your expenses will also go up, at the same time that government agricultural financial support declines and credit becomes increasingly tight.

Over the past few years, farmland prices have gone up significantly in some areas, creating a farmland bubble. While prices have gotten overheated in some states, farmland that is productive will continue to be in demand due to rising agricultural exports in the Aftershock. Therefore, farmland prices will hold up better in the Aftershock. In the shorter term, the huge rise we've seen in farmland prices recently (see Figure 8.2) is a setup for a farmland bubble pop or at least a correction as we head into the Aftershock.

With real estate values down during the Aftershock, farmland will sell mostly on a cash basis, based almost entirely on the value of the agricultural business. For owners of farmland and those looking

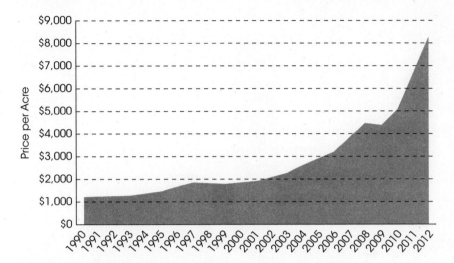

Figure 8.2   Farmland Prices Up Dramatically since 1990
Iowa Statewide Farmland Values prices are up significantly since 1990, looking a lot like a
bubble, and will likely see a downward correction in the next few years.
Source: Mike Duffy, Iowa State University.

into it, the land value itself will be far less important than the value
of the commodities produced on the land.

Some Final Thoughts on Real Estate: Where
Do Home Prices Go from Here?

Even now, smart people continue to make the same mistakes as
before. They see that home prices have risen in some areas and
they want to get a "bargain" before home prices rise even more.
They don't see that the recent rebound in real estate is being
driven largely by stock market gains, which in turn are being driven
by unsustainable massive money printing and unsustainable irra-
tionally positive investor psychology.

As long as most people don't see this, their mistaken idea that
home prices will continue to rise will be somewhat self-fulfilling
because increasing demand leads to higher home prices. But home
prices are still higher than is justified by underlying fundamental
economic drivers. So, like it or not, in the future the overall trend
for home prices will be to go down, along with all the other bubbles
in our multibubble economy.

A big factor that will help depress demand for real estate, and
therefore will push home prices down in the future, is the big drop

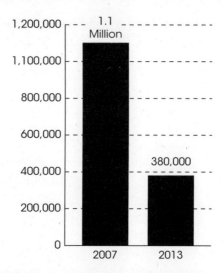

Figure 8.3 New Household Formation Has Dropped Sharply Since the 2008 Financial Crisis
The number of new households formed in 2013 was less than half the number of households formed in 2007, before the 2008 financial crisis.
Source: U.S. Census Bureau

in household formation since the financial crisis (see Figure 8.3). That means far less Americans are seeking a new place to live, opting instead to stay in their parents' homes or with roommates. That's a big drop in demand for housing. If it keeps up—and it will because there aren't enough good paying jobs to turn it around—the drop in household formation will eventually push down home prices.

Keep in mind that bubbles don't rise and fall in a straight line because psychology is so involved and because the government will do many things to try to stimulate home buying and support prices. For these and other reasons, as we mentioned before, it is hard to predict the exact timing of the next drop down, but you can be sure that projections and proclamations by various economic experts that falling home prices are a thing of the past are mostly conjecture.

You will notice that there is never much of a reason given for the deep faith that home prices will continue to rise from here. They don't say why home prices will keep rising, or offer any analysis based on the fundamental forces driving real estate prices. Perhaps they just "feel" it has to happen. After all, home prices normally go up, and so any decline has to be just a temporary aberration. This sounds a lot like what Wall Streeters might have said a few years ago.

Instead of doing a careful analysis of the economics behind the asset values, they simply relied on the fact that, in the past, stock prices and home prices went up, so in the future, they will have to go up, too. Apparently, they don't listen to their own disclaimer: "Past performance is no guarantee of future results."

The positive projections by real estate experts that tell us that home prices will only go up from here are optimistic conjecturing at best, and pure cheerleading at worst. Either way, they are telling people what they want to hear because that's what gets the biggest audience. By the way, we like to hear it, too. We also own houses. But if you are going to keep or buy a home, please keep your expectations about the future realistic.

Rule 3: Avoid Bonds and Most Fixed-Rate Investments as Interest Rates Rise

Remember what we said at the start of this chapter: these rules are for the long term, not necessarily immediately. Right now, interest rates are still low, although they moved up in 2013. That small increase in interest rates created a drop in bonds that caught many people by surprise.

Because low interest rates have much more room to go up than to come down, we see little upside left for bond prices in the future and we see gradually increasing downside risk.

Even before the bubbles pop, just a moderate rise in interest rates will have a terrible effect on bond prices (see sidebar). As inflation continues to rise, higher and higher interest rates will devastate the value of all fixed-income securities—with longer-term bonds falling the most as interest rates rise.

Here's a good way to think of the relationship between rising interest rates and falling bond prices, and how the risks of short-term, mid-term, and long-term bonds compare to each other. Imagine a very long seesaw. On one end of the seesaw are interest rates, and at the other end are bond prices. As interest rates go up, all bond prices go down. However, because this is a very long seesaw, the long-term bonds that are way out at the far end of the seesaw go down in price the most, while short-term bonds that are much closer to the fulcrum, don't go down as much. Short-term and mid-term bonds are at less risk than long-term bonds to movements in interest rates, although all bond rates will fall as interest rates rise significantly.

Moderately Rising Interest Rates Equal Sharply Falling Bond Prices

Think U.S. Treasury bonds are a safe investment? Sure, the U.S. Treasury may not default on bonds in the next couple of years, but bonds can still lose a lot of value if inflation shows up and forces interest rates to rise. To give you some idea of how much a Treasury bond can lose with relatively small increases in interest rates, we offer you the following example. Let's assume you just bought a 10-year Treasury bond that is earning 3 percent. If the interest rate rises from 3 percent to just 4 percent, your bond loses a whopping 12 percent of its value. Here's what happens if interest rates go even higher than 4 percent:

Interest Rate	Lost Bond Value
5%	18% lost
6%	25% lost
7%	31% lost
10%	46% lost
15%	63% lost

But even owning less risky short- and medium-term bonds will be tricky because you will need to sell them well before all bond prices drop. The other problem is that short-term bonds are not especially profitable, due to their very low interest rates. Ideally, if you want to invest in bonds and other fixed-rate investments in the short to medium term, you need to be very aware of when to pull out or have a money manager who understands the coming Aftershock and knows what to do and when to do it.

When the Aftershock hits, asset values across the board will fall and most of our bubble wealth—much of it currently in bonds—will go to Money Heaven. That will greatly constrict the supply of capital and further raise the price of borrowing money, pushing interest rates even higher. The government will have little choice but to print even more dollars, causing even higher inflation and higher interest rates.

Bottom line: the bond market will be decimated in the Aftershock. Prior to the Aftershock, long-term bonds will be the riskiest.

Will Municipal Bonds Be Safe?

Municipal bonds, which include state, local, and special tax districts for baseball stadiums and the like are increasingly in the news. Analysts are comparing California to Greece. But so far, the threat to municipal bonds is still relatively small. Most of the trouble muni bonds are having now is due to special circumstances that are compounded by the slow economy. The Detroit bankruptcy clearly highlighted fears in the muni market, but generally Detroit is being viewed as a special circumstance.

Overall, the muni bond default rate has more than doubled recently, but if your bond holdings are in a diversified bond fund, these defaults will have little impact. Besides defaults, rising interest rates are also a problem. Small interest rate rises will be a bigger threat to long-term municipal bonds than to shorter-term bonds. With default rates and interest rates still low, there is no major threat in the short and medium term.

However, the longer-term outlook for munis is not so great. State and local governments have taken on massive amounts of debt that they can pay only if the economy recovers. In fact, the amount of debt states and local governments owe has ballooned since the early 2000s from $1.1 trillion to $3.0 trillion in January 2014, according to usDebtClock.org.

Detroit was not bailed out. But later on, when there is any major threat of default by a major state or local government, the federal government will almost certainly bail out the muni market before it becomes a significant crisis for the market. Guaranteeing debt and opening a borrowing window at the Fed for states and localities could avert any major meltdown in the muni market. That will work for a while. But the problem is that the ability of the federal government to continue to bail out defaulting municipalities is not limitless. At some point, they won't be able to do it anymore.

So, short term, there is no need to panic about your municipal bond holdings, but given that we know how this movie ends, you may not want to hang onto them for too long.

Where's the Best Place to Stash Cash?

The cash you get from selling your stocks, real estate, and fixed-rate investments obviously has to go someplace. Right now, you are pretty safe with just about anything short term, such as money markets, short-term government bonds, and so forth, although these have very low interest rates and don't pay very much. However, as we move closer to the Market Cliff, you will need to be much more careful about where you put your cash.

Keeping cash in money market funds of banks and corporations that may fail is clearly not a great idea. Your money market accounts are likely heavy with Treasury bills.

But when the Aftershock hits, even short-term U.S. government debt will be problematic, which means you should be moving heavily toward precious metals, such as gold and silver (see Chapter 9), and similar inflation-driven investments, such as some foreign short-term debt instruments, as pressure on the dollar and government debt increases.

Clearly, this is a dynamic situation. We are no longer in a "set it and forget it" investment environment.

How Long Must We Follow These Three Rules?

We know that as the collapsing multibubble economy falls, the last bubbles to burst will be the dollar and the government debt bubble. The exact timing of when the dollar and government debt bubbles will pop is hard to nail down. It could occur as early as 2015 but more likely in three to five years.

Increasingly negative investor psychology will be key. After we go over the Market Cliff, inflation and interest rates will rise and there will be a significant decrease in the amount of foreign capital flowing into the United States. Instead of borrowing massive amounts of foreign money, we will have to print massive amounts of money, further pushing up inflation and interest rates, and further devastating U.S. asset values.

Therefore, you have to follow our Three Rules until after the dollar and government debt bubbles fully pop, or you will very likely lose a lot of money.

Letting Go Is Hard to Do

We understand that quitting stocks, bonds, and investment real estate is not easy. It's tough to just give up on investments that we have come to know and love, investments that have provided so well for us in the past—so supportive and so comfortable. It's almost like giving up on Mom and Dad. These investments have served us so well over the past few decades; how can we just walk away? Everybody invested in stocks, bonds, and real estate, and usually everybody did very well. The world just doesn't seem right without them. And if leaving Mom and Dad isn't bad enough, moving to alternative investments may feel like moving to an orphanage.

Actually, you will be able to make much more money with alternative investments (see Chapter 9) than you could with stocks, bonds, and real estate in the past, but that will be much harder to do than in the easy glory days of the rising real estate and stock markets. Also, few investors will join you in the alien world of alternative investments that go up when the economy goes down. Instead, a lot of people are going to be very upset. Pursuing safety and profits in such as strange investment environment just won't feel the same as the rising bubble economy. Easy bubble money felt so good and hard Aftershock money, while very good, won't feel the same.

In most economic situations, reading what *not* to invest in is pretty useless because you probably wouldn't invest in it anyway. You would invest in typical stock mutual funds and some basic real estate just like everyone else. However, in a bubble economy, what not to invest in can be one of the most important financial decisions you make in your lifetime. That's because the losses on stock, bonds, and real estate will be so large.

At this point, especially with the dollar bubble yet to pop, you have to be very careful about what investments you hold. There was a great line in the old television show *M*A*S*H* that essentially said, "In war, there are two rules. Rule number 1 is that young men die. Rule number 2 is that doctors can't change Rule number 1." The same logic can be applied to this falling multibubble economy:

Rule 1: No matter what happens, all bubbles eventually pop.

Rule 2: No amount of optimism can change Rule 1.

Being optimistic about your stock, bonds, and real estate investments will not change their future value. We have to deal with the reality we have, not the reality we want.

If you are still not convinced that we are in the middle of a bursting multibubble economy, please re-read the first half of the book. However, if your head says, "This book makes sense," but your heart says, "I want my bubble back!" then take a few deep breaths or have a few stiff drinks or take a nap but, whatever it takes, get over it and get on with your new life in the new economy. Don't spend too much time wishing for the good times to magically return. They won't. It's time to wake up and change your thinking. You still have time to protect yourself. In a few years, you are either going to look like a genius or you are going to be kicking yourself for waiting until it is too late. It's really up to you.

What to Do if You Sort of Believe Us but Not 100 Percent

You don't have to believe us entirely to start protecting yourself now. You needn't change your investments completely and all at once, but you do need to change, and you need to continue to change as our analysis starts looking more and more correct to you.

Hindsight is 20/20, but times like this call for more than hindsight. Right now, what you need is foresight. We are trying very hard to offer that to you. Listen to what we are saying, and keep your eyes open for more evidence that what we are predicting is in fact actually happening. In time, you will believe us partially, and then you will believe us fully. The sooner that happens, the better it will be for you.

Even if you think we are completely wrong, you should still wait until you see real estate values going back up again for at least one year before you invest. Waiting at least a year before buying real estate will be easy because prices move slowly and you won't miss much by holding off for a while.

With stocks, we suggest a slow withdrawal from the market while it is going up. You can never lose money making a profit. The more you don't believe us, the more slowly you should go. Think of it as diversification.

However, if you think we might be partially right and also partially wrong, then do what Bob's friend did and only take half our advice. That would certainly be a prudent course of action for any reasonable person. For example, you could sell 10 to 30 percent of your stocks with every 1,000-point drop in the Dow. You may later end up like Bob's friend, wishing you had done more, but better to do half than do nothing. More sophisticated investors can employ a hedge strategy, increasing their hedging as they see the stock market and overall economy continuing to go down.

Even if you don't believe us fully now, try to be very open to changing your mind. If what we are saying seems to become increasingly true, then increasingly move in the direction of our suggestions. This show's not over by a long shot, and you still have time to adjust your positions. Moving gradually may mean you could take some losses, but that's okay. It's not always smart to go 100 percent with any one way of thinking. Just keep your eyes and your mind open. And be sure you make adjustments along the way.

At Some Point It Will Be Time to Sink or Get Out of the Boat

The Aftershock is not right around the corner. Because timing is difficult, we cannot guarantee exactly when it will happen, only that it will. If you want to follow our long-term advice for the Aftershock before the Aftershock happens, then you will have maximum long-term safety, but you will also miss out on possible short-term profits and could even see some short-term losses. If you don't want that, then don't follow our long-term advice for the Aftershock until you see more evidence that we are closer to the Aftershock. But understand that the closer you push it, the greater your risk of going over the Market Cliff. In the shorter term, you will have the potential for profits, and in the longer term your potential for loss is ever increasing.

So it's up to you. You are going down a river that ends with a waterfall (Market Cliff). It's up to you to decide to stay in the stay boat with everyone else and squeeze out a little more enjoyment of being in the boat for a while longer, with the hope of jumping out of the boat at just the right time before the boat goes over the waterfall and sinks. Or get out of the boat sooner and miss out on the rest of the boat ride, both the good and the bad.

Ideally, we all would love to do both—stay in the boat as long as we can and also get out of the boat before it's too late. Theoretically, that is certainly possible, but in practice it's very hard to actually do. If you push your luck, stay in the boat too long, and go over the Market Cliff, don't blame us. However, if you decide to get out of the boat early to maximize safety, please don't blame yourself for missing a bit more of the boat ride before the fall. As we said earlier, perfect timing is impossible.

What Else Can I Do to Protect Myself?

In addition to the three big rules for long-term investing (stay away from stocks, real estate, and fixed-rate investments), there are other actions you can take to avoid losing money before and during the

Aftershock. Much more of this is covered in *The Aftershock Investor*, Second Edition. We include a few items here to give you some ideas.

Credit Card Debt

Pay off what you can, especially adjustable-rate loans, which will go up greatly in cost as interest rates rise. Even fixed-rate credit cards have clauses in their contracts that, under certain circumstances, allow interest rates to increase. So pay these off, if you can.

However, if your credit card debt is quite high relative to your income and assets, you might want to consider not paying your credits cards at all. When the bubbles pop, many credit card companies will go out of business. In fact, with the new credit card laws going into effect, credit card companies will go out of business even faster when so many people cannot make their payments. After the bubbles pop, you will likely still owe your credit card debt balance to the government but at that point, who knows when they will get around to collecting it, and in any case, high inflation will rapidly destroy the debt. They will have many other emergencies to deal with first.

Not paying your credit card debts will significantly harm your credit score, but after all the bubbles pop, credit scores are going to be pretty lousy all around, and few people will have the need for a high credit score.

Other Loans

As with credit cards, pay what you can and try to get rid of these, if you can afford to do so. But if money is very tight, you might be better off saving some money for a rainy day or to take advantage of some of the investment ideas in the next chapter.

If you can, refinance all adjustable-rate loans to fixed-rate loans, including any home equity lines of credit, car loans, and personal loans. Lock them in now at the lowest fixed rates you can get.

Student Loans

If you have a job or think you can get one, keep paying your student loans so you can maintain your credit score and be able, perhaps, to buy a car to get to work.

But if you have no job and don't expect to get one anytime soon, your credit score may not matter as much to you. Student loans come with very aggressive collection actions, so be prepared to be pursued. But if you can't pay, you can't pay. You can talk to the lender about possible deferment or restructuring of the loan, or you can just let it go. Even people who are paying back their student loans now may find themselves stopping that later, when they make less income. As we mentioned before, after the bubbles pop, credit scores won't be as important as they are today because many Americans will have very poor scores. Even the U.S. federal government will have a very poor credit score!

Reduce Spending

One of the hardest steps to take to protect yourself and your future is to reduce spending—not starting next month or next year, but right now. Not many people like downgrading or contracting their lifestyles without a really good reason or future reward. Luckily, you have one: the less you spend, the more money you will have available for some of the investment ideas in the next chapter. Not only that, as the recession continues and the economy does not recover, you will need some cash on hand for emergencies, such as losing your income or your home. Cutting spending is the quickest way to put some money aside. Please start today.

Hang On to Your Job

See Chapter 10 for details about which careers and employment will do relatively better than others. But keep in mind that even if you are in one of the "safer" job sectors, like health care or education, that doesn't guarantee you work. Many positions even in these sectors will be cut and some people in safe positions will be replaced.

Consider spending some time now making yourself more marketable in a safer job sector, or adding skills within your chosen field, or looking for ways to make yourself irreplaceable in your current job. If you decide to change jobs, don't quit your current employment before getting your next position lined up.

Rethink Retirement

For those approaching or in retirement, the coming multibubble pop could not happen at a worse time. After a lifetime of working hard, raising a family, accumulating wealth, and planning for one's golden years, it may feel like the plug is being pulled on all your expectations. Putting some real gold into those "golden years" will take a new kind of retirement planning—with new knowledge, courage, and actions that very few financial planners can help you with. We devoted an entire chapter to this subject in *The Aftershock Investor*, Second Edition. This is too important a topic for us to quickly summarize here, other than to say that the advice for protecting and growing assets in this and the next chapter doubly apply to retirement.

Remember, Your Net Worth Is Not Your Self-Worth

It's never a good idea to equate your personal worth with your net worth, but in a booming, multibubble economy on the rise, it may not cause you too much harm. However, in a bursting multibubble economy on the way down, this bad habit may come back to haunt you. Most people will see their net worth fall dramatically in the months and years ahead. Reading this book can help minimize your losses and maximize your gains, but please don't focus so much on your wallet that you forget what really makes life so worthwhile. We are not being corny when we remind you of what you already know: *it's not really about the money.*

As much as this book focuses on money, and as much as everyone will be terribly focused on money over the next few years, the best advice you may get won't be financial. Be sure to focus on your family and friends. Your family will need your support, and your friends may need you now more than ever—and you may need them more as well. Mutual support is the key to a good life in both the best of times and the worst of times.

Your networth is not your selfworth—and same for others, too. Remember the size of your wallet is not as important as the size of your heart.

CHAPTER

9

Cashing In on Chaos
BEST AFTERSHOCK INVESTMENTS

There are enormous amounts of money to be made before and especially during the Aftershock—far more than during the three decades of the bubble years because the bubble money is not sustainable and will disappear just as the bubbles disappear when they pop. In fact, we predict that far more "real" (non-bubble) money will be made in the Aftershock than the amount of "real" money made in the past three decades combined. Of course, it won't come close to matching the total amount of *bubble* money made during the past three decades, but most of that money will go to Money Heaven, along with a lot of real money. Money that goes to Money Heaven is not coming back.

Plenty of Profit Opportunities, but They Will Feel Quite Uncomfortable, Even Scary at Times

Gone are the days when you could just sit back with a glass of wine or a six-pack of beer and watch TV, knowing that by the end of the year your house would be worth 10 to 20 percent more than at the start of the year even though you didn't lift a finger to improve it.

Gone are the days when you could just buy a set of stocks or mutual funds that everyone else buys and watch them rise 1,400 percent in 25 years, or if you chose higher-growth stocks, watch them grow 2,500 percent or more. No need to be a stock-picking genius or a high-risk, high-judgment venture capitalist to make ridiculously high returns. In fact, for most investors, it was better if you didn't use any judgment at all and just chose index funds, as John Bogle, the founder of Vanguard Funds (the second largest mutual fund company in the United States), correctly advised. Back then, you could just sit back and watch the stock market automatically take your investments to tremendous heights while you did absolutely nothing.

Those good old days are beginning to come to an end. Going forward, good judgment and taking risks will be critical to making money as we get closer to the bubbles popping, and even more so in the Aftershock. In fact, good judgment and taking risks will be critical to simply *holding on* to your money in the future. Without smart thinking and some risk-taking, your money will go straight to Money Heaven, along with just about everyone else's money in the coming years. This journey is not for the faint of heart.

"We were wondering if now would be a good time to panic?"

This Economy Is Evolving; Your Investments Should Evolve, Too

The investment environment is changing but it's not as if a bomb is going to drop and the next day inflation and interest rates will be sky high. This economy is evolving over time—rather gradually at first, then faster as we go over the Market Cliff, and much faster when the bubbles pop and the Aftershock begins. But even if we never have an Aftershock, this economy is evolving forward, not cycling backward to the former, easy bubble-money days.

Therefore, your investment portfolio must evolve, too. No longer can you set up your portfolio once and leave it alone for decades, like we used to be able to do years ago. Now your investments, with one or two exceptions, must continue to change along with the changing economy.

To do that you must have the *correct macroeconomic view* of where we're headed. Without the correct macroeconomic view of the evolving economy, even your most well-thought-out investments will eventually get crushed. We made a strong case in Chapters 1 through 7 for what we believe the future macroeconomic environment will be like. If you don't correctly judge the future environment, you will likely lose most of your money—as will most everyone else.

At the very least, you need to *prepare for lots of volatility*. We think there will be a multibubble pop and Aftershock at the end of this volatility, but even if there isn't, you need to at least be prepared for volatility in the future and the likelihood of diminished returns from traditional investments.

And we also believe you need to *invest for the long term* because the short term is just too hard to accurately predict. Investor psychology, government actions or inactions, and unusual political events can have major impacts on the short-term course of the financial markets.

Even more annoying is that certain events or actions may have little effect on the financial markets, while others will have major effects, and we can't tell ahead of time which will be which. Sometimes events will have a major positive effect because investors mistakenly *hope* that they will have a major positive effect. Later, when investor psychology turns more negative, the same or similar events may have a negative effect. For example, the Fed's massive money printing is currently having a positive impact on the stock market. Later, when inflation rises, continued money printing will eventually have a negative impact on the stock market due to fear of it creating even more inflation.

All this adds up to one thing: if you are going to try to invest in such a changing economy, your investments are going to have to frequently change, too. Our last book, *The Aftershock Investor*, Second Edition, discussed our views on active portfolio management in great detail. For now, in this chapter, we are going to review some key highlights from that book for how to make money as we evolve toward the Aftershock.

Three Goals of an Evolving Aftershock Investment Portfolio

The three goals of an evolving Aftershock portfolio are sensible and straightforward:

1. Capital preservation
2. Limited volatility
3. Reasonable returns

Goal 1: Capital Preservation

What we mean by capital preservation is protection against a long-term decline in the stock and bond markets and high inflation down the road. Those are the real threats to your hard-earned wealth.

The fact that stocks are not good long term doesn't mean that they have peaked today. In fact, because of continued money printing, stocks could easily go even higher. So capital preservation does not mean you must exit the stock market immediately, although you could and that would certainly provide full protection from the coming Market Cliff. Or, you could stay in the stock market a while longer with the goal of making money.

Timing is always an issue in investing, and it's hard to time the market. We'll talk more about how to handle the timing issue later in this chapter.

Goal 2: Limited Volatility

Minimal volatility isn't too hard to define, although exactly how little volatility you want depends on your financial tolerance for volatility. Also, there's no free lunch. To get higher returns you will have to accept somewhat higher volatility. But you can shoot for a happy medium that is less volatile than the stock market but still gives you returns that are comparable to a modestly rising stock market today.

Some people don't like that goal. They want to profit on every upswing and be protected from every drop. That is a lovely fantasy, but it is not very achievable. Instead, the idea is not so much to beat stock market returns, although you may still do that, but to avoid big drops. *It's better to be defensive for the longer term than greedy in the shorter term* because we can't know exactly when we will hit the Market Cliff. That doesn't mean you can't make some profits along the way. It means that aiming to maximize profits is not as good as aiming to maximize safety, especially the longer you stay in the market.

What you want is reasonable returns and limited exposure to what is potentially a big downside in the stock market and bond market. That's your biggest threat over the next five years. Maybe not this year and maybe not next year, but within the next five years, which is far more important for most investors, and that's what you need to focus on.

Goal 3: Reasonable Returns

Reasonable returns are harder to define in part because the definition of "reasonable" varies based on the context of the times. For example, six or seven years ago, it was very reasonable to expect a 5 percent return on a safe bond. Today, that kind of a return is typical of a low-quality junk bond, and therefore going after a 5 percent return today is very risky. If you are getting a high return, you are likely taking a high level of risk. In conventional investing, this is called the *risk-adjusted rate of return*, which is often expressed as the Sharpe ratio (the higher the Sharpe ratio of an investment, the better the rate of return you are getting relative to the risk you are taking).

Of course, we are seeing certain investments as risky long term that the market is currently not seeing as risky. So our risk-adjusted rate of return would be different from standard investing analysis. Nonetheless, the concept is correct, and we are advising a lower rate of risk taking now for most people, and that will result in a lower rate of return. But it's better than losing your money. Also, you can make very high returns as we near the Aftershock, but you will be taking more risk and will get higher volatility.

Reducing Risk with a New Kind of Diversification

In the past, risk was reduced with broad diversification, but only within one or two asset classes, such as stocks and bonds. What we are suggesting is to reduce risk, not by diversifying only within one or two asset classes—which does nothing to protect you from the risk of these markets falling—but to reduce risk by diversifying *across multiple asset classes.* Merely owning a well-diversified range of seats on the *Titanic* is not as good as also having some seats on an entirely different boat, preferably one that is less likely to sink! Having multiple asset classes is like having a fleet of boats, not just one or two.

Often, the best way to diversify across multiple asset classes is to use exchange-traded funds (ETFs). These are very similar to an index mutual fund in both cost and structure. ETFs tend to be relatively cheap since they are not managed like normal mutual funds. And, depending on the asset class, ETFs may be the only way to buy and sell some investments, such as gold, within a brokerage account, making them more convenient than directly trading the asset itself.

When maximizing diversification across multiple asset classes, here are some assets to consider:

- Stocks
- TIPS (Treasury inflation-protected securities)
- ETFs for foreign currencies
- ETFs for commodities
- ETFs that short stocks
- ETFs that short bonds
- Gold ETFs
- Physical gold and silver

Stocks

As we made clear in the Chapter 8, we don't recommend stocks as a long-term buy-and-hold. You will need to move out of stocks well before the overall market goes way down.

But, in general, going long in the stock market will continue to be a better money maker than bonds or real estate, for as long as direct and indirect government intervention to support the market continues, and for as long as investor psychology remains strong.

We have been saying for many years that continued money printing by the Fed could push the stock market back up to and even higher than previous highs. That is exactly what happened, and it could easily keep happening with continued massive money printing and continued positive investor psychology. But keep in mind that we have to have both money printing and upbeat investor psychology. Money printing alone will not do it. We have to have those good animal spirits to keep the party going.

The key to protecting yourself is to get out of stocks before investor psychology turns firmly negative and we go over the Market Cliff. For some, that might mean exiting now or soon. For others who want to take their chances, there are still opportunities to profit on stocks in the short term.

High-dividend stocks provide a short-term buffer against the volatility of the current market and a decent dividend income as well. Options include pharmaceutical, health care, consumer staples, and electric utility stocks. The ETF tickers for these categories are PPH, XLV, XLP, and XLU, respectively. Electric utilities stocks perform somewhat like bonds and are down in 2013. They may not do as well in the future as they did in the past, in part because, like bonds, they will fall as interest rates rise. Therefore, we favor consumer staples and pharmaceuticals, as of this writing in January 2014.

TIPS

Treasury inflation-protected securities, or TIPS, are bonds that are adjusted for inflation. The principal of a TIPS increases with inflation, as measured by the Consumer Price Index (CPI). The coupon rate does not adjust for inflation, but the principal does. So they are somewhat inflation protected. We say *somewhat* because a TIPS is adjusted by the CPI, which is not a particularly accurate measure of real inflation.

Daily prices are influenced by investors' expectations of future inflation, which are fairly low right now. TIPS become most effective when investors are expecting inflation to rise in the future. Hence, they perform more like a regular bond currently and have not been particularly good investments in the past year, although they did quite well in 2011. Nonetheless, they will do better than a typical long-term bond, which is not adjusted for inflation, as we get closer to the Market Cliff.

The ETF TIP holds longer-term TIPS with an average maturity (as of this writing in early 2014) of about 8.5 years. The ETF STPZ holds shorter-term TIPS with an average maturity of about 2 years. Like all shorter-term bonds, the shorter-term TIPS funds will have less volatility but also have less potential for price appreciation than longer-term TIPS.

Foreign Currencies

These are a trickier category because they are fairly volatile, especially with the European debt crisis, so the dollar could be stronger for a while longer. Therefore, we see foreign currencies as a longer-term play. There is probably too much volatility now for most people to work with this asset category and not enough upside to make it worthwhile.

However, longer term, when inflation rises and foreign investors become wary of the United States as a safe haven, the dollar will fall, and foreign currency will become a good buy. It's hard to invest in any given currency because it can be affected by country-specific issues. However, a good and relatively stable one for the future will likely be the Canadian dollar. The ETF for investing in the Canadian dollar is FXC.

Another currency option in the future (not now) is to short the dollar index just prior to the full bubble pop. The dollar index is a basket of foreign currencies measured against the dollar. As the dollar index falls in the future, the short will go up. The ETF for shorting the U.S. dollar index is UDN.

Commodities

In the longer term, there will be downward pressure on most commodities due to the declining global economy. Short term, there will also be downward pressure due to a slowing Chinese economy. Since the financial crisis of 2008, China's growth has been the primary supporter of commodity prices. Offsetting some of the long-term downward pressure on commodities prices is that they generally adjust fairly rapidly for inflation.

Agricultural Commodities

Because people will continue to eat, agricultural commodities will be one of the best long-term commodities and is also likely to do relatively well short term. Short term, it won't face the same downward pressure from slowing Chinese demand as will metals or oil. Long term, the falling dollar will help support agricultural prices since agricultural goods are easily exported and will fall in price for foreigners due to the falling dollar. DBA is an ETF that holds a diversified basket of agricultural commodities.

Metals Commodities

Nonprecious metals, such as copper, steel, and zinc, will feel the full brunt of a slowdown in the world economy. These metals are heavily used in construction and the manufacturing of durable goods. Both sectors will be hit hard in any downturn. Although there may be short-term opportunities in these metals, they are not good long-term Aftershock investments.

Oil and Natural Gas

Oil is in an unusual position because we will likely be a net oil importer for some years to come. That means that when the dollar falls, the price of oil will go up in dollars. Even with past increases in U.S. oil production, we will likely only produce around 7 million barrels of oil per day in 2013, according to the U.S. Energy Information Agency. Since we consume about 18 million barrels of oil per day, we will be an importer for some time to come.

Even if the United States can increase production by 500,000 barrels per day for the next 10 years—and that is a big assumption—we will still be a net importer. Of course, consumption will decrease in the Aftershock, but it is likely that the price of oil will still be governed by the imported price of oil for some time. That will hold up the price of oil produced in the United States or imported into the United States, but the global price will fall due to falling demand.

USO is an ETF designed to track the movements of West Texas Intermediate crude oil. It is one way to invest directly in oil. There will be a lot of volatility in investing in oil over the next few years and, hence, is not one we highly recommend, although we do think the long-term outlook for oil in the United States is good. Investing in oil company stocks is another way to invest in oil, but it is primarily an investment in stocks, which will do very poorly when the Aftershock hits.

Natural gas is also in an unusual position because we import very little natural gas. In fact, we now import less than 5 percent of our annual natural gas consumption (almost entirely from Canada). So, the price of gas won't be determined as much by the fall in the dollar as will imported oil. However, the cost of producing gas in the United States is rising. Rising production costs will push natural gas prices up over time. UNG is an ETF that tracks the price of natural gas futures. Because it is based on futures, it is not always a good reflection of daily natural gas price movements.

Long term, we are very bullish on natural gas prices. We are also bullish in the short term since drilling for natural gas has fallen over 70 percent since 2008. The lack of drilling should produce upward pressure on natural gas prices. Already the price of natural gas has doubled from its lows in spring 2012. In fact, it was the best performing commodity in 2013, up 26 percent.

Coal

The world consumes a lot of coal now, and demand for coal will continue for quite a while because there won't be as much competition from other forms of energy in the depressed world economy. Subsidies for alternative fuels will dry up, and demand for coal will remain strong, at least until economies rebuild and alternative energy sources become more economically viable.

Who will fulfill the steady demand by the world for coal? U.S. coal will be relatively cheap for the world to buy because the dollar will be down against other currencies, and therefore U.S. coal will take over a larger share of the world coal market. Coal will be one of the few industries that will do very well in the United States after the bubbles pop.

ETFs that Short the Stock Market

Short ETFs or inverse ETFs are simple to buy and sell, but difficult to profit from in the current market, especially while so much money printing is still occurring. Inverse ETFs are also rebalanced daily, so that's a technical issue that means they don't always follow the longer-term trend. Hence, they are best used when the trend is strongly in your favor, and that can be hard to predict.

In the shorter term, inverse ETFs can be most effective as a hedge, or "insurance," against some long positions in stocks.

In the longer term, there will be a time when these can be used to make money, but it won't be until we start to see real weakness in the stock market. If you do use inverse ETFs in the next couple of years, don't be afraid to take profits. Markets can move against you quickly, and you can quickly lose whatever you have gained. But if you are using inverse ETFs mainly as insurance, this is less of a concern. One of the most popular inverse stock ETFs is SH, which shorts the Standard & Poor's (S&P) 500.

Please be especially careful with 2X or double-short ETFs. These are leveraged, so you can make twice as much money, but you can also lose twice as much money. Plus, the technical problems with daily rebalancing can have a greater negative effect on tracking long-term trends with leveraged ETFs than nonleveraged.

ETFs that Short Bonds

The same issues that apply to inverse stock ETFs apply to inverse bond ETFs. Bonds will likely turn bad earlier simply because interest rates have fallen so low that even a modest upward movement could damage bonds quite a bit and create nice gains for inverse bond ETFs. That change has already occurred.

The bull run for bonds is now over, but there is a limit to how low they will fall in the short and medium term because the Fed will limit that fall for as long as they can. So we don't expect bonds to go over the Market Cliff in the near future.

One of the most popular inverse bond ETFs is TBF, which shorts the 20-year Treasury bond and is not leveraged.

Gold

Gold is a key ingredient for successful investing before and during the Aftershock. For thousands of years, gold has been viewed as a universal store of value, and that sentiment continues today, although the price of gold in the short term can be quite volatile.

As discussed in detail in earlier chapters, rising inflation and interest rates (caused by massive money printing and increasingly negative investor psychology) will have a very negative impact on stocks, bonds, real estate, and other interest-sensitive assets. Rising inflation and high interest rates will also pop our two remaining bubbles: the dollar and the government debt bubbles.

But there is one asset that rising inflation and rising interest rates generally do not push down: gold. Therefore, by default, when most other assets are falling, gold is going to look increasingly attractive as people around the world begin to bail out of their sinking investments and pile into the gold lifeboat. Gold will be seen as a safe haven when the U.S. and world bubbles pop.

A key reason that gold will do so well as the other bubbles fall is its very limited supply. Worldwide, only about 2,500 tons of gold are currently mined each year plus only about another 1,600 tons of gold per year are recycled, according to the World Gold Council.

While most Americans have yet to warm up to gold, the rest of the world (about 90 percent of the gold market) is not only comfortable with buying gold, they will surely pile into gold when the U.S and world bubbles pop. At that point, many Americans will want to buy gold as well, further pushing up the price.

Gold has had a remarkable run in the past dozen years, although it declined sharply in the spring of 2013 possibly in part to some downward manipulation in the price of gold (see Appendix). But even with the 2013 drop, gold is still up more than 300 percent from 2000 to 2013 (see Figure 9.1).

There is also good reason to believe that, while demand for gold futures (paper gold) fell in 2013, which pushed down the price demand for physical gold is quite strong (see Figure 9.2).

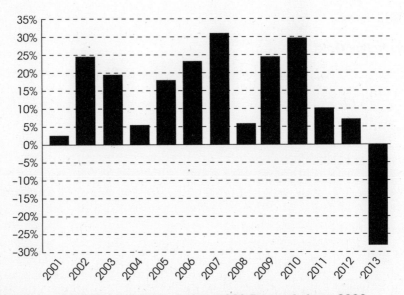

Figure 9.1   Gold Has Increased about 300 Percent since 2000
Even with the recent drop in gold prices in 2013, gold rose every year from 2000 to 2012, for a total rise of more than 300 percent from 2000 to 2013.
Source: Bloomberg.

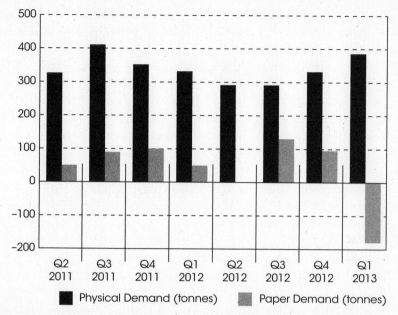

Figure 9.2   Demand for Gold Futures Down, Demand for Physical Gold Up

Physical gold buyers continue to increase their holdings, while demand for gold futures (paper demand) has fallen.

Source: World Gold Council.

How to Buy Gold

There are several options for participating in the gold market, including:

- Physical gold
- Gold individual retirement accounts (IRAs)
- Gold ETFs
- Gold-mining stocks
- Leveraged gold

Physical Gold

You can buy physical gold from a local coin shop or from a reputable online dealer. When buying physical gold, we suggest buying gold bullion coins since they have the lowest premium over the spot price of gold. The easiest coins to trade are the Canadian Maple Leaf, American Eagle, Austrian Philharmonic, and South African Krugerrands.

Coins are usually one ounce in weight, but also come in smaller half-ounce and tenth-ounce sizes. We suggest buying one-ounce coins since they have the smallest markup. You can buy these from local coin shops, but they will be a bit more expensive per ounce than buying online. However, there are no shipping and insurance charges at the coin shop. Some states may charge sales tax or, like Maryland, may require that you buy at least $1,000 worth of gold in order to be tax exempt.

You can find local coin shops in the yellow pages or online. Getting to know a local coin dealer now may help you later when you want to sell some coins. It's often cheaper to buy bullion coins or bars online or by phone. You can simply type "gold bullion" into the search bar of your favorite Internet search engine and investigate your options. Or go to the website for the U.S. Mint (www .usmint.gov) to search for reputable gold dealers.

Online outlets and retail stores require certified checks or cash to buy gold, or will ask you to wait until your check clears your bank before they ship or let you pick up your gold. Keep in mind that retail coin stores often charge a higher sales commission than a gold ETF, often $30 or more per ounce.

One of the problems with physical gold is that it can be lost or stolen. Hence, we suggest you keep it in a safe-deposit box at a bank or in a lockable safe at home.

Another option is to store your physical gold in a gold depository, such as Monex in Newport Beach, California. This is often preferred for larger quantities of gold. The depository issues a certificate of ownership that allows you to easily sell the gold whenever you wish or to take delivery of your gold at any time.

Gold IRAs

In the last few years, regulations were changed to allow for the ownership of physical gold (and silver) in some IRAs, including Roth IRAs. Some of these IRAs also allow other investments and some only allow precious metals. There are many companies that now facilitate the setup and maintenance of gold IRAs. Please check carefully for various fees that may make this retirement investment less appealing in the short term, although high fees will become far less of a consideration in the longer term when gold rises substantially.

Gold ETFs

An easy way to add gold to your Aftershock portfolio is with ETFs (exchange-traded funds). Gold ETFs are traded like stocks on the

New York Stock Exchange with the price roughly tracking one-tenth of the price of an ounce of gold. The first and most popular ETF is GLD and is a product of State Street Global Advisors. Its competitor is IAU, which is very similar.

A different type of gold ETF is PHYS, which is actually a closed-end fund, rather than an ETF. It holds physical gold in Canada. However, GLD and IAU also hold physical gold. GLD holds its gold in London. They actually list on their web site the serial numbers of the 400-ounce gold bars (London Good Delivery Bars) that they hold.

Many people prefer to buy gold ETFs because they offer:

- A way to buy and sell gold within a brokerage account, which more people are familiar and comfortable with than they are with coin shops and online gold sellers.
- Easy to buy and sell with a few mouse clicks or phone call.
- No storage needed.
- No insurance or other fees.

Gold ETFs have some tax disadvantages and expenses, but their trading convenience and small entry point make them quite popular with all types of investors, especially because they can be bought and sold through brokerage accounts, just like stocks. Also like stocks, ETFs can be bought on margin.

Gold ETFs are safe for now, but could become less safe in the future, particularly in the Aftershock, at which point owning only physical gold might be best.

Gold-Mining Stocks

Gold-mining stocks have the advantage of multiplying the profits that a gold-mining company can derive from mining gold. Hence, they can rise faster than the price of gold itself because multiple of earnings can be made from selling gold. Revenues rise as the price of gold rises, but operating costs do not. Therefore, as gold prices go up, gold-mining companies can do very well. That's the upside.

However, the downside of gold-mining stocks is that they can also go down faster than the price of gold. So, in general, gold miners are more volatile than gold.

Gold-mining stocks can be affected by three key issues that are outside of the price of gold. The first is the overall stock market, which, when it falls, will tend to take everyone down, at least for a while. The second issue is that each gold-mining company faces the same company risks that any company can face. (As Mark Twain said, "A gold mine is a hole in the ground owned by a liar.") Third, many mining companies, particularly the larger ones, are not pure gold plays. They often get the majority of their revenues from other metals, such as iron and copper.

In 2013, gold-mining stocks took a beating. GDX, an ETF index of gold-mining stocks, fell about in half from its peak in October 2012 to late 2013. Why did the gold miners fall more than physical gold? Because they have a high beta: they go down faster and up faster than gold itself. Also, even when the miners are generally on the rise, not all gold-mining stocks will perform equally.

Because the gold miners have come down so much recently, they are becoming a better and better value as prices drop. However, they could become a better value so be careful in the short term.

Later, many gold-mining stocks will go down temporarily when the stock bubble fully pops in the Market Cliff, but then do extremely well—in some cases, even better than the price of gold itself.

So there is a lot of money to be made in gold-mining stocks in the long term if you are aware of the risks we just mentioned. Currently, these are not performing well. But in the longer term, when the stock market falls and gold rises, there will be even better opportunities to buy gold-mining stocks. Rather than risk money on one mining stock, another option is to purchase a diversified fund or ETF that holds a variety of gold-mining stocks, such as the ETF GDX.

Gold-mining stocks may be more attractive if your investment vehicle allows investments in gold-mining stocks but does not allow direct investment in gold. But remember, great care is needed to avoid the downward pressure of a collapsing stock market on gold-mining stocks.

Leveraging Gold

One thing we've seen in recent years is that leveraging (borrowing money to fund part of the purchase of an investment) can light a fire under the growth of your assets. Hedge funds and private equity funds used leverage to create astounding returns for several years. But that fire can also burn you, as the hedge funds and private equity funds certainly found out.

The same goes for leveraging gold. There is no quicker way to make money on gold, and no quicker way to lose it. The greater the price volatility, the greater the risk, because even if you are right in the long term, you can be squeezed out by margin calls in the short term due to sharp short-term declines in the price. The price may jump back to its high very quickly, but you may have lost much of your money in the dip if you couldn't make the margin calls on your highly leveraged gold investment and had to sell your position at a low price.

Because we believe there will be greater volatility in the beginning of the gold bubble, we suggest you keep your leverage more limited in the early stages. However, as the gold bubble begins to take off with the dollar bubble pop, you could consider increasing your leverage.

If you decide to buy gold on margin, the amount of margin you can get is controlled by the government, like any brokerage account. But, depending on the volatility of gold, you can leverage three to five times. With a 3× leverage, you can get $30,000 worth of gold for $10,000 cash. There are also significant interest costs and fees associated with leveraging.

Gold now and in the future will likely be highly volatile, so be careful. We can't tell you how much leverage to use, since the amount of leverage you can take on is very much a factor of your wealth and willingness to take risks. All we can say for sure is that for most people leverage is like alcohol: use it in moderation.

What About Silver?

We have been focusing on gold, but much of this discussion applies to silver as well, which is why we recommend buying one-ounce standard (meaning well-recognized) silver coins.

Silver is different from gold in that it is a hybrid investment. It is both a precious metal investment and an industrial commodity. About half of silver's production each year is consumed for industrial purposes, heavily electronics. That means that it is also much more vulnerable to downturns in commodities prices caused by economic downturns. That bodes poorly for silver.

However, silver is also cheaper and easier for many people to buy and is very much considered a monetary asset. Even our coins were made of silver up until 1965. So we expect silver to keep following gold, but in a severe economic downturn, silver will not track gold as well as it does now, given that industrial demand is a big part of silver demand.

However, one offset to the downward pressure that will come from falling industrial demand is that silver is heavily mined as a by-product from other metal mining, most notably copper. In fact, over 70 percent of silver production is as a by-product. So when demand for commodity metals, such as copper, falls, so will production of silver. This will help offset some of the downward pressure on silver.

In general, silver tends to be even more volatile than gold (see Figure 9.3) and we expect that to continue for the next few years.

However, we expect both gold and silver to do very, very well in the longer term. There may be times when one outperforms the other, but at the height of the Aftershock, gold will be king and silver will be prince. Regardless of which precious metal you personally prefer, the world thinks of gold as number one and silver as number two (think of the Olympic first- and second-place medals).

Short-Term versus Long-Term Gold Investing

The big problem with a very large allocation of your portfolio in gold for the short term is the price volatility. However, if you are investing in gold for the long term, then short-term volatility doesn't really matter.

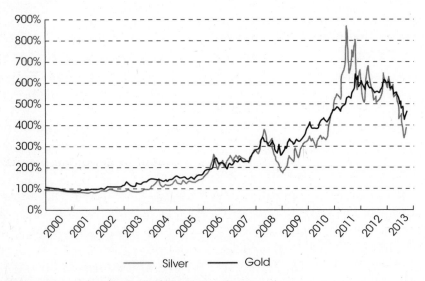

Figure 9.3   Silver More Volatile than Gold
When gold goes up, silver tends to go up a lot more, and when gold goes down, silver tends to go down a lot more. Silver is down more than 50 percent since its highs in 2011, unlike gold, which is down 30 percent.
Source: Bloomberg.

As the Aftershock comes closer, and you are more convinced that it is coming, you should increase your gold holdings accordingly. But buy some now even if you aren't very sure of the Aftershock. It could easily go down for a while after you buy it, but best to get your toes wet now so that you will feel more comfortable buying gold in the future.

Don't sweat the short-term volatility in the price of gold or try to pick just the right entry point. Any price we pay for gold in the short term is going to look like a bargain to us in the longer term. In the shorter term, we can expect to see continued ups and downs in gold, in part due to possible manipulation (see Appendix) and other short-term factors.

Even if you think you cannot afford to buy gold, you probably can. Start by putting even just $20 or $50 dollars aside on a regular basis. When you have enough to buy one gold coin, go to a local coin dealer, buy one, and bring it home. Then start putting aside some small amount of money again. Even if you end up with only a few, later in the Aftershock you will be very happy you did.

Timing Is Everything before the Bubbles Pop, but It Won't Be Perfect

By "timing" we don't mean *perfect timing* for when to enter or exit markets because that is impossible. For example, as we explained in Chapter 4, if you want to exit the stock market at the *perfect* time, you would have had to get out in 1999, prior to its fall in 2000, and then put your money in gold before its massive rise. That way you would have avoided the long period after 2000 until now when the market has fallen relative to inflation, but have cashed in on the massive gains in gold since 2001. Too late for that now. You are not going to get in at the perfect moment or get out at the perfect moment, so please forget about that.

When we say "timing" in this context, we are talking about getting in and out of assets in a way that maximizes your odds of *approaching* the three idealized goals mentioned earlier: preservation of capital, minimal volatility, and reasonable returns.

Notice we said "approaching." We are rarely going to fully reach these goals. Instead, the strategy is to approach these goals by paying close attention and been willing to move quickly.

Attempting to describe this kind of timing in any book is challenging. Optimal investment management could easily require you to change your portfolio allocation mix as often as quarterly, monthly, or even more frequently, depending on what is going on in the world and the markets at the time.

There are some longer-term Aftershock investments, such as gold, that can be held through the shorter-term ups and downs, if that is part of your longer-term strategy. But most of the other investments we mentioned earlier will need to come and go in your portfolio, depending on the changing economy—and perhaps more important, depending on *changing investor psychology*, which ultimately determines all market movements.

So trying to advise you about the timing of these sorts of moves in a book is impossible—which is why we have monthly newsletters and other services.

Aftershock Investing after the Bubbles Pop: Gold, Foreign Currencies, and Foreign Bonds

When we said that investing just before and during the Aftershock was going feel uncomfortable, this is what we meant. With the bubbles falling and the Aftershock close, the time will come to switch to three categories of assets that Americans typically do not own in significant amounts, if at all.

Gold in the Aftershock

We've already talked about how to buy gold. What we would like to add here is just how important gold will eventually become in your postbubble Aftershock investment portfolio.

We are not "gold bugs." We simply are reporting to you what our objective analysis indicates. And all indicators point to a very big rise in gold in the Aftershock. After the Market Cliff and after the full multibubble pop, you will no longer want to own stocks and U.S. bonds. Instead of these, the lion's share of your new Aftershock portfolio will be gold and perhaps other precious metals.

A key reason that gold will do so well in the Aftershock is that it is not inflation or interest rate dependent, unlike stocks, bonds, and real estate. Gold is one of the few remaining assets that will not be brought down by rising inflation and interest rates. Quite the contrary, investors worldwide will pile into gold as a flight to safety, when those other assets fall. In time, this will create a gold bubble, as more and more money rushes into gold, and gold prices explode.

Even prior to the Aftershock, gold is a great Aftershock investment because it will take advantage of a falling dollar, a falling stock market, and a falling world economy. As other asset values decline, people will want to put their money somewhere. They will want to buy something, preferably something of rapidly rising value that has a long tradition of acceptance and demand during difficult times. That is gold. As demand continues to rise for gold, and then rapidly rises even more when the other bubbles pop, the price of gold will shoot up. The rising gold bubble is your very best bet for profits during the Aftershock.

As we mentioned earlier, scarcity is important. Compared to other assets, such as stocks and bonds, the amount of gold now available in the world is relatively tiny. Surely, more gold will be mined in the future to satisfy growing demand, but rapidly increasing demand will far outpace supply, pushing up the price. Huge and growing demand, plus relatively tiny supply—you do the math.

As we have already said, we are not gold bugs. In fact, gold just might be the silliest of all investments. Think about it. People spend tons of capital, time, and effort to haul a bunch of rock out of the ground at enormous expense and smelt out tiny bits of gold from the rock, melt them together, and then do absolutely nothing with it—just put it in an expensive vault. How much sillier can you get?

But in the coming years, silly gold will be a truly smart and spectacular Aftershock investment. Huge amounts of money will be made—and lost—in gold. Gold is a rising bubble on its way to becoming one of the biggest asset bubbles of all time. Second only to the fall of the dollar bubble, the bursting of the gold bubble many years from now will be quite impressive, as well.

Gold is an excellent investment for these crazy times because it not only takes advantage of the falling stock market and falling dollar; it benefits from the overall falling world economy as well. Gold is an investment opportunity that is custom made for the crazy times ahead. Silly times call for silly investments? Well, sort of.

Here are some not-so-silly reasons why gold will be a super-smart investment in the Aftershock:

- The gold market is very, very small compared to the stock and bond markets. Even a small shift of capital out of these markets and into gold will dramatically boost its price. And a large inflow of capital into gold will have a very huge, positive effect, indeed.

- The gold market is much more of a world market than U.S. stocks and bonds. Foreign investors can buy stocks and bonds, but in many countries buying gold is easier. Hence, gold has a much greater world demand. For example, India and China are the world's biggest consumers of gold, buying almost 40 percent of the world's gold consumption annually—about four times as much as the United States. However, neither China nor India are large consumers of stocks and bonds. There's not a stockbroker on every corner of town, but there is often a gold dealer. Therefore, the ease with which worldwide investors can buy gold will also heighten its appeal.

- Gold is viewed much more positively as an investment in the Middle East and Asia than it is in the United States. Hence, for those countries, which are the biggest consumers of gold, its acceptability as a good investment will push up the price of gold when their economies tank even worse than the U.S. economy.

- It is very difficult to rapidly increase gold production. Gold mining will not be able to keep pace with demand for many years. When demand for gold goes up, so will the price.

- Gold has traditionally been seen as an inflation hedge in the past, and in this case will be an extraordinarily good hedge against inflation in the near future, so high inflation often drives gold purchases. Inflation will be very high in the United States and also in major European and Asian nations.

- All of the world's stock and bond markets will be under severe downward pressure. Some stock and bond investors, especially in the Middle East and Asia, will move out of stocks and bonds and toward higher gold holdings over the next few years, driving up the price.

- Just as we predicted in 2006, as the world's banking system comes under increasing stress, gold will have increasing appeal.

- Dollar-based investors receive a double benefit by buying gold. That means if you buy gold with dollars, you are taking advantage not only of the price rise in gold, but also the fall of the dollar. As an example, if gold goes up four times, and the euro goes up two times against the dollar, your net increase is eight times.

If Gold Could Do So Well in the Bad Gold Environment in the Past, Imagine How Well Gold Will Do in a Much Better Gold Environment in the Future

The most compelling reason to believe that gold will shoot up in the future comes from gold's recent past. Despite a downturn in 2013, gold is still up more than 300 percent in the past decade, a period of time when the environment for gold was not very gold favorable, including:

- Low inflation
- Very good bond market
- Good stock market
- Okay dollar
- Low investor anxiety

Now imagine the reverse of every condition listed above, as we will have in the Aftershock:

- High inflation
- Down bond market
- Down stock market
- Fallen dollar
- High investor anxiety

If gold could rise 300 percent in the past when all the lights were red for gold, imaging how fast gold will rise in the future when not one but *every* light turns green for gold. Surely, that will push gold much, much higher in the Aftershock.

Foreign Currencies in the Aftershock

While not in the same league as gold, another way to profit from the falling bubbles just before and during the Aftershock is to buy foreign currencies that will rise relative to the falling dollar. Foreign currencies may also lose buying power compared to their previous values due to rising inflation in their own countries, but they will not be as inflated as the dollar. Therefore, their values will not fall as deeply as the dollar. So, *relative to the dollar*, these currencies will do well.

The major foreign currencies, such as the euro, yen, Canadian dollar, and Swiss franc, can be easily bought and sold using exchange-traded funds (ETFs). For example, the euro ETF trades under the symbol FXE. Each share of FXE sells for about the price of 100 euros. You can buy this ETF just like a stock through your normal brokerage account. Other currency ETFs include FXF for the Swiss franc, FXC for the Canadian dollar, and FXY for the yen.

Each currency is affected by its government's policies, so they don't move in tandem. A most obvious example is the euro, which is negatively affected whenever the European debt crisis flares up.

We think the Eurozone will likely see significant economic problems among its members. However, despite these problems, we expect the euro to survive the coming Aftershock and, in the long run, rise along with other foreign currencies as the dollar falls. In the meantime, there could be some significant volatility due to what will be an ongoing European debt crisis.

As always, timing is everything. In the short term, buying and selling currencies can be highly risky, and we don't recommend highly active currency trading unless you really know what you are doing. Even then, you may lose money if you sell when you should hold, or hold when you shouldn't have bought in the first place.

Another good reason to hold off on currency investing is because the dollar has been strong in 2013 and could remain strong in 2014. This is specially true in relation to the yen, whose government policy is to weaken the yen to encourage exports. The dollar is also strong against many merging market currencies (Brazil, Turkey, India, even China). The dollar has done well against most other currency other than the euro, which held up best against the dollar in 2013.

Please also be aware that changes in the value of currencies relative to each other will be manipulated by central banks, which adds an additional level of volatility and risk. Also, central bank manipulation can be effective in the early stages of a major foreign exchange collapse but can fall apart suddenly when market pressures become greater than the central banks can handle. This means you may be running up against significant manipulation against your positions until the central banks can't manipulate anymore and then the price moves very quickly and very massively in your favor, but only during a very short window. The key is not to miss that window because that's where most of the money will be made.

If you want to diversify the risk of being involved in any single currency, you can buy an ETF called UDN that rises when the dollar falls against a basket of currencies known as the U.S. Dollar Index.

Foreign Bonds in the Aftershock

You can also buy foreign currencies through bond funds that invest in foreign corporate or government debt. These are fine currency investments in that they also pay interest and diversify your foreign currency holdings. However, like any U.S. long-term corporate or government bonds, they will lose their value when interest rates rise. So be careful with bond funds because when interest rates rise, their values will fall significantly. Hence, you will need to exit them before interest rates climb. Like any bond fund, you also have to be careful about default risk, especially with debt-troubled European countries and some emerging markets.

One other issue to be aware of is that if inflation is significantly higher in other countries than the United States, the value of the dollar in nominal terms would rise. However, the inflation-adjusted value of the dollar would still be falling. To offset the effect of inflation on your currency investments, you will need to invest in short-term debt instruments of that currency rather than in the currency itself.

Again, this is an issue only when inflation begins to hit in other countries, but it is an important issue. You can't invest in currencies at that point; you will need to invest in short-term debt instruments of those currencies so that you will receive interest that offsets the rise in inflation.

Putting It All Together: Aftershock in Action

So far, we have thrown an awful lot at you. We've told you this recovery is 100 percent fake, how the first four bubbles (real estate, stocks, private debt, and discretionary spending bubbles) in our multibubble economy have already begun to pop, and how two more bubbles (the dollar and government debt bubbles) will also eventually pop, after stocks and bonds go over the Market Cliff and inflation and interest rates rise due to massive money printing by the Fed. We also told you how the Aftershock will impact the rest of the world, what to do to limit your losses, and now, in this chapter, how to maximize potential gains.

What we cannot tell you in a book is specifically how you can put these macroeconomic Aftershock ideas into action in your own life. We certainly do not want you to panic because that does little good, and you still have time to get ready for what's ahead. Instead, without knowing your unique situation, we would like to help you with your personal task of trying to prepare in a way that is right for you.

Toward that end, here is a summary of some ideas about how you might pace some of our recommendations, with the full knowledge that only you can decide if and how fast to implement such personal steps.

When to get out of stocks. Selling high is always better than selling low, so one option is to begin to slowly exit stocks while the market is still in pretty good shape. It is true that with the Fed printing massive amounts of money, the stock market could continue to rally. It is also true that this won't go on forever, and since it is hard to get the timing perfectly right, you have to decide if you would rather be a bit too early or a bit too late in getting out of stocks.

As we have already mentioned, this may not be too easy with stocks held in retirement accounts, although it is worth exploring your options. For stocks under your direct control, you can slowly move out. You may miss out on some short-term profits, but you will also miss out on a big part of the coming downturn.

When to get into gold. The trouble with trying to decide when to buy gold is that it's easy to feel insecure. Gold is a very volatile asset, and often the day after you buy it, the price goes down. Conversely, the day after you decided not to buy it, the price goes up. One thing we have noticed about buying gold—which has risen by more than 300 percent in the past decade—is that each time we buy it, we worry that we could have waited and gotten it cheaper, and then after we own it for a while, another regret kicks in: we wish we had bought more! Whenever you buy gold, as long as it is before the dollar bubble pops, most of the upside will still be ahead. So if this is an investment you want to participate in, try to relax into this investment and buckle in for a bumpy ride.

Rethink retirement. If even one-tenth of what we are predicting comes true (and it will be far more), most conventional retirement investments are headed for real trouble. If you have any belief in what we have described in this book, retirement accounts and plans must be revisited—the sooner the better. But you needn't panic because it can be done in stages, with increasing changes made as you see more and more that we are right and your confidence in our predictions grows. Even if that takes you until what we would consider the last minute, you can still make some of the moves necessary to protect some of your assets.

Get real about real estate. In general, the time to get out of real estate (other than perhaps your primary residence that you plan to stay in for quite some time) is before prices start to fall again. You can still take some time to sell, but don't put it off for too long. Once real estate falls again, it is not coming back any time soon. Decide and act before you get burned.

Cut spending low and keep your job. We've already covered this more than you may have liked, but it bears repeating. Cut spending now and hang on to your job for as long as you can. Invest wisely, and later you will have the means to pick up a lot of mad bargains when others cannot.

A Final Note on Investing: Dumb Luck Is Still Important

Of course, as in past money-making periods, much of the money in the future will be made through dumb luck. The money will be made by people who didn't really see what was coming but, for a variety of reasons, happened to take one or more of the right actions that lead to a profit.

Gold is an obvious example. Many people will hold gold because they were naturally inclined toward gold for cultural reasons, or to avoid taxes, or because they thought the end of the world was near. These people will make a lot of money in the future. But gold is also a bubble. Hence, many of the people who will make money in gold through dumb good luck will also lose it through dumb bad luck because they won't know when to (or even that they should) get out before the gold bubble pops.

Other people will be lucky if they happen to live outside the United States and they have the capital to invest in the United States after the dollar bubble falls and U.S. investments become very cheap for foreign investors. It won't be that they planned it; it's just that they live outside the United States. The dumb luck of living outside the United States when the dollar pops will have to be combined with good judgment in investing in the United States, but there is still a large component of being in the right place at the right time due to plain dumb luck.

To help you make some of your own luck, please take a look at *The Aftershock Investor*, Second Edition (Wiley, November 2013), because it contains much more of our investment advice than we can squeeze into this chapter.

Got Macro?

We did not write our series of books in order to get you to buy something from us. All our current products and services grew out of reader demand over many years. For those who want to prepare for, not just read about, the coming Aftershock, we offer the following:

You are welcome to visit our web site, www.aftershockpublishing. com, for more information as we approach the Aftershock. While you are there, you may sign up for a two-month free trial of our popular **Aftershock Investor's Resource Package** (IRP), which includes our monthly newsletter, live conference calls, and more. Or you may reach us at **703-787-0139** or info@aftershockpublishing.com.

We also offer **private consulting** for individuals, businesses, and groups. Please contact coauthor Cindy Spitzer at **443-980-7367** or visit www.aftershockconsultants.com for more information.

Through our investment management firm, **Absolute Investment Management**, we provide hands-on, Aftershock-focused asset management services on an individually managed account basis. For details, please call **703-774-3520** or e-mail absolute@aftershock publishing.com.

10

Aftershock Jobs and Businesses

The economic cheerleaders want us to believe that if we will just be patient and wait a little longer, strong job growth will soon return. While we have had good job growth in 2012 and 2013, it has not been of good jobs. As pointed out in Chapter 1, most new hires have been for part-time jobs, and many people who lost and would like to return to full-time jobs have been forced to work part time.

If you lost one good-paying, quality job and replaced it with two lower-paying, lousy jobs, the government statistics still counts that as two new jobs. But it isn't much improvement for you. Quality matters. That's why average household income is still 6 percent lower than in 2008.

As of this writing in January 2014, overall new job creation has been less than impressive: averaging about 200,000 jobs per month. That sounds pretty good, until you realize that we need to add at least 150,000 jobs per month just to keep up with population growth. So we have not made up for all the 7.5 million jobs lost in the Great Recession.

How many of the 200,000 new jobs per month we are creating are good jobs? Only about 5,000 per month are manufacturing jobs, according to the Bureau of Labor Statistics. The picture is a bit brighter for jobs in construction and real estate, which are growing at about 12,000 per month, at least for now. Jobs related to oil and gas account for only about 800 per month.

Even in health care, our best job sector, which has increased employment for 124 months in a row, there are signs that job growth may be cooling down. New health care jobs averaged 19,000 per month in 2013, down from 27,000 per month the year before.

Among working-age Americans, employment is not growing much, and most new jobs are not especially good jobs. If this is any kind of recovery, it is one without much good job growth, and that kind of "recovery" is no recovery at all. Strong and sustained quality job growth is essential to any significant future economic growth— not only for the country but for most people's personal economies, as well. Slower job growth means less income for many Americans and less tax revenue for federal and state governments, which is not conducive to strong future growth.

Finding and keeping a good job in this evolving economy of falling bubbles will become increasingly challenging as time goes on. Much of this you can do nothing about, but you do have some control over which jobs you try for and what you can do to keep your current job or prepare yourself to move to another potentially more secure job before the falling bubbles fully pop.

While the pressures on the slow-growing job market will continue and increase, all jobs and businesses are not created equal; clearly, some will fare better than others as the various bubbles continue to pop. The purpose of this chapter is to give you an overview of what is happening with jobs and businesses, and what to expect next.

The Rising Bubble Economy Created Huge Job Growth; Now the Falling Bubble Economy Means Fewer Jobs

As the conjoined real estate, stock, private debt, consumer spending, dollar, and government debt bubbles all rose in tandem from 1980 to 2000, the U.S. job market boomed, adding a whopping *40 million* new jobs during this time period. New employees were in such high demand in the late 1980s and 1990s that employment agencies and headhunters could hardly keep up.

But when the Internet bubble popped in 2000, much of that strong job growth began to unwind. Then the housing bubble pushed up job growth again, but nothing like it was in the 1980s and 1990s. So when the real estate bubble popped, jobs related to real estate—like jobs in construction and real estate sales—took an immediate and lasting hit.

But our job problems didn't end at the edges of the real estate landscape; we had other falling bubbles as well. Because the rising real estate bubble was so key in driving up the private debt bubble and the consumer spending bubble, when real estate began to pop, much of the hot air escaped from those other bubbles, too. With less home equity to tap into and rapidly tightening credit, consumers naturally spent less, which only made matters worse for businesses and jobs.

So, along with the decline in housing-related jobs, big job layoffs were seen across the board, from the airline industry to shopping mall closures. And because the falling bubbles have not been entirely reinflated despite massive government stimulus to temporarily support them, many of those bubble-driven jobs have not come back. Most of the nonfarm jobs created during the rise of the real estate bubble are now gone.

The bottom line is, even with the new jobs that are being created by the massive government stimulus since 2008, we have had a very big hole to climb out of. While the number of jobs from 1980 to 2000 increased by 40 million, there was zero net job growth from 2000 to 2010. In fact, we lost almost 200,000 jobs (see Figure 10.1).

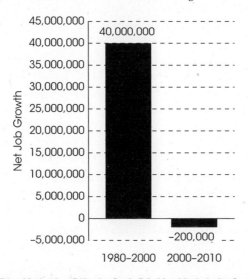

Figure 10.1   A Big Hole to Climb Out Of: No Net Job Growth from 2000 to 2010
From 1980 to 2000, 40 million new jobs were created. However, from 2000 to 2010, we actually lost 200,000 jobs.
Source: Bureau of Labor Statistics.

Conventional Wisdom about Future Job Growth Is Based on Faith that the Future Will Be Like the Past

As with stocks, bonds, real estate, life insurance, and nearly everything else, conventional wisdom (CW) faith in future job growth is derived from the assumption that what we had before (during the rising bubble economy) we will surely have again. CW loves to extrapolate trend lines—at least the trend lines they like. When things are going well, CW sees more great growth ahead; when things are going not so well, CW says don't worry, the previous good trend line will naturally return very soon. For CW, good trend lines always continue, even if they happen to get temporarily sidetracked for a while.

For example, five years ago when the number of government jobs was growing significantly, CW said government job growth would always be strong. CW says all good job trends last forever. Not only that, CW also likes to believe that whatever is the current popular area of discussion—such as green jobs or nanotechnology jobs—will have strong job growth in the future. The CW winning formula for future jobs is the current trend line (or the recent past, if that looks better than today) plus whatever is in fashion at the moment.

One of the reasons that CW feels so confident about its views about the future is that extrapolating trend lines has worked pretty well for CW in the recent past. Naturally, in a rising multibubble economy, most positive trend lines have been remarkably reliable, and it has not been all that difficult for CW to be right on many near-term positive predictions in the recent past. This, along with the need to ignore unpleasant facts that threaten the status quo, has become the strong foundation on which CW now rests its firm faith that all good trends, including all good job growth trends, never end.

While this may sound like a bit of an exaggeration, if you look back at CW over the past three decades, you will see almost all the CW-oriented analysts and economic cheerleaders continuously telling us that everything is basically very good and will continue to be very good, even if we have a little down cycle occasionally. You never hear them say that a currently good trend is unsustainable because it is based on an unsustainable rising bubble economy. At this point, rising bubbles are considered both the norm and our American birthright. And, naturally, that will always include lots of good American jobs.

Even when CW acknowledges that many U.S. jobs have been moved overseas in recent years due to cheaper labor costs, there is no acknowledgment of how the rising U.S. bubbles created many jobs or how falling bubbles could take them away.

Why Conventional Wisdom on Jobs Is Wrong

Just as for stocks, bonds, real estate, life insurance, and nearly everything else, CW's views on future job growth are wrong for the same reasons that CW is wrong about all the rest: good past trend lines *cannot* be extrapolated into the future indefinitely. The future is not the past. Not even the present is the past. Good trends do not continue forever because *markets always evolve*, and this is certainly true for the job market as well.

The U.S. job market has always evolved over time, driven by real underlying fundamental economic drivers, not the latest fashionable interests. For example, back in the 1800s, 9 out of 10 Americans were actively involved in growing food, either for income or to feed themselves. However, as farming technology changed and more manufacturing jobs were created, farming jobs evolved and the numbers of people working on farms declined. Today, only 3 percent of Americans are involved in growing food.

There are countless other examples of how the job market has evolved over time, based on the evolution of technology and the economy. In our current recession, unless the economy goes back fully to how it was before, the jobs are not going to come back fully to how they were before. Since economies never go backward, only forward, jobs evolve forward as well.

As discussed earlier in the book, the combination of slowing productivity growth and coming Aftershock is moving us toward to a new economic reality that we have not experienced before. It certainly will not move us back to the old rising multibubble economy, no matter how badly we may want our bubbles back. Once these jobs are lost, it is hard to bring them back without fundamental changes to the economy.

Does Government Stimulus Create Jobs?

The answer is most definitely yes! The stimulus of massive borrowing and massive money printing *does* lead to more jobs—as long as you keep pouring in more and more stimulus money to keep those new jobs going. But not long after the stimulus ends, so will the jobs. Why? Because big government stimulus does nothing to change the underlying reasons that jobs declined in the first place; therefore, when the heat of the stimulus is withdrawn, the positive impacts of the stimulus will cool down quickly. That might not be the case in a normal, healthy economy going through a rough patch. In that case, a big temporary stimulus might help to get things back on track. But that won't work in a falling bubble economy. As soon as the stimulus is withdrawn, we are soon back to where we were before or worse.

Remember what we said earlier in the book: Try as we might, a falling bubble cannot be turned into a rising bubble for very long, if at all. We may be able to keep the bubbles from falling further temporarily, but not forever. Bubbles eventually pop.

In the short term, the current government stimulus programs (massive borrowing and massive money printing) are helping to slow the rate of job loss, and they may even create new jobs in some areas, but the stimulus alone will not be enough to permanently save us from the deteriorating jobs market. Even additional "incentive" programs, such as tax credits to encourage employers to hire more employees, are likely to have limited impact. Until demand returns because the fundamentals of the economy change, the job market will continue to experience slow growth.

What's a Savvy Aftershock Investor to Do?

As we said at the start of this chapter, *not all jobs are created equal*; some jobs will do better than others, depending on what sector they are in. So understanding how each job sector will fare in the future (explained in this chapter) is key to understanding which jobs will likely hold up best as the bubbles continue to fall.

Although job opportunities in the Aftershock will not be the same as in the recent past, there are similarities to what has happened since the financial crisis and what will happen as we get nearer to the Aftershock. The best job prospects are in the medical industry, while the capital goods industries, such as construction and manufacturing, will be hit very hard. Figure 10.2 shows what has already occurred.

While the bubbles are still partially inflated and the government is still pumping in stimulus to keep them afloat, now is a good time to start planning your next move, whether it is a move to a new job in a different sector or the same sector you are already

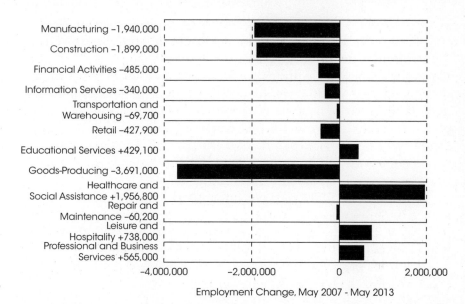

Figure 10.2   Gains and Losses by Types of Jobs, May 2007 to May 2013
Health care jobs have done the best, while manufacturing and construction have done poorly,
as will be the case in the future.
Source: Bureau of Labor Statistics.

in, or a new way to make yourself more valuable to your current
employer or your customers.

But before we get to the details about each job sector, there
are two important points to keep in mind, whether you are an
employee or a business owner. First, keep your eyes open. Don't
believe everything you see and hear from the economic cheerleaders about the so-called recovery. We don't have one.

Second, please understand that this is not the recession of the
late 1970s and early 1980s. What we have now is a falling multibubble economy, not just a typical economic slowdown. Don't expect
big improvements to come quickly.

Some General Considerations for Employees and Job Seekers

- Understand that the overall economy and the job market are
  both evolving over time. A job that seems secure today may
  not be around in a few years. There is no need to panic, but
  now is the time to prepare for the changes ahead (see details
  about the job sectors below).

- Be willing to move from one job to another or from one job sector to another, but do not quit any job without having another one lined up.
- Consider your options for getting some extra job training, technical certificates, or academic degrees if they will help you move to a better-paying or more secure job, but *only* if this can be accomplished fairly quickly, such as in one to three years. Don't start a 10-year program and expect to be done with it before the Aftershock hits (for more details, see the section on college, later in this chapter).
- If you lose your job, consider taking a lower-paying job or doing temporary work, consulting, or even an internship (see the internship sidebar later in the chapter). Don't hold out for many months, waiting for the same job that you just lost to magically rematerialize. The further the bubbles fall, the less likely that will happen.

Some General Considerations for Business Owners

- Consider selling your business if it is in one of the more dangerous sectors of the economy (see details in the next section).
- If you were already planning to sell your business in the future, move up your time frame and sell it sooner, rather than later. It takes a fair amount of lead time to sell a business. Start now, before many of your potential buyers figure out what you already know about the future economy. The longer you wait to sell, the harder it will be to find a buyer and the lower the selling price, if you are able to sell it at all.
- Get as much cash as possible. If you must hold the note, make sure it is very short term. Try to keep it to less than five years—two to four years preferred. The more time that goes by, the less likely your buyer will be able to make your payments. Collect as much as you can up front.
- If you want to keep your business or start a new one, look for ways to cash in on or at least survive in the falling bubble environment (more details on this later in the chapter).

The Falling Bubbles Will Have Varying Impacts on Three Broad Economic Sectors

In assessing the impact of the falling bubbles, we find it helps to think of the U.S. economy in terms of three broad sectors:

1. *Capital goods sector*—cars, construction, major industrial equipment, and so forth.
2. *Discretionary spending sector*—fine dining, entertainment, leisure travel, high fashion, jewelry, art, collectables, cosmetic surgery, and the like.
3. *Necessities sector*—basic food, shelter, basic clothing, energy, basic health care, basic education, and so on.

In a normal economic downturn, we would expect to see the capital goods sector slow significantly, the discretionary spending sector decline somewhat, and the necessities sector to be mostly spared. But this is not a normal economic downturn. The impact of the Aftershock will be felt by all sectors, even the necessities sector. This time, all three sectors will suffer significant job and business losses, with the capital goods and discretionary spending sectors performing worst, and the necessities sector faring better, but not entirely spared. All three sectors will have some safe jobs and profitable businesses, but competition for these will grow as time goes on.

Right now, there are still jobs available but not as many as needed. Even with the creation of some new jobs since the 2008 crash, jobs have not been coming back equally in all sectors, as shown earlier in Figure 10.2.

The Capital Goods Sector

In the Aftershock, high interest rates, coupled with a big economic slowdown, will be very bad news for the capital goods sector, including autos, construction, major industrial equipment, and so on. Rising inflation and rising interest rates will make borrowing money very expensive for consumers and businesses. This will have a very negative effect on the capital goods sector, which depends on its customers' having access to low-cost capital. High interest rates will also add to the reasons why full economic recovery will take far longer and be far more difficult than in previous recessions.

Many Jobs in the Capital Goods Sector Will be Lost.

Jobs in capital goods industries will be the worst hit in the coming Aftershock. If you have one of these jobs now, there probably isn't a lot you can do to protect yourself other than to gear up to move on to a job in another sector. Your best bet may be to rethink your career now with an eye toward joining an industry that will do better when the bubbles burst. We certainly don't recommend quitting one job until you have another in hand, but we also don't recommend waiting too long to make a move, if you want to do so.

If a major career makeover is not your style, you may want to consider making a move to a more stable area within your current industry. For example, if you work in the construction industry—which has already taken a terrible hit and is not coming back any time soon—you may find that moving into repair-oriented work, rather than new construction, will keep you busy while others sit at home. Of course, many construction workers will also get this idea after the bubbles fully pop, so the sooner you begin your transition toward repair work, the better. Most types of maintenance and repair work, such as automobile repair, will be in increasing demand, as people buy far fewer new cars and instead try to hang on to their older cars for as long as possible.

Most Businesses Will Fare Poorly in the Capital Goods Sector.

We won't dress it up for you. The bottom line for business owners in the capital goods sector is not pretty. If you can sell now and get out, you probably should. No one can predict exactly when the Aftershock will hit, but even if it takes another two or three years, the marketplace for your business is unlikely to improve much during that time. The value of capital goods sector companies will not rise much under current conditions and will fall in value later, as unemployment continues to rise and the economy continues on its slow-growth or no-growth track. So if you have a business in the automotive, construction, industrial equipment, or any other capital goods industry, the longer you wait to get out, the more vulnerable you will be to significant losses.

As with selling homes and commercial real estate, your pool of potential buyers will get smaller and smaller as time goes by, so the sooner you go fishing in that pool for a possible buyer, the better. Selling any business takes time. Start now. Don't wait until the economy gets worse and most of your potential buyers have figured out that they should not own a business in the capital goods sector.

What will you do after you sell? Options include using your proceeds to invest in the kind of Aftershock portfolio discussed in this book. You can also be on the lookout for unexpected business opportunities in the Aftershock (discussed later in this chapter). If you decide to just hold it all in cash while you think about what to do next, be careful where you put it. Banks will be vulnerable leading up to and in the Aftershock, and the Federal Deposit Insurance Corporation (FDIC) will likely cover up to only $100,000 per bank account. Also, as inflation rises, the buying power of your cash is evaporating.

The Discretionary Spending Sector

As the economy continues to fall, Americans are not going to run out to the mall every night after work (if they have work) and squander their very limited cash and even more limited credit on high-priced designer handbags or the latest CDs. Discretionary spending on things like travel, restaurants, and entertainment is, well, discretionary. Many items and activities that we may currently still enjoy will simply be left off our shopping lists after the bubbles continue to fall and eventually fully pop. Over time, this will slow many businesses to a crawl and force others completely out of the game, further driving up unemployment.

But discretionary spending will still hold up better than the capital goods sector of the economy because some people will still have money, and they will keep spending their money, but they will spend at a lower level than before. So, instead of discretionary spending disappearing altogether, the people who can still spend will simply buy lower-priced discretionary items. For example, instead of shopping for designer handbags at Saks Fifth Avenue, they may downgrade to Walmart or Target.

The restaurant business will face this trend as well. As the bubbles fall, fewer people and businesses will spend money on eating out. That will certainly affect all restaurants. But some people and businesses will have money to eat out and will be quite happy to go to restaurants, as long as they don't have to spend as much as they used to. So the restaurant industry will continue to be a huge industry in the United States, but business will begin a long-term shift toward the lower end. For example, Mexican and Chinese restaurants will continue to survive and will gain increased market share, while high-end seafood and steak houses will be much harder hit.

To a large extent, this same trend will happen throughout the discretionary spending sector. Instead of brand names, we'll want bargains. We will still want to buy some stuff that we don't absolutely need, but we will buy less of it and we will want it at lower prices.

Because consumer spending drives more than two-thirds of the U.S. economy, any decline in consumer spending has a big impact on the overall economy. This is a new situation for the United States. Back in the 1920s, when the nation was much less wealthy and was heading into the Great Depression, consumer spending represented a much smaller portion of our overall economy. So when the stock market bubble crashed in 1929, and the economy took a major downturn, the large dip in consumer spending back then had a much smaller impact on the overall economy because it just didn't make up that large a part of the economy. Other industries took a big hit, but people still had to eat basic food and buy basic clothing, so most of these industries just kept on going.

We are in a different situation today. Much of what we currently buy (and that keeps our economy going) we can easily do without. We may not like to skip the latest, high-priced fashions, but if we have to, we can easily shop at lower-end and discount stores. We can also survive quite nicely without $100,000 kitchen makeovers, complete with granite countertops and stainless steel appliances. As incomes and assets evaporate, Americans will learn to manage without these pricy pleasures.

While the discretionary spending sector will be hit less hard than the capital goods sector, the fact that discretionary spending has become such a big part of the current U.S. economy means a downturn in this sector will greatly accelerate the popping bubbles and make our postbubble recovery even harder.

Jobs in the Discretionary Spending Sector Will be Hit Hard.

We've already mentioned how the slowdown in the discretionary spending sector will harm many businesses in the restaurant, retail, and home improvement industries. The travel industry has already taken a big hit, and that will continue as the bubbles fall. Leisure travel will be especially stalled, while more Americans will travel to locations that are closer and cheaper—such as into their living rooms to watch TV. Major entertainment destinations, such as Orlando and Las Vegas, will hang on due to liquidation of assets and to foreign visitors coming to spend their more valuable currencies in our cheaper playgrounds. Once the dollar bubble fully falls and the Aftershock begins, leisure travel by Americans going overseas will face the double whammy of minimal discretionary spending and a dollar that has fallen dramatically against foreign currencies.

Business travel will suffer as well. Domestic business travel will decrease as the bubbles continue to fall and companies become more interested in cutting costs. Overseas business travel will be hit by high costs and the low value of the dollar, so only the most important overseas trips will continue. Once the Aftershock hits, our imports will be way down and there won't be much need for business travel overseas at that point.

If you are currently employed in the discretionary spending sector and are in a position to retrain for another career, this would be a good time to look for a job elsewhere, such as the necessities sector.

Businesses in the Discretionary Spending Sector Will Also Fare Poorly.

Most businesses in this sector will experience some downturn as the bubbles continue to fall, and in the final pop and Aftershock, many will not survive. Businesses that have the best chances of survival during these increasingly leaner times will include low-end restaurants, low-end clothing stores, discount shops, used clothing and household furnishing stores, and businesses that cater to local or inexpensive travel.

If you own a business in the discretionary spending sector, you might want to give some thought to selling it. If you were already thinking of selling your business, you may want to move that time frame up and sell sooner rather than later. Waiting until many business owners start to realize that they need to sell will not be a good time to put your business on the market. Lots of sellers and not many buyers will mean prices will go way down.

In addition, you will be fighting against some demographics. Many businesses are owned by aging Baby Boomers, and as they get closer to retirement, they will become more risk averse and more likely to want to cash out of their businesses. Having more businesses for sale when you want to sell your business will make it harder for you to find a buyer. If you wait too long, you may risk facing the coming price drops.

Some Limited Good News: The Necessities Sector

Here is where we actually agree (somewhat) with conventional wisdom. Jobs and businesses in health care, education, and the government will do relatively better than in the other sectors. But even jobs in the necessities sector—such as health care, education, agriculture, government service, and utilities—not every job will not be perfectly protected before and during the coming Aftershock.

Historically, many of the jobs in this sector don't pay very well, and they will pay a bit less after the bubbles pop, when there are more workers available than jobs. But if you have a job in this sector, at least you have a job, and it will be much more reliable than most other jobs as the bubbles fall and later in the Aftershock. Even at lower pay, necessities sector jobs will be a godsend for families with a spouse who used to make more money than his or her mate but is now unemployed. The lower-paid, still-employed spouse, working as a nurse, teacher, medical administrator, or other necessities sector employee, will likely retain his or her job and be able to carry the family through the worst of the downturn.

But please understand that even in this sector, not all jobs will be equally protected. Many necessities sector jobs will not survive in the Aftershock. Why? Because they may not be "necessary" enough. So even in this sector, you will need to plan ahead.

The necessities sector is composed primarily of health care, education, utilities, basic food, basic clothing, and government services, usually run by government or other nonprofit entities. The private companies that supply these government and nonprofit entities have the potential to survive, as well. Of course, as the bubbles fall and eventually pop fully, the necessities sector will also take a hit because it currently contains a larger portion of discretionary spending (spending on high-end items within the necessities category) that will eventually be cut. So even within this relatively good sector, some jobs will not stay.

Health Care Jobs and Businesses.

Health care is a very strong element of the U.S. economy, and it will continue to be the best bet in the necessities sector as the bubbles fall and fully pop. But there will still be some negatives, especially as unemployment rises and health care revenues decline in the Aftershock.

Even now, in late 2013, jobs in the health care sector are not growing as fast as they were in 2012. Hospital hiring has slowed the most.

When the Aftershock hits, all job sectors will be negatively affected. Health care capital goods, such as radiology machines and hospital construction, will not do very well. However, businesses providing services and supplies to the health care industry will continue to do okay, even though they, too, will experience some downturn.

Health care services jobs that will do the best include:

- Nurses
- Primary care doctors
- Psychiatrists
- Nurse practitioners
- Physicians' assistants
- Medical technicians, support personnel, administrative staff, and others involved in primary care medicine (not specialties)

Health Care Could Become 20 Percent of the GDP When the Bubbles Pop

Health care will be one of the safest havens for business owners and workers before and during the Aftershock. Currently, the huge health care industry accounts for about 16 percent of the nation's GDP. As other industries decline, especially in the discretionary spending and capital goods sectors, the more stable health care industry will naturally take up a larger percentage of our economy. We've seen this before on a smaller scale. For example, during the oil bust in the 1980s, the percentage of the Houston economy represented by non-oil industries grew dramatically.

Add to this an aging population with increasing demands for health care, and it is quite possible that health care could take over a staggering 20 percent of our economy after all six of the bubbles pop. And that's even if we have what could be a 50 percent cut per person in medical care costs, primarily by limiting procedures and reimbursable rates.

So not only will the safest jobs and businesses be in health care in the Aftershock, but also that the nation's hopes for regaining significant productivity growth in the postbubble economy will lie with dramatic productivity advancements in the health care field.

Specialists and their supporting staff and services will not do well, with surgeons taking the biggest hit due to falling demand. Elective procedures, such as cosmetic surgery, already had a downturn during the financial crisis. If you can, transitioning out of these kinds of nonessential medical jobs into more basic areas of health care would be ideal.

Government Jobs and Businesses.

After health care, the next best positions in the necessities sector will be government service jobs, such as police and firefighters. As in past recessions, government services will still be needed. However, unlike in past recessions, in the Aftershock, government services will have to take deep cuts when the government can no longer borrow money after the government debt bubble pops. Before the Aftershock, government service jobs will hold on and may seem protected, but they could be pulled out from under you later, when things get worse.

This will be particularly true for private companies that have contracts with the federal government or states. Businesses and individuals who supply capital goods or construction services to the government will be hit. Road construction and maintenance, and transportation in general, will do poorly as the money for these expenditures dries up. Businesses that can make the switch to repair work and repair-related services will fare far better.

Education Jobs and Businesses.

Along with health care, the demand for public education will continue, so businesses that supply education or health care products or services to the government will benefit from strengthening their marketing and business ties to these areas and increasing their percentage of sales in these sectors.

Jobs in education will be more secure than in, say, the restaurant business (discretionary spending sector), but do not make the mistake of thinking that *all* education jobs will be fully protected as the bubbles fall. As tax revenues drastically drop at both the state and local levels, funding for education will fall. Long term, jobs at primary and secondary schools will hold up better than those in higher education. Some number of elementary, middle, and high school math and science teachers will still be in demand, but as class sizes expand, many math and science teachers will not find a job.

Music and art teachers will face more layoffs, along with extra-curricular personnel. Once the bubbles are fully popped and the Aftershock begins, we may find that seniority and union member-ship won't matter much. Instead, if you want to get or keep a job in education, you will need to be very good at your job, be willing to teach more classes to more students, and be loyal to your school's administration.

The picture for higher education will be tougher. Strong departments in practical fields, like engineering and computer science, especially at top colleges and universities, will fare bet-ter than those in "soft" departments (sociology, English, etc.) at liberal arts schools. Don't count on tenure to save you if your department has to take big budget cuts. If you are lucky enough to be retained in a strong department, be prepared to teach more classes for less pay.

Broader Job Trends.

One of the obvious job trends as we near the Aftershock will be growth in cash businesses and jobs. Expect that jobs in restaurants will increasingly be paid with cash and many people will be able to find temporary jobs or consulting jobs that pay cash and will be willing to work at lower rates. The underground cash economy will likely grow substantially, as it has in other countries experiencing a major economic downturn. Jobs in repair, as we mentioned earlier, will be more resistant to the downturn and are the type of jobs that can be easily paid for in cash.

Also, another current trend that will continue into the Aftershock, and especially afterward, will be higher pay and growth in demand for highly skilled blue-collar jobs. Although highly skilled blue-collar workers will be hurt like most job seek-ers, this area will still offer reasonable pay and decent opportu-nities even during the Aftershock. This is especially true if these skilled jobs also involve difficult working conditions, such as being an electrical lineman who has to repair electrical lines in storms. Such jobs will continue to pay relatively well and there will be decent demand, mostly because many people with skills don't like those kinds of jobs. Even now, there are lots of vacan-cies for these types of jobs and significant turnover in many of them. Although conditions will tighten considerably in the future, this will still be an area for employment simply because of the skills required and many people's unwillingness to work under bad conditions.

Free Internships—Not Just for College Students Anymore

Free internships have been a good route for college students to potentially get a paid job by working for free. For the student, an internship provides an opportunity to get a foot in the door of an employer, as well as getting some on-the-job training. For the employer, the internship offers a chance to get to know the intern in the work environment before deciding to hire or fire, while also getting some work out of them for free, making the internship an effective win-win for both parties.

While not in favor now, in the future Aftershock, unpaid internships for adults who are not college students will become more common. In an increasingly tight job market, workers who are willing to work for free for a period of time will have a competitive advantage. Like college students, they will have the chance to get their foot in the door, while also gaining training and on-the-job experience. The value to the potential employer is obvious: free labor.

As the bubbles continue to fall, and even more so after they fully pop in the Aftershock, unpaid internships for non–college students will become increasingly common.

If there is a job you are going after now and they don't currently offer an unpaid internship, there is no harm in suggesting one. The company may not be set up to accept your offer, but you never know. Everyone likes a freebie.

Should I Go to College?

For high school students or recent graduates, planning to go to college still makes sense. Even though the economy may be falling during that time and you will likely emerge from college in a difficult work environment with fewer jobs and business opportunities than before, it is still a good idea to get a college education if you can. The longer you wait, the less likely you are to go back to school, and a college degree will still mean something, even in the Aftershock.

However, spending too much on college is not a good idea. In figuring the costs and benefits of continuing your education, it is important to be realistic.

In general, the financial value of an expensive four-year college degree in the liberal arts has been going down recently, while the value of a two-year college degree in a practical field, or a diploma or certificate of completion from a trade or technical school, has gone up.

While additional education is no guarantee of landing employment, it will definitely increase the odds of getting a job after you graduate and will also improve your chances of getting a higher-paying job. Obviously, you will do better picking a field in the more favorable job sectors mentioned earlier. If you already have a secure, full-time job, going back to college may not be worth it, unless you can get your degree in a year or two.

Opportunities after the Bubbles Pop: Cashing In on Distressed Assets

In nearly every industry in all three sectors of the economy, there will be some opportunities to benefit from falling asset values. Just as high-priced office furniture from bankrupt dot-com companies ended up at auction sales for pennies on the dollar after the relatively small Internet bubble popped, there will be countless auctions of every description after our multibubble economy pops. Opportunities to make large profits by buying, selling, and servicing distressed businesses and other assets will actually become one of the good sectors in the postbubble economy.

As always, timing will be key. One of the biggest mistakes many people will make is buying distressed businesses or other assets too soon. In this very unusual economic downturn, involving the fall of multiple bubbles, we will face very high interest and inflation rates that will take a lot longer to come down than anyone might imagine. It will be easy to mistakenly think the worst has passed and the time is right to start buying up distressed businesses and assets, when actually the price of these bargain properties will likely fall *even lower*. For maximum profits, think years, not months. Many people in the real estate market are making this mistake right now. They think that because an asset has lost 25 to 50 percent of its peak value, it is a bargain. That is true only if it is not going to fall farther.

That said, there can be some shorter-term opportunities to "flip" a distressed asset even before the Aftershock hits and assets fall even further, if you can find a willing buyer.

Once the Aftershock hits, the servicing of distressed assets and businesses will be an instant and long-term winner. People and companies who buy, restructure, manage, and resell distressed businesses and other assets will have the opportunity to make huge incomes and profits, including:

- Accountants and financial analysts involved with forensic accounting and distressed properties accounting.
- Consultants, bankers, managers, and others involved in the acquisition, restructuring, and management of distressed businesses and other assets.
- Bankruptcy attorneys.
- Liquidation companies and auction houses.

"We're still the same, great company we've always been, only we've ceased to exist."

Dig Your Well before You Are Thirsty

The title of Harvey MacKay's excellent book *Dig Your Well before You Are Thirsty* makes a lot of sense in these pre-Aftershock days before the full bubble pop. Now is the time to network among colleagues or make new connections that you can draw on later, as needed.

Now is also the time to show your boss (or your customers) just how great an employee (or business owner) you really are. Make yourself indispensable before any downsizing or pullback occurs. And, of course, never leave a job or income source before having another one in hand.

If you find yourself without a job or other income, don't allow pride to stop you from taking whatever you can get in a reasonable time period, while you continue to look for better work. This will not be a good time for holding out for something better.

If you do find yourself temporarily out of work, please remember, as we always say, your net worth is not your self-worth. And perhaps more important, please show that same respect to others. In tough times, judge people not by the size of their wallets, but by the size of their hearts.

11

Understanding Our Problems Is the First Step Toward Solving Our Problems

W hen people start talking about the financial crisis or the very slow economy, there is always a tendency to want to blame someone. The usual suspects are Federal Reserve chairmen, past and present, individual investment bankers, all investment bankers, Congress, the president, and so on. Although all of these people share blame, some more than others, for our economic problems, it is usually only a partial answer. We could change the Fed chairman, but would that make that much difference? We could put some investment bankers in jail—and maybe they should go—but is that really the heart of the problem? We wish it were so easy, but it is doubtful that such changes will really turn the fundamental economy around.

The real culprit is more important than any of these individuals or groups of individuals. The real culprit is economists. What we are witnessing now is a *fundamental failure of the economics profession*. Understanding this failure and how to resolve it will create a powerful tool for solving our current and future economic problems.

If You Don't Understand Why an Economy Grows, You Can't Understand Why It Doesn't Grow

The fundamental failure of economics goes beyond simply not seeing the crisis before it happened, or not warning of it, or not telling us how to prevent it. The even bigger failure is a fundamental lack of understanding of how the economy works. Economists don't really know why an economy grows—whether it's the United States or China or Japan. Hence, they can't tell you why it stops growing. Yes, economists can certainly tell us if an economy is growing and where it is growing, but they can't really tell us why. They don't understand economic growth, so they don't understand the lack of economic growth either. (*Hint:* It has to do with productivity growth, as we'll explain shortly.)

Of course, no one really cares if they don't understand how the economy grows, as long as it's growing. Nobody gets mad at economists because the economy is growing 10 percent per year; they get mad at economists when it stops growing—hey, man, we need you to solve this problem, and quick!

Of course, since they don't really know why it was growing, they don't really know how to get growth going again. When it's growing, all a good economist has to do is agree that the economy is growing and will continue to grow, as most economists did. For that, they were richly rewarded with good academic positions, research grants, and other favors.

In fact, we have certainly spent more money on economists and economic research in the past 30 years of the bubble economy than we have for all of previous history. During the bubble economy the resources devoted to economics have ballooned enormously from previous decades, not just in the United States but in Europe and Japan as well.

It's truly been the golden age of economics. The only problem in this golden age is the almost complete lack of major economic breakthroughs from all this economic research. That wasn't true before. We have had big economic breakthroughs in the past century, but the past 30 years have been among the least productive of the past 100 years, despite enormous increases in funding.

You Need to See the Big Picture before You Start to Focus

This is partly because a lot of money can be spent researching very narrow or obscure issues. There is nothing wrong with that— as long as you also research and understand the bigger picture as well. In true sciences, like chemistry or geology, these narrow or obscure issues can often be very beneficial in the advancement of, for instance, chemical or geologic knowledge. That's because these additional bits of research are tied very closely to strong fundamental scientific theories of chemistry or geology. The smaller details fit into a bigger picture. In economics, research on relatively narrow issues is not very useful because it is not tied to a strong overall understanding of economics. When you don't understand the big picture, looking at the little picture doesn't really help.

In geology, if we did the same thing, it would be like having thousands of people study the Appalachian Mountains to understand how mountains form. However, if you don't understand continental drift, even if you put tens of thousands of people on studying the Appalachians, you're not going to understand how mountains form. Beautiful mountains, yes. A lot of well-funded research, definitely. But breakthroughs in understanding? Not a chance.

Understanding continental drift may involve looking at the Appalachian Mountains, but that's not the focus. The focus is more on fundamental concepts of how *all* mountains are formed, and what could be driving the evolving nature of those mountains—which, of course, involves recognizing that those mountains are evolving. Unless you are studying the Appalachian Mountains as simply a springboard for a broader understanding of geology and how mountains form, you will get nowhere. You need to understand the big picture to understand the Appalachians.

It may be comfortable to have thousands of other very focused, very scholarly researchers with you in your Appalachian Mountain research, but it isn't going to lead to any big breakthroughs for the geology profession in understanding how mountains are formed. Lots of money spent and no insights gained.

This, unfortunately, it the current state of economic research.

But to better understand why the economics profession has hit a brick wall in its ability to form an accurate big picture about economic growth, despite the enormous increases in funding, we need to tour through a brief history of the economic breakthroughs in the past. For anyone who wants more, we strongly suggest that you read Robert Heilbroner's book, *The Worldly Philosophers.* It's the runaway best book on the history of economics. It's also easy and enjoyable reading and a great book for noneconomists.

Key Breakthroughs in the History of Economic Thought

We're just going to review seven major breakthroughs in economic thinking over the past few centuries to give you an idea of how we got to where we are and to guide us in what needs to be done in the future. There were other key insights in economic thought developed during this time, but these breakthroughs basically shaped the structure of economic thought today.

Breakthrough 1: Free Markets

We begin with Adam Smith and the concept of free market competition. His support of free markets and opposition to business monopolies set up by the monarchy was a foundation for modern economic thought. Much of the power of Smith's work is due to his focus on some aspects of property rights (the rights of monarchs to establish a monopoly in a market) and how these rights are an important part of economics. By focusing on certain aspects of property rights he vaulted economic thought forward. The definition of *property rights* that we use is simply "the way in which society determines who gets what resources."

Smith's most important written work, *The Wealth of Nations*, was first written in 1776, an auspicious time for questioning the wisdom of monarchical rule in the British Empire. He was effectively one of the democratic revolutionaries who helped others to question the value of the monarchy in general and more specifically, in their interference with free markets. To a large degree Adam Smith's work is the start of modern economic thought.

What Adam Smith missed was a focus on the evolutionary aspects of economic growth and specifically, the evolution of the forces that were changing property rights. (Economic growth *evolves* over time, as other aspects of society, such as science, technology, and politics, evolve. We will have much more to say about this in other books.)

Breakthrough 2: More Focus on Economic Evolution and Property Rights

Karl Marx was instrumental in the second major breakthrough in economic thought, more for what he focused on than for his actual theoretical insights. With his publication of *The Communist Manifesto* in 1848, he continued Adam Smith's focus on property rights but added an evolutionary element to it. He attempted to construct an evolutionary theory of property rights. He just wasn't correct about what that evolution was.

Part of the reason that Marx had such difficulties in figuring out the correct evolution is that he couldn't look into the future. His view of economics relied very heavily on Utopian Socialism, which viewed economic activity through a lens on the past—a much more agricultural-based economy with many small craftsmen, rather than a modern industrial economy with large corporations. His model was heavily based on an agricultural economy with the land-owning nobility holding ever more and more land. Marx incorrectly transferred his model to the rising industrial sector. He had no real understanding of productivity and how it impacted agricultural and industrial development.

Marx also focused on the role of capital in society, which is important, but again he was more focused on capital as land and the rent that it produced, as opposed to a return on the investment of capital, which is so critical to modern industrial society. However, his lack of understanding of the role of capital and its return was a key factor in forcing economists to develop a viable theory of what determined the return to capital, meaning what determines the level of profits and interest rates.

So Mr. Marx made a good effort at trying to understand the evolution of the economy and the key concepts of property rights and capital, but ended up not fully understanding them due to his focus on a past economic model, which was the predominant model at the time. It would be clear to an astute observer, however, that the economy was rapidly moving away from this model. But, his work motivated other economists to develop an adequate theory of capital.

Breakthrough 3: Understanding Supply and Demand (the Beginning of Microeconomics)

Economic thought had a third breakthrough—the development of the combined model of supply and demand. This was not as easily attributable to one person. Prior to Marx, concepts of supply and demand developed separately. Adam Smith had led the way with work on supply and supply-based pricing. Other later work developed a competing price model based solely on demand. After

Marx, these concepts were combined into a unified theory of supply and demand. This combined supply-and-demand concept was an excellent basic theory and was a good start at understanding how markets worked. It was the beginning of modern microeconomic theory.

However, it was based on an abstraction of an idealized nineteenth-century grain market. For it to be used in a real economy, there had to be unrealistic constraints, which severely limited its applicability to the real world.

For example, free entry into a market, as defined in the free market economic model, is critical to a true free market, but it rarely exists at the required level in most markets today. Just as the government can establish and maintain a free market, it can destroy a free market by declaring monopolies in markets to benefit friends and supporters. Adam Smith opposed this type of government destruction of free markets, and that opposition was a key motivation for developing his theory of free markets. Free markets don't benefit the individual businessmen participating in them (that's why they wanted the king to grant them monopolies), so there is a natural tendency to thwart the free market to gain extra profits.

The government's role in establishing and maintaining free markets and free entry into those markets was not well understood at the time and is still not well understood. And that's just one example of the problems underlying supply-and-demand models of the economy. So theories of supply and demand are an important breakthrough, but they are often highly constrained in their applicability to the real world. Overall, this breakthrough is a good idea in principle, but poor in actual real-world execution.

As you can see at this point, economics was suffering in part from an overall lack of an integrated theory. Instead, economics was a collection of theories and concepts. These concepts were usually developed by economists observing economic behavior in everyday life and abstracting that behavior into more general and theoretical concepts with broad application. That's a good way to take a first step, but it isn't an overall integrated theory. And, in particular, economists were still not focusing on key issues such as property rights, technological evolution, and information dynamics (the way people learn). That also means those concepts were certainly not part of an accurate, integrated theory of economics, which is critical for good economics.

Breakthrough 4: Understanding the Role of Capital and the Payment for Capital

As mentioned earlier, Karl Marx helped future economists focus on capital. This led to the fourth major breakthrough in economic thought, which was an understanding of the role of capital and the payment for capital in a modern economy. In particular, this meant understanding interest payments as compensation for the "time value" of money and as compensation for the riskiness of an investment. In addition, economists began to better understand the idea that investors get (or want to get) compensation for taking business risks. They better understood the concept of *return on investment*, which was fundamental to the financing of the modern industrial economy.

However, theories of risk and returns need to be integrated with a better understanding of property rights to be fully applicable to the real world. Overall, this breakthrough has merit—like theories of supply and demand, a good idea in principle but poor in actual execution.

Breakthrough 5: Macroeconomics (Monetary and Fiscal Policy)

The fifth breakthrough in economic thought was the development of the modern concept of macroeconomics. Modern macroeconomics is in part an attempt to solve some of the earlier problems just mentioned with theories on supply and demand, which did not allow for a number of variables, such as the occurrence of recessions or depressions.

Macroeconomics was developed to deal with these problems in a more sophisticated way than simple supply and demand theories, which proved totally incapable of explaining what happened. As mentioned earlier, supply-and-demand theories were abstractions of an idealized nineteenth-century grain market. The influential British economist, John Maynard Keynes, created a more sophisticated bit of abstraction by looking at how governments had funded wars in the past through borrowing money. Monarchs had often borrowed money in the past to fund wars. Keynes broadened the concept to how governments could borrow money (run a deficit) to stimulate the economy, or conversely to run a budget surplus to reduce economic activity. Decisions involving governmental borrowing and spending are called *fiscal policy*.

In the same light, a more modern macroeconomist, Nobel Prize winner Milton Friedman, looked at how governments printed money, which is called *monetary policy*. Again, printing money was something that monarchies had done to finance wars in the past, so Milton Friedman abstracted this concept and applied it more broadly to the whole economy as a means of stimulating or reducing overall economic activity. This also led to a much clearer theoretical foundation for the causes of inflation.

Thus, the creation of the concepts of both fiscal and monetary policy (how governments borrow and print money and its effects on the economy) was the foundation of modern macroeconomic analysis.

However, since macroeconomics is based on abstraction, it cannot handle what will soon become one of our key tools for getting out of the mega-depression: targeted stimulation. To integrate the ideas of macroeconomics with real-world activities necessary to effectively run an economy requires a fundamental understanding of economics as a more complete and unified science.

The fact that economics has both a microeconomic theory and a macroeconomic theory illustrates this fundamental problem mentioned earlier—that the field of economics does not yet have an integrated comprehensive theory. Having two separate theories with no integrating larger theory to connect them strongly suggests that neither theory is completely adequate. The inadequacies of these economic theories are a big part of the reason why economics profession has failed us so completely in understanding or warning us about the Aftershock ahead, let alone helping us prevent or solve it. These inadequacies will become painfully obvious when the Aftershock hits.

Breakthrough 6: Mathematical Models

In the post–World War II period, economists developed ways to represent the equilibriums suggested by the supply and demand model, as well as fiscal and monetary policy, through systems of equations. The system of equations could be solved so that the model provided an equilibrium solution. Due to the many fundamental theoretical problems we discussed earlier, these models have been less successful than was hoped in representing real world economies, but they do represent an important step in introducing more mathematics into economics.

Reaching a *static* equilibrium is not what real economies tend to do. In the real world, an economy behaves less like a seesaw that is seeking its static equilibrium balance point and more like the weather—constantly changing and seeking *dynamic* equilibrium. As will be discussed later, for these fluctuating systems, numerical simulation models, based on better fundamental analysis and assumptions, are the preferred way to create a viable mathematical model of the economy. Just as with better analysis and understanding of the ever-changing weather, more accurate analysis and understanding of the behavior of a dynamic economic system yields more accurate and useful information.

Breakthrough 7: Empirically Tested Mathematical Models

Another major postwar breakthrough was the use of econometrics, which allowed a statistically based empirical validation of an economic theory or model. A model that could be empirically tested is a big step in the right direction, but when tested it turns out that the models don't work that well. Models that produce a high correlation of multiple model inputs with model outputs may test well statistically, but correlation does not imply causation. So, for example, while high home prices might be correlated with high demand, that does not mean high demand is the cause or the only cause of rising home prices, which may also be impacted by many other factors, such as property rights. These other factors cannot be measured or analyzed correctly with current econometric analysis.

In other words, causation is complicated. It involves many interacting factors, as one would expect it would, given that we are talking about complex human behaviors within complex social systems that are continuously changing over time.

To some degree mathematical models can be modified to produce whatever results you want them to produce. But manipulating the model and the assumptions to produce a desired outcome is not the same as revealing truth. As Mark Twain so aptly said, "There are lies, damn lies, and statistics." The fact that the numbers "work" doesn't make it accurate in practical terms.

Nonetheless, empirically tested mathematical models are a good step in the right direction because they move the field of economics closer to becoming a science. However, economists are using the wrong mathematical approach and empirical approach. The econometric approach will need to be replaced by an empirical approach based on scientific experimentation.

Although there have been minor improvements to microeconomic and macroeconomic thinking, as well as to econometric modeling, in the past 30 years, there have been few major breakthroughs. We are still trying to improve and advance economic thoughts by relying on these limited concepts, and naturally it's not working very well.

In Tribute to Lawrence Klein—Pioneering Economist, Entrepreneur, and Friend

Lawrence Klein died on October 20, 2013, at the age of 93. He was one of the pioneers of econometrics. Econometrics allows the creation of a mathematically based empirical validation of an economic theory or model. He was a Nobel Prize–winning economist and a professor of economics at the University of Pennsylvania. Coauthor Dr. David Wiedemer was one of his students at Penn.

Dr. Klein began using his early mathematical modeling techniques just after World War II to predict that the United States would not enter a recession postwar but would instead grow rapidly. This was quite contrary to what most economists were thinking at the time. They thought the massive cut in government expenditures after the war would almost certainly force the economy into recession.

That, of course, did not happen. Just as Klein's econometrics predicted, the economy did grow rapidly. So he was an economist who was right when other economists were quite wrong. And his predictions weren't just opinions, but were based on his theories of more scientific and practical mathematical modeling.

Not only was he a gifted academic economist, but he also worked hard to apply his research to the real world and helped found Wharton Econometrics. The company pioneered in the use of econometric modeling for businesses. The company grew steadily and was ultimately bought by IHS, one of the largest information companies in the world. To this day it remains the preeminent provider of econometric models to both business and nonprofit organizations.

He was an unusual person and an unusual economist. He was a true pioneer in economics at a time when pioneering innovations in economic thought have become increasingly scarce. He was also a successful entrepreneur who helped found a business that successfully applied his economic theories to the real world. That is a rare combination indeed.

The economics profession, and Dave, will miss him.

Economics Needs a Breakthrough Big-Picture Idea like Geology Needed Continental Drift

Almost 30 years ago, the evolution of economic thought essentially came to a stop with the introduction of mathematical models. Despite the massive resources spent since then, we have had few major breakthroughs. There has been a lot of research, lots of funding awarded to think tanks, lots of John Bates Clark awards for best economic scholars under 40, lots of tenured professorships given, lots of Nobel prizes awarded, lots of highly regarded articles published in the *American Economic Review* (one of the most prestigious academic economic journals), but no significant breakthroughs.

Why?

It would seem, based on all these prizes and funding, that the profession is having a breakthrough every day! But it's not, and that's why economists are having such problems dealing with understanding the causes of the recent Great Recession or forecasting the coming Aftershock. In fact, all the activity and prizes almost seem designed to distract everyone from the glaring lack of real breakthroughs. Like cheerleading in the financial markets, it is cheerleading in the economics profession.

Using the earlier analogy of thousands of geologists studying how the Appalachians were formed with no real breakthroughs on understanding why mountains in general form, we could give out thousands of tenured professorships, print thousands of articles in prestigious journals, and give out lots of prizes for great work on studying the Appalachians, but it still won't help us understand what created the Appalachian Mountains.

Unless, of course, you have someone like Alfred Wegener, who is willing to take on the status quo view of geology and come up with a radical and useful new idea like continental drift. Of course, when a big breakthrough like continental drift occurs, you don't need thousands of people studying the Appalachians anymore. Alfred has figured it out. The other guys were just wasting their time and need to go home despite all their prizes and funding. And of course, no one likes that, so there is great resistance.

Not that there isn't plenty of new work to do. The new model of continental drift not only provides a powerful new understanding of geology; it also opens up a huge window of potential new research to more fully develop the new model. But very likely it won't be something that most Appalachian scholars will want to do or know how to do. That will be for a new generation of geologists to fully run with and develop, now that geologists have the breakthrough basic understanding of continental drift.

What the field of economics needs is a breakthrough like continental drift and a person like Alfred Wegener. See the sidebar for some background on Alfred Wegener and his heroic struggle against the status quo academic leadership to bring an enormously important breakthrough to geology, for which we award him the ABE Award for Intellectual Courage.

ABE Award for Intellectual Courage: Alfred Wegener

Alfred Wegener created the greatest breakthrough in modern geology, the theory of continental drift. However, he wasn't even a geologist. He received his PhD in Planetary Astronomy from Humboldt University in Berlin in 1905. He was also interested in climatology. His lectures, "The Thermodynamics of the Atmosphere," became a standard textbook in meteorology. Obviously, he had no problem getting support when he wasn't attacking the status quo.

However, with continental drift, he was attacking the status quo head-on. He had reasonable but not overwhelming evidence for his continental drift idea. He had noticed the obvious fit of North America to Europe and South America to Africa. He tried to prove this theory that the continents were once connected by doing research on fossils and geology. He found identical fossils and identical rock strata on both sides of the Atlantic.

After 1912 Wegener publicly advocated the theory of continental drift, arguing that all the continents had once been joined together in a single landmass and had drifted apart. In 1915, in *The Origin of Continents and Oceans*, Wegener published the theory that there had once been a giant continent, which we now call Pangea.

Reaction to Wegener's theory was almost uniformly hostile, and often exceptionally harsh and scathing; Dr. Rollin T. Chamberlin of the University of Chicago said, "Wegener's hypothesis in general is of the footloose type, in that it takes considerable liberty with our globe, and is less bound by restrictions or tied down by awkward, ugly facts than most of its rival theories."

Needless to say, no one was interested in helping him prove or disprove his theory. They simply dismissed his groundbreaking ideas out of hand without even wanting to understand them or discuss them.

In fact, reaction to his ideas was so strongly negative that after the American edition of Wegener's work was published in 1925, the American Association of Petroleum Geologists organized a symposium specifically to criticize his continental drift hypothesis.

However, by the 1960s the evidence for Wegener's theories of continental drift became overwhelming. Despite all of the efforts of highly credentialed status quo defenders, Wegener's ideas succeeded because they were right. He revolutionized geologic thought and became the father of modern geology.

So Why Aren't We Getting an Alfred Wegener or a Breakthrough Idea like Continental Drift?

It's an interesting question, and, as we alluded to before, it's very much related to that huge increase in funding for economists and economic research during the bubble economy. Life has been good for economists during the bubble economy. Partly as a result of the stock and housing bubbles, universities have had no trouble raising tuition enormously—way beyond the rate of inflation. This allowed them to increase or maintain professors' salaries. It also allowed professors to spend less time teaching. Theoretically, they should have been spending more time researching, but the reality is often quite different, and what they were researching hasn't been very productive.

Economists Have Become Academia's Version of Financial Cheerleaders

Once professors are given tenure, it is almost impossible for them to be fired. Tenure amounts to total job security. Rewards in academia are not solely monetary. They also include quality (or ease) of life. Yearlong sabbaticals are easier to get when the university has a lot of money. Well-funded retirements are also a great perk. Because of all of this, the status quo has been very good for most economists, and most people naturally don't want to threaten it. People in that position don't want to see the status quo changed and have an inherent bias against ideas that would threaten the status quo. Hence, explanations of the economy tend to be biased in support of current ways of thinking and not to favor new ways of thinking that are vital for breakthroughs. The result is that economists became academic cheerleaders—the academic counterparts to financial cheerleaders. And when you are a cheerleader, there is no hope of making a breakthrough.

In a sense, they are right to become economics cheerleaders. The alternative of having the bubbles pop is not good for them. A final popping of the bubbles would result in huge funding cuts for economists at universities and research centers, since both will be badly hit by government cutbacks in spending (due to the dollar and government debt bubble collapse) and huge drops in philanthropic giving (part of the discretionary spending bubble that will pop). In such an environment, it will be hard to protect economists from cost cutting, especially since they won't be seen as contributors to a solution. Their obvious lack of understanding of the economy prior to the Aftershock will certainly be very noticeable during the Aftershock.

Economists really don't want to think we have a bubble economy for very good reasons. Their jobs are especially vulnerable to a bubble pop.

The Demands to Get Tenure and the Rewards of the Good Life after Tenure Have Delivered a One-Two Punch to Creative Economic Thought

Although the life of many economists has been good, the life of someone trying to become one has not. In particular, it has become increasingly rigorous, requiring increasingly high levels of mathematical skills to gain tenure at a major university. The intense rigor required and the narrow areas of acceptable, well-funded research are effectively freezing out people with a high degree of creativity that could have something valuable, like continental drift, to offer. Sure, the selected few can publish highly rigorous, highly mathematical articles, but they don't have the focus or opportunity for a lot of creativity.

Of course, math should be a key part of economics, but we must have a good model to apply the math to. Doing a lot of math when you don't have a good model for how the economy works is fairly useless. Once you have a good model, then math becomes quite useful.

However, with the intensity of focus and rigor required to gain tenure, you are effectively selecting *out* the potentially most creative economists, who might create such a new model. You get people who don't question the status quo because they can't. They aren't able to do so because they are highly focused on the enormously rigorous task of trying to get tenure, not on solving the fundamental questions of economics that would create real breakthroughs. Creating real breakthroughs is just an unnecessary and highly risky distraction from getting tenure.

So it is a two-pronged problem of a good life after tenure and a very difficult, highly focused, and rigorous path to get tenure that is making economic breakthroughs increasingly difficult.

We should add that this "breakdown in breakthroughs" is affecting not only the economics profession but other sciences as well, such as biology and geology. The most important science—physics—which is the mother of all sciences, is facing this same issue. Without movement forward in physics, the other sciences are inherently limited as a result.

Interestingly, Lee Smolin, an American physicist now living in Toronto, recently wrote a book called *The Trouble with Physics*. It describes how physics has hit a brick wall in breakthroughs (sound familiar?). Despite massive funding, the past 30 years have been some of the least productive years in the past century for breakthroughs in physics (sound familiar?). And the same concerns he has about the academic community in physics are found in other academic fields. We gave Lee Smolin the ABE Award for Intellectual Courage in the first edition of *Aftershock*, and we give it to him again in this third edition (see sidebar describing Lee Smolin's work).

So the problem is not just in economics, which makes sense because the reasons we gave for the unwillingness to question status quo thinking in economics would affect all academic departments to some degree.

ABE Award for Intellectual Courage: Lee Smolin

Lee Smolin is one of those unusual academics and intellectuals who can spot a major problem and write very coherently about it. His book, *The Trouble with Physics*, is one of the best critiques of the current physics communities ever written. He points out, very convincingly, that the physics community, after decades of very impressive breakthroughs, has come to a virtual standstill since the early 1980s. In his many years of teaching and researching at major academic institutions, such as Princeton, Yale, and the Fermi Institute at the University of Chicago, he has seen the physics community become overly focused on string theory as the theoretical basis for breakthroughs in our understanding of physics.

More important, the physics community has not allowed or encouraged much discussion on other theories that might bring greater insight into the problems physicists are having such trouble solving. And string theory hasn't gotten physicists anywhere in almost 30 years. The inability of this academic community to encourage and create alternative theories that may answer their questions is a serious problem.

What does this have to do with the bubble economy? Not much directly, but it has a lot to do with the current state of economics. In many ways, economics is facing a similar problem. Although there was much progress made in the decades prior to the 1970s in a variety of areas including Milton Friedman's work on monetary policy and John Maynard Keynes's work on fiscal policy, as well as advancements in econometrics, very little has been accomplished since. The economics community has not been very encouraging or creative about major new approaches to understanding our economy. These failings are much more apparent to us than those of the physics community since they affect our pocketbook, but the failings of both communities are very similar.

Most important, any movement to make economics a real science, as opposed to a social science, has ground to a halt. In the end, for economics to be a real science, it has to be directly tied to the mother of all sciences, physics. If physics is having a problem, all sciences will have a problem, including economics, which needs to truly become a science. We should all share Mr. Smolin's concern about physics because it affects all the sciences and, ultimately the same problems affecting the mentality of the physics community are likely affecting other sciences as well, just as we see similar patterns in economics. Hats off to Lee Smolin for his important insights and his enormous courage.

Where to Now? Answer: Economics Needs to Move from Being a Collection of Competing Philosophies to Being a Unified Science

Given the long-standing lack of innovation and the all-consuming demands of gaining tenture and maintaining funding, we haven't had a real breakthrough in economics in many decades, and no new breakthroughs from the economics community are likely to come in the near term. So what do we do? How do we get economics moving on the right track so that it can solve our economic problems? Where should economics go for more breakthroughs? How do we improve economics?

First, we need to realize that we need a massive paradigm shift. It's not a regular paradigm shift, such as moving economics from being nonmathematical to being mathematical. The paradigm shift needed is much more fundamental. Economics needs to move from a philosophical approach to a more scientific approach. There is a reason that Robert Heilbroner's great book on the history of economics and economists is called *The Worldly Philosophers*. Past economists have been philosophers first and economists second.

They look at the real world and then make an abstraction of it to try to better explain how the real-world economy works. As we mentioned, an economist might develop an idealized nineteenth-century grain market to better explain how an actual market works. It's an abstraction of the real-world economy.

As philosophers, economists have fallen into various philosophical camps: Communists, Capitalists, Socialists, and so on. Or they follow a certain philosophy of an economist or group of economists: Keynesian, Austrian, Marxist, and so on.

As mentioned earlier, two of the great breakthroughs of twentieth-century economics—greater understanding of fiscal policy (government borrowing), led by John Maynard Keynes, and monetary policy (how the government creates money), led by Milton Friedman—are to some extent abstractions of how governments have financed wars for centuries, through either borrowing money or printing money. These abstractions were then turned into macroeconomic theory.

Although there have been some breakthroughs in creating a better philosophical understanding of how the economy works over the past 200 years, we have not had a big breakthrough in developing a more scientific understanding of the economy.

Imagine the field of medicine before Louis Pasteur and after Louis Pasteur. Before Pasteur, a nonscientific philosophy could be very important to medicine, such as the concept of spontaneous generation for the creation of or adaptation to diseases. Spontaneous generation is not scientifically based. However, using a more scientifically based model of diseases that includes an understanding of the impacts of viruses and bacteria created a revolution in medicine. This understanding was developed by more than just Pasteur, but the key is that medicine changed from being a philosophy of various opinions on how diseases were created to a very scientific understanding of what really caused diseases. This had a huge impact on the development of medicine and the degree to which medical science could help solve health problems in our society.

This is the kind of paradigm shift needed in economics if it is to move from competing philosophies to a real science that can properly analyze and understand our real economic problems and thus help actually solve them.

So what has to happen to make economics more of a science? As we just mentioned in the analogy to continental drift and as we talked about in *America's Bubble Economy* and *Aftershock*, we need to look at economies not as static systems but as continuously *evolving* systems. It is not simply cyclical; it is evolving. As we say in our many presentations to investors and financial professionals, the economy of the 1850s is not like the economy of the 1950s. The economy of the 1920s is not like the economy of the 1990s. Thirty years ago China wasn't even a consideration in our economy. Now China is the world's second-largest economy and very important to our economy. All economies *evolve;* they don't just cycle.

And economies do not evolve in a vacuum. They evolve as society evolves, including systematic changes in technology, politics, and science. All of these factors will continue to change and evolve. We don't cycle back to the technology, the social systems, the political systems, or the world economy of the 1850s. We continue to evolve. When you look at a short period of time, such as five years, this evolution is not very obvious. But when you step back and look at a period of 100 years or 150 years, the idea that economies evolve becomes blatantly obvious.

Equally obvious from this big-picture point of view is the idea that the various evolving parts—science, technology, economics, and politics—are actively impacting each other and therefore are evolving together. (We introduced this idea in our first book, *America's Bubble Economy*, in 2006, and we look forward to writing more about it in the future.)

Four Key Elements for Making Economics More of a Science

To make economics more of a science, we need to further develop the idea that the economy is *evolving*. We propose four new areas to focus on to help create a better and more unified field of study that, like weather forecasting, will help us better understand what is happening and what may happen next.

Information Dynamics

Information dynamics is a theory of learning, psychology, and the costs of learning. We need to bring an understanding of learning into our understanding of both production and consumption. We also need to understand that learning is inherently an evolutionary process. Over time, consumers learn more about what they want to buy and how much they are willing to pay for it, and producers learn about how to increase profits by refining their products, advertising, production efficiencies, and other factors. Learning is extraordinarily important to economic growth. To better understand this learning, we need to better understand how the human brain learns in general, as well as the psychology of how specific groups of people (of various ages, backgrounds, motivations, etc.) learn.

A full understanding of how the brain learns is probably quite a ways off; just recognizing the importance of learning in both production and consumption and focusing on this issue is an important breakthrough toward making economics more of a science. The recent interest in behavioral economics makes a tiny step in this direction, but what is needed is to add information dynamics founded in neurobiology to help us understand the deep scientific linkages, and hence the need for a scientific and experimentally based economic analysis.

Better Understanding of Technological Change

Technological change is inherently evolutionary, with more advanced and evolved technologies building on past technologies. For example, you need to have breakthroughs in producing electricity before you can develop integrated circuits.

At first, such an understanding of technological change would seem hard to develop. Focusing only on those technologies that improve productivity significantly makes it a bit easier to develop. There are only a small number of technological changes that make major improvements in productivity, and it is important to focus on these key technological changes because productivity growth drives economic growth. Again, the close connection with engineering and science also shows how economics will eventually have a very strong scientific and experimental basis.

A Theory of Property Rights

We define property rights as the rules a society uses to allocate resources. These are both governmental rules and nongovernmental rules. Governmental rules include laws, taxes, incentives, regulations, and the like. Nongovernmental rules are social and business rules, such as who is more likely to be admitted to college or hired for a job, how businesses reward or limit employees, and so on. In short, property rights help determine who gets what resources and how much they get.

Property rights, like information dynamics and technological change, are inherently evolutionary. Property rights evolve over time. In the United States, we moved from being a monarchy to a democracy. That was a big change and over time greatly affected our economy. But, more important, it was an evolution, not just a change. That means we are not going to cycle back to a monarchy.

The concept of property rights is very important to economics because it is an important part of production and consumption. For example, companies need capital to increase production. Governments control the banks and the capital markets, so they have a very direct impact on production.

As another example, it was no coincidence that when the United States moved from being a monarchy to a democracy, the country became a leader in the support of free markets. Monopolies had long been created by monarchs and dictators as a way to bring in revenue for themselves. This monopoly privilege of the monarchy is what Adam Smith was essentially attacking in his writings on free markets.

In the period from 1800 to 1850, court rulings by path-breaking jurists such as John Marshall and changes in laws increasingly destroyed government-granted monopolies. The United States led the world in its support of free markets. U.S. citizens saw monopolies as being beneficial to a few (which they were) and harmful to the growth of business and to individual citizens. With the vote, they had the power to change that aspect of property rights.

In a more recent example, when the U.S. Army took over Japan after World War II, it established a new property rights system that dramatically changed Japanese production of goods and services. And, again, it wasn't just a change; it was part of an evolution that dramatically increased Japanese productivity and economic output. Since this evolution occurred, Japan is not going to cycle back to its pre–World War II property rights system.

Property rights do not evolve by themselves; they are generally forced to evolve by other changes, particularly technology. For example, when military technology moved from swords to guns, property rights changed. The people with the guns ultimately forced their property rights system on the people with swords. Their ability to create and utilize new technologies was part of an economic evolution that extends way beyond just military technologies and affects other important technologies and social and business property rights.

Understanding how property rights evolve is a key element in making economics more of a science. Since the theory of property rights has as it basis both information dynamics and productivity theory, it, too, becomes a very scientific and experimental theory.

A New Methodology for Economic Analysis and Predictions

Currently, the mathematical models used to analyze the economy and make predictions are not adequate, which is a nice way of saying that the methods are wrong.

Without getting too detailed, current economic modeling assumes that you can reach a state of equilibrium. Economists change various inputs in an equilibrium model and see how it affects that equilibrium. But, in fact, reaching static equilibrium is never the case in the real-world economy. The economy is constantly changing.

A better mathematical method to analyze the economy and make predictions would be to use numerical simulation models. These are the same models used to predict weather patterns or how our continents will move across the Earth. If we used our current inadequate econometric models to predict the weather, we would never know what to expect next.

One of the key advantages of numerical simulation models is that they can be tested scientifically by seeing how well they predict what has already happened in the past. For example, a good numerical simulation model of continental drift should accurately show how North America got to where it is today. If the model keeps showing North America where South America is, you know it's wrong and have to modify it, so that it ultimately shows how every continent got to exactly where it is today. That takes a lot of work and a lot of money, but it's worth it because you are creating a model that accurately predicts continental drift in the past and hence can reasonably accurately predict where continents will drift in the future.

Increasingly, numerical simulation models are being used in all the sciences, from geology to physics to chemistry and biology. They are also used in technological research, from oil drilling and production to nuclear weapons testing. They are being used because they work. Increased use of numerical simulation models will be an important part of future breakthroughs in all the sciences.

For economics, developing numerical simulation models will be far more expensive than current econometric models. However, the advantage is that they work. It's better to put more money into something that works than less money in something that doesn't.

Being able to make models that properly predict what we know happened in the past and that can make accurate predictions about the future that can be tested is a key test of any good scientific theory. Hence, it is a key element of making economics more of a science.

Where Do We Stand Today in Making This Transition?

So where do we stand today in advancing our knowledge of these four key elements for making economics more of a science?

Well, fortunately, a few people are concerned that current economic theory needs to change. This has been especially true since the failure of the economics community to foresee the popping of the U.S. bubble economy. Hence, some people refer to this focus on developing a new theory as the search for a postcrash model.

A physicist, Doyne Farmer, from the Santa Fe Institute, recognizes the limits of current mathematical models of economics. He believes we should be using numerical simulation models in economics. He is moving in the right direction, but his proposed model leaves out property rights, information dynamics, and technological evolution. Hence, such a model is guaranteed to be quite incomplete. It is also telling that such a non–status quo idea comes from a physicist and not an economist.

A psychoanalyst, David Tuckett, from University College London, is doing work on bringing more psychology into understanding market gyrations. It's good to bring more psychology into economics, but without a full understanding of information dynamics, of which psychology is definitely a part, this will lead to a dead end. Again, it is also telling that such a non–status quo idea comes from a non-economist.

The Economics Profession Does Not Want to Make This Transition

Economists resist change for many reasons. Most economists don't believe there is anything all that fundamentally wrong with their current economic theories. Yes, they say some tweaking may be needed, but there is no need for an entirely new theory.

Even worse, some economists, like Roman Frydman of New York University, think we can never forecast the economy with any accuracy. We're tempted to respond with, "What the hell are you doing in economics then?" It's like a manager who tells you that his business is unprofitable because it never could be profitable, so don't blame him.

So part of the problem in economics, as we mentioned before, is that economists are pretty happy in their current positions as professors and hence in their current thinking that no fundamental change is necessary. Sounds a lot like the management of General Motors in the 1980s and 1990s, doesn't it?

Mark Gertler, who previously worked with Ben Bernanke but is now with New York University, feels that the economics profession is highly competitive, and if you have a better idea in economics, it is going to win out. We agree with Mr. Gertler in the long run, but it's not going to happen the way Mr. Gertler thinks.

That's because getting a job in economics requires that you think the way other economists do—from a fundamental standpoint. Not that you can't have disagreements in economics. You can and are highly encouraged to have lots of little disagreements. But in raising questions about the *fundamentals* of current economic thinking, you will find little support. Hence, it will be hard to get tenured as a professor.

Just as we all know that in Communist Russia, even though the competition to be an economist was fierce because these were highly respected and sought after positions, the people who were hired for those positions were probably not the ones who were fundamentally critical of the Communist system in favor of competition. Don't expect people who are pleased with the current way of thinking to be very eager to hire someone who is not.

Hence, if you really want to advance economic thinking, you are probably best off not depending on the economic profession for a job. You shouldn't leave the profession—quite the contrary, you should be very active in thinking about how to improve economic thought. But, what you can't do is rely on the economics profession for a job, or you will naturally be forced to think like the other economists and not focus on the need for a fundamental change in their way of thinking.

A great recent example of a scientist who faced enormous decades-long skepticism over his ground-breaking Nobel prize–winning medical research work by much more highly credentialed status quo academics was Barry Marshall. For his struggle against the status quo, we give him the ABE Award for Intellectual Courage (see the sidebar).

ABE Award for Intellectual Courage: Barry Marshall

Through great persistence and personal sacrifice, Australian physician Barry Marshall took on the medical establishment in the 1970s and 1980s, and despite tremendous resistance to his paradigm-shifting discovery, his "crazy" idea eventually prevailed.

Dr. Marshall was interested in gastroenterology, especially stomach ulcers. Through careful study and observation, he noticed that many of his ulcer patients had a mysterious spiral-shaped bacteria near the site of their ulcers. Dr. Marshall wondered if these bacteria might be causing the ulcers—an idea that was completely at odds with the prevailing status quo thinking that "knew" stomach ulcers were caused by excess stomach acid brought on by diet and stress.

Marshall did a great deal of research that convinced him of the role of these bacteria, eventually called *Helicobacter pylori*, in causing ulcers. He also noticed that bismuth, a component of Pepto Bismol, killed this bacteria and gave temporary relief to patients, further convincing him of the bacteria's causative role.

When he presented his findings at a medical conference in Brussels in 1983, the highly credentialed supporters of the status quo were *very* skeptical. He had limited credentials and was attacking the status quo—two big strikes against him. So his groundbreaking research was ignored.

But Dr. Marshall persevered and found considerable success in treating patients with a combination of bismuth and antibiotics. Lacking much support or funding for expanded research, as a last resort the doctor finally drank a bottle of the bacteria himself! Sure enough, he began to get an ulcer. He had so much faith in his

(Continued)

carefully reasoned theory that he was willing to use his own body to prove it was correct.

In 1986, Dr. Marshall was invited to the University of Virginia to further his research, and after a decade of further work, his theory became more widely accepted. In 1996, the FDA finally officially approved the treatment of ulcers with antibiotics. And later, after returning to Australia, Barry Marshall was awarded the Nobel Prize in 2005.

While his observations were objective and his conclusions were correct, for decades Dr. Marshall research was first ignored and then vehemently opposed. Barry had to overcome enormous opposition from highly credentialed medical scholars to do his work. Not to be overlooked, the sizable industry performing ulcer operations would be eliminated if ulcers could be easily cured by simple antibiotics. All Dr. Marshall had going for him was the correct understanding of the problem and dogged persistence to see it through.

Fortunately, after much struggle, the truth won out. He overcame all the highly credentialed opposition and lack of interest from leading medical research institutions, such as Harvard and Yale. It wasn't easy, but millions of ulcer sufferers around the world have Barry Marshall to thank for greatly improving their lives.

The Solution to the Lack of Interest in Making Important Changes in Economics: The Coming Aftershock

We will have a lot more to say in future books about the four key areas described earlier for developing economics into more of a science and for using that science to solve some of our real problems. There are many questions to answer within each of the four key areas, and nothing will move forward significantly until other economists become motivated to focus on them.

What will provide that motivation? It will take some time, but we believe the coming Aftershock will help to speed up the timetable—a lot. That's because right now it's not that obvious that the field of economics is totally lost. The economy is doing okay, as are economics faculty and researchers at major universities and research institutes. There has been no significant loss of funding for economists.

However, once the Aftershock hits, it will be quite obvious that economics has failed miserably. Not only that, there will be a whole lot less money to go around for universities and economics research institutes. And since economists had a lot to do with creating the Aftershock through their lack of understanding of the economy, there won't be a lot of sympathy for paying them when funding is extremely tight. Unlike now, poor performers will not be rewarded in the Aftershock. There will simply be no more money for it, and it will be quite obvious that they were poor performers.

Hence, eventually a new group of economists, albeit a much smaller group and much more poorly paid, will take the place of the current well-paid, underperforming group. That group will be desperately looking for solutions to the economic problems of the day and will have a huge incentive to justify their meager pay by showing some positive results from their research. It will be these people who will not only be willing to question the fundamental concepts of economics but extremely eager to do so since it is so obvious that those concepts have failed. In addition, the economists will desperately want to do something to show their work is worthwhile and they deserve to keep their jobs.

So, in this way, what Mr. Bernanke's friend Mark Gertler said will come true. The good ideas will win in the end because economists will be highly motivated at that point to abandon current thinking and to find a different theory of economics that helps solve our economic problems. A meltdown in the economics profession may not be what Mr. Gertler had in mind, but it certainly will work by dramatically changing the incentives for supporting fundamental changes in economic thought.

A meltdown in the economy and in funding for economists may not be the only solution to our current economic problems, and it certainly isn't the best solution, but it is a solution. Most important, it will work and is quite feasible to implement in the real world—in fact, in time it will be unavoidable.

CHAPTER 12

Our Predictions Have Been Mostly Accurate, So Why Do Some People Still Dislike Them?

Most economists and financial analysts did not foresee the global financial crisis of 2008 and 2009, and most still do not see the coming Aftershock, nor will they agree with many of the ideas and predictions in this book. How come? Why do most people not see what seems pretty straightforward and obvious to us?

The reasons lie in the six psychological stages of evolving denial we told you about in Chapter 6. We were in the first stage (Denial) for a long time, and more recently we have been in the second stage (Market Cycles), in which most experts believe if we just wait long enough things will get better—in fact, if you try really hard, you can believe things are already getting better right now! What is so compelling about the Market Cycles stage of denial is that it is so *comforting.* It helps us cope with our anxieties by insisting that all will be well again soon. This comforting stage is being strongly promoted and maintained by both the cheerleaders, who say all is great right now, and the comforters, who, unlike cheerleaders, admit we have problems but say the solution is at hand—or could be if we would just do A, B, or C (none of which will actually save us).

So we have both cheerleaders and comforters hard at work, keeping us from facing facts and really getting prepared for what is ahead. Naturally, both cheerleaders and comforters do not like our books because we are saying that the economy is not in a down cycle as they say, and our economic problems will not simply cycling up and down.

"I want my bubble back."

Toles Copyright © 2008 *Washington Post*.

Understanding why some people react negatively to our book is important for understanding why the bubble economy occurred in the first place and for seeing where we are in the progression of those six psychological stages. The roots of the antagonism to our ideas are grounded in the very strong desire to hang on to the many benefits of the rising-bubble status quo and the very strong psychological need to hang on to the comforts of the known and rewarding past. The overwhelming desire for, and the reassuring comfort of a rising bubble economy makes almost everyone—even the authors, at times—want to deny these problems until we have absolutely no other choice but to face them and solve them. Until then, most people want to maintain the many comforts and benefits of the status quo.

Therefore, it's important that we not only be able to analyze and predict what happens with the economy, but be able to analyze and predict the reactions people will have to our predictions because that tells us a lot about how our country will react to and handle the coming Aftershock. It's somewhat unusual for a book to look at why people might not like its ideas but, in this case, quite essential to a good understanding of what is happening with the economy and how it is evolving. It is also important for our readers to understand where other people are coming from so that we can better understand why so many other people might say we are wrong—and why you should resist being one of them.

Here are some of the main reasons why many people will not accept the validity of our books' predictions until after they occur.

It's Not a Cheerleading Book

Most people want a highly plausible cheerleading book that says everything is okay, or it will be soon, even if we hit some rough patches along the way. They want good news, but they also want the good news to be plausible, meaning that it has to be based on some kind of seemingly rigorous analysis. The analysis itself can be terrible, but as long as it seems rigorous (i.e., complicated), and it supports the idea that things will get better soon, that's what they want to hear.

Ideally, this good-news analysis should also square with conventional wisdom. The analysis can't be too optimistic, or it will sound like fantasy. It has to be very cognizant of current problems while being fundamentally optimistic that the economy, stocks, and real estate will all inevitably go back up.

Alan Greenspan was a master at this. He was the perfect cheerleader because he was optimistic but always sounded well reasoned and quite plausible. Greenspan never talked too much about any fundamental economic problems, except with very long-term issues, such as the long-term cost of Social Security and Medicare. However, he always brought up some negative short-term issues that made his overall optimism seem well considered. Even when his views didn't square with reality, people still loved to hear them.

As an aside, it is quite interesting that since retiring, Greenspan has become much more outspoken about the deeper problems in the economy, particularly related to the ballooning national debt, the origins of the real estate bubble, and the vulnerability of the dollar. That, of course, does not get much media coverage. Not too many people want to hear from an old cheerleader who is no longer beating the drum for what they consider to be well-reasoned optimism.

In place of the earlier cheerleader Greenspan, we then had Federal Reserve Chairman Ben Bernanke and most recently Janet

Yellen, who both have been furiously printing money, temporarily boosting the stock market and providing short-term stimulus to the economy. As a result, people have been feeling more bullish and giving the cheerleaders some temporary ammunition. *The Federal Reserve is currently the biggest weapons supplier in the cheerleaders' war on rationality.*

Even when cheerleading analysts and economists are proven wrong time and again—for example, when the housing market did not recover and the economy did not turn around in 2009 and 2010—these people still retain a lot of credibility. They sound rigorous, and they are trying to be optimistic. The audience that wants cheerleaders still likes what cheerleaders are selling.

In this group, nobody likes a bear, least of all when that bear is right.

It's Not a Complex Book (Although It Is Based on Complex Analysis)

For some readers, a really complicated, hard-to-understand book or research paper is best. It makes the reader (and the author) feel as if they know something that very few people can understand. This makes readers feel really smart. It also obscures the upsetting truth about the economy. This group may not want a cheerleading book, but they also don't want to be too fundamentally critical of the economy or its future prospects. For example, this group might like to read about a detailed analysis of complicated credit default swaps and the intricate ways they might threaten the economy, even though the real threats to the economy are simpler and much more fundamental.

Many people in this group are very threatened by the real economy since many of them will lose their jobs in the Aftershock, including many economists and financial analysts and other professionals. But here's a question: If the people writing these complex research papers and books could not predict or even talk about something as big and important as the financial crisis that hit in 2008, exactly how good is their complex analysis? What good did their analysis do if it could not even warn us that so many banks would fail and the U.S. stock market would lose half its value?

If these people cannot protect us from such a huge occurrence, what exactly can they do for us? The answer is: they keep us relatively happy and in the dark. They don't draw their power from accuracy; they get it from having a certain level of credibility (at least for now), based not only on their academic, business, or government credentials, but also on group denial.

These analysts and economists don't want to see the reality of the economy because if they did, they would have to ask, "How did so many smart people make such terrible mistakes?" Maybe because they weren't so smart? But if that is the case, then what will happen to Wall Street, and what does that say about economists and politicians and their super-smart advisers? It says that they are quite likely to fail and to take the economy down with them. That is really painful for all of us. It is much more comforting to think of these folks as credible and smart for as long as we can than to look at this logically and say they are not so credible or so smart.

For example, the biggest mistake made in the run-up to the 2008 financial crisis was that people on Wall Street *and* Main Street *and* in Washington all thought that it was perfectly fine for housing prices to go up 100 percent or more while people's incomes only went up a few percent. That was a pretty basic economic mistake to make, don't you think? The idea that the fundamental problem was caused by Wall Street gods gone greedy or caused by too-risky credit default swaps is just wrong. The fundamental problem was bad investment judgment at a very basic level. Home prices cannot go and stay up 100 percent or more while incomes do not equally rise. This was very bad investment judgment by most people, from the least financially sophisticated to the most financially sophisticated people in America.

Our analysis in 2006 in *America's Bubble Economy* was quite different. We looked at the fundamentals driving the housing market rather than hoping that huge price gains were well justified and would keep on coming. The analysis was spot-on and even televised nationally, when Bob Wiedemer said in February 2008 on CNBC's *Squawk Box* that homebuilding stocks would go down even when almost every other financial analyst felt that, for some reason, they had already gone down enough, were certainly at the bottom of the cycle, and would naturally go up.

Now we are making an even bigger mistake than before, when we were blaming Wall Street. Now we are making the catastrophic mistake of ignoring the future consequences of allowing the Federal Reserve to massively increase the money supply, which will create high inflation and high interest rates in the longer term, in exchange for the temporarily boosting the stock market, economy, and lending in the short term.

Supposedly brilliant analysts writing brilliant research papers are simply not seeing this threat, just as they did not see the problems that would eventually arise from the real estate bubble or all the rest of the bubbles. Even right up until the financial crisis of 2008 and after it, these "smart" guys were clueless and unprepared. People at the very top of the financial world were not very smart about their investments that they should have been extremely smart about. Instead, they bankrupted (or effectively bankrupted) some very impressive commercial banks and investment banks that had previously survived the greatest of our nation's financial difficulties for more than 100 years.

It's absolutely amazing that these people had such poor investment judgment that they couldn't even survive in an economy with some of the lowest unemployment levels, lowest inflation rates, and lowest interest rates in our nation's history. It was an absolutely phenomenal misjudgment in the face of these easy-to-see facts. Clearly, this shows the power of not wanting to face facts and that despite being "masters of the financial universe," these people were not very smart at what they should have known best. And now they are doing it again by ignoring the future negative impacts of massive money printing by the Fed. Instead, they are thrilled by the stock market rally that the massive money printing is helping to create. As long as they are getting what they want now, people can suspend logic and believe almost anything.

In the more distant past, Wall Street has shown great skill and innovation due to the fine efforts of some very impressive people, such as J. P. Morgan and Charlie Merrill. But these great skills were not on display by the Wall Street of the past decade. That these supposedly impressive financial managers had such terrible judgment inevitably raises the question of how well the economy will do in the future. And it makes a very uncomfortable statement about the way our society is structured and about the people who are running it. It's not just bad or evil individuals that are causing us problems; it's something much more profound that is affecting our economy: bad judgment that only rewards us in the short term and ignores the longer-term price.

The ideas in our book make people uncomfortable. If it's really that simple to understand our economic problems, then a lot of people in positions of power are not doing their jobs and cannot be very smart. That's a painful fact to face.

Once the Aftershock hits, most of these folks will lose their current credibility. At that point, we won't need any more highly respected, inaccurate cheerleaders; we will need some highly accurate thinkers! Including some of the readers of this book.

It's Not a Crazy Book

Crazy books are just cheerleading books in disguise. They propose crazy economic or financial theories that aren't real. Some of these books are far more critical and radical and more "doom and gloom" than we are. They might say much more critical things about our country. They might be far more critical of individuals such as Alan Greenspan or the Wall Street Titans. But they are so silly that they aren't very threatening. Hence, by being so implausible, they are effectively cheerleading for the status quo. Many crazy books, therefore, become quite popular forms of entertainment.

Timing is everything. Unless the time is right for a critical mass of society to begin to accept the new ideas in a basically accurate book, it will be rejected. Instead, many people will prefer a crazy book because it is far less threatening. Our book is not a crazy book and lays out a very reasonable and rational analysis of our current economic situation, including how it started and where it is headed. For that reason, many people who would like a crazy book of course will not like our book.

It's Not an Academic Book

In addition to the reasons discussed in the previous chapter about why many economists don't like the ideas in this book, they also don't like the book because we are not playing by their rules. In most academic circles, an author has to be published in a refereed (peer-reviewed) journal to have any credibility; otherwise, academics aren't going to be very interested in the book. That actually makes a lot of sense in some ways because there are plenty of crackpots out there, and this is a good way of filtering them out. However, a problem arises when the academics are fundamentally wrong in their analyses, and someone outside the inner circle has something of merit to say. Then the policy becomes a real negative because academics are not exposed to different viewpoints (in part because they don't want to be).

In addition to the problem of exclusivity, academics often have the problem of a narrow focus. A narrow focus is good—in fact, it is absolutely necessary for good analysis—but only if you have a solid understanding and a good theory of what is going on in the broader context.

For example, if you don't understand continental drift, trying to study small changes in the Appalachian Mountains isn't going to improve your understanding of how they were formed. Without a good overall theory to provide a larger context, a narrow focus is just a way of avoiding the hard work of developing a good overall theory that explains what is really going on.

This is what many, if not most, economists do. They spend decades focusing narrowly, while the larger context goes unexplored and misunderstood. Clearly, we can't all be big-picture thinkers. But equally clearly, someone has to do it, and they need to do it as accurately, rationally, and objectively as possible.

It's Not Suggesting Armageddon

One of the most common themes we see in some financial books that many people seem to like is that, rather than present an honest assessment of the problems we will face, they say that our financial problems will result in financial Armageddon. That might be combined with another Armageddon theme that says that a financial collapse will result in violent unrest across the world. Another lighter version would be the "end of capitalism" or the rise of dictatorships in the United States and/or other currently democratic countries.

As with the crazy books, some people prefer reading Armageddon books because reading them is much more comfortable than facing the reality of a fundamental change in people's economic, social, and political lives. They retreat to the fantasy of Armageddon because, even if they have some extra food stored in their basements, they know that Armageddon is not really going to happen, and reading about it is a good way to avoid dealing with changes in society or the economy that they would rather not see. *Pretend Armageddon* is simply a more comfortable alternative for some people than what our book predicts.

It's Not a Reality-Denying Book

All of the preceding reasons why people don't like our book boil down to this one common denominator: it does not help people deny reality. Other books, in one way or another, more strongly support the status quo by saying so directly or by being so off base or by adding so much meaningless complexity that they offer no real threat to the status quo. This book threatens the status quo in a fundamental way because we are saying that our problems are knowable, relatively simple, caused entirely by us, and cannot be reversed.

The inevitable future consequences of the current Bubblequake and coming Aftershock will force big changes on our businesses, our government, and our society. Like the aftermath of the Revolutionary War in the United States or World War I in Europe, the aftermath of the Aftershock will alter the status quo.

We are daring to say that we have made some big economic mistakes in the past, that we will go through a difficult time (the Aftershock), and the final result will be a much better and wealthier society than we have today—but one that will be fundamentally very different.

Us versus the Comforters: How *Aftershock* Stacks Up against Other Bearish Books

On the surface, the book you are now holding in your hand may seem (to people who haven't read it) like just another "doom-and-gloom" economics book. In fact, *Aftershock* is substantially different from any other book currently available.

Some books have correctly predicted that our economy is heading for trouble. To varying degrees, each has contained some partially correct insights, forecasts, and advice. Many have offered some truly bad investment ideas. And many others have provided some very good investment advice, but for wrong or incomplete reasons.

The reason for this is that most bearish books, while recognizing that all is not well, do not fully analyze the problem but instead provide a degree of *psychological comfort* to those who benefit from the status quo (which is most of us). This allows readers who are observant enough to see that we have serious problems to think about these problems while still maintaining a feeling of safety. We all like the feeling of safety, and that is the primary thing that books written by comforters give us.

Obviously, we don't have the space here to analyze the details of all the bearish economics and finance books on the market today. Instead, we'd like to take a closer look at three popular books, *Crisis*

Economics (Penguin, 2011) by Nouriel Roubini, *Aftershock* (Vintage, 2011) by Robert Reich, and *Crash Proof 2.0* (John Wiley & Sons, 2009) by Peter Schiff. We chose these three, not because they are the worst or the best of the bunch, but because these well-received books have attracted a lot of attention and therefore serve as good models against which we can compare our predictions and our entirely unique perspective. In their own unique ways, each has been written by what we call a comforter.

Crisis Economics *by Nouriel Roubini*

Nouriel Roubini is a popular bearish economist, sometimes referred to as "Dr. Doom," the same moniker Henry Kaufman earned when he was chief economist at Salomon Brothers. Fundamentally, Mr. Roubini sees our current problems as being the result of a financial crisis (as indicated by the title of his book) that was caused by too much debt, heavy use of leverage by financial institutions, and inadequate regulation of those institutions. He believes that with better regulation of financial institutions to prevent them from making large numbers of excessively risky transactions, along with less debt, we will be able to solve the current problems and avoid future financial crises.

One might wonder why, with a name like Dr. Doom, we would call Nouriel Roubini a "comforter." To understand this requires realizing that a comforter is not a cheerleader. A cheerleader says all is well; a comforter says all could be well again, if only we would just go back to doing things as we did (or should have done) before. Dr. Doom, therefore, is a comforter. He is part of a larger group of comforter economists, such as Paul Krugman and Ben Bernanke, who strongly suggest that we look to the past, specifically the Great Depression, as a guide for how to deal with our current financial ills. Based on what worked, or would have worked, in the past, they suggest similar remedies of stronger regulation and greater fiscal stimulus. They also suggest that we should not greatly reduce the money supply as we did in the Great Depression. We completely agree. They also don't see major problems in tripling the money supply. We completely disagree.

We also differ strongly from Mr. Roubini in that we see our economic problems as being caused by a set of multiple interacting bubbles that are beginning to pop (as described in 2006 in

America's Bubble Economy) and are now putting strong downward pressure on two much more important bubbles, the government debt and dollar bubbles (the Aftershock).

We don't see a lack of financial regulation as being the *core* problem, nor do we see printing money as the solution—in fact, printing money is pumping up both the dollar and the government debt bubble. Unlike some comforter economists, we believe we are in an entirely different situation from the Great Depression. Continuing to think that we can solve our current problems by using techniques from the Great Depression shows a fundamental lack of understanding of our current situation. It is much like the general who always wants to fight the last war, instead of taking on the current reality. The last war is the war the general knows best and is most comfortable with, not this new situation.

Unlike us, Roubini does not see any threat from future inflation. He also did not and still does not think gold is a good investment. We disagree strongly on both counts.

Unlike Roubini, we see the financial crisis as a result of the popping of the housing and consumer spending bubbles, which popped the private credit and stock market bubbles. The financial crisis was not a cause of the problems, but much more a symptom of much deeper underlying problems—the popping of our multibubble economy. Roubini and the other comforter economists still do not recognize the full magnitude of the problems caused by the two biggest bubbles, the government debt bubble and dollar bubble.

In general, the comforters tend to believe that our problems are more limited to excessive financial debt, financial risk taking, and lack of financial regulation than to a fundamental problem with a multibubble economy that is still in the process of popping—clearly a far less comfortable problem to recognize. It is far more comfortable to think that all we need is more regulation as we've done in the past and more government stimulus, which seems like something we've done in the past, even though it certainly is not at the same level that we've done in the past, given the magnitude of the increase in deficit spending and the magnitude of our accumulated debt.

The bottom line is that both the analysis of the problems and the kinds of solutions offered are much more comfortable and comforting than the actual economic situation we are in, as we have described in our books. This is a key part of why Roubini gets so much attention: He gives us a comfortable message, and he does so with greater credibility than most economists who did not foresee any problems. He did foresee some problems, so he now has some credibility, and his comforting message is relatively easy to digest.

Aftershock *by Robert Reich*

Robert Reich was Bill Clinton's Labor Secretary. He is considered a leader of liberal thought, so we thought it was important to include his book in a review of the most recent books on the economy and how we differ from them.

In the fall of 2010, Robert Reich published a book surprisingly called *Aftershock,* one year after our *Aftershock* came out. Yes, we did complain to his publisher about using our title, but they refused to change it. We're not sure why he calls his book *Aftershock* since he doesn't really describe any aftershock to the financial crisis. Maybe he just liked the eye-catching title. It is a good title—we can attest to that.

In terms of his book, Reich's primary thesis is that the rich have been getting an increasing proportion of the wealth in the nation, creating the greatest income inequality since the stock and economic boom of the 1920s. The lack of income for the middle class has forced them to take on too much debt to maintain an adequate standard of living. That came crashing down in the financial crisis of 2008, which is causing a lack of consumption now and, hence, a very sluggish economic recovery.

His basic prescription for improving the economy is more progressive taxes to reduce income inequality. In addition, he supports more unemployment compensation and other welfare-type support for members of the lower class, as well as more health and education spending to help the middle class with health expenses and to better train them for new jobs. All of this, he says, will stimulate the economy and encourage more spending by the middle class, which will further boost the economy.

Reich, like Roubini and others, is a comforter who looks to the Great Depression for an understanding of what is happening and what to do about it. Unlike Roubini, Reich does not focus on more regulation and instead sees the remedy as more Depression-era thinking that calls for more welfare and progressive taxes. Both are comforters because they are telling us we can solve our problems by looking to the past.

We differ with Reich in several ways. We see growing income inequality as primarily a result of, not the cause of, our economic problems. Income inequality increased as our multibubble economy rose. When those bubbles pop, the income inequality caused by the bubbles will be reduced because a lot of rich people will no longer be rich (unless they follow the advice in this book!).

We also don't feel that the middle class was forced by economic circumstances to take on too much debt. The debt related to the financial crisis for both the middle class and the upper class was much more related to the rising asset bubbles, particularly real estate, than any need for a better standard of living. Pushing up bubbles took a lot of borrowed money.

Most important, we see the basic problem that underlies the slow economic growth as being a *slowing of productivity growth* since the 1970s. Fundamentally, we see increasing productivity growth (not decreasing income inequality) as the key to growing the economy. Income inequality is always going to be higher during a rising asset bubble or during periods of high economic growth. Reducing income inequality is not the key factor for creating real economic growth; productivity is. Hence, our prescription for future growth is to *increase productivity*.

Unfortunately, most of the focus in the economy now is on maintaining the asset bubbles and not on increasing productivity. The popping of these asset bubbles will likely be an important part of getting the government and the public more focused on productivity growth than on maintaining the bubbles. Once all the bubbles pop, our only alternative for growing the economy will be to increase productivity. Until then, we are ignoring this.

Increasing productivity will not be easy and will take fundamental reforms to our government and the economy that will likely take time, just as real productivity growth has always taken time in the past. That is not as much fun as a rising bubble economy, but it works. Greater spending by the government to boost the economy, which is fueled by borrowing money and printing more money, will not result in higher economic growth, either. All such borrowing and printing will do for us is preserve the bubbles for a little while longer and make the final popping of the bubbles that much more devastating.

Crash Proof 2.0 *by Peter Schiff*

The third book we've chosen to look at is *Crash Proof 2.0* by Peter Schiff, which we actually like more than most others. But, again, just like the other authors, Schiff is a comforter. He is a "Back to Basics" thinker (one of the six psychological stages discussed in Chapter 5), who would like us to return to the gold standard for the dollar, significantly cut federal spending, and get rid of the Fed.

Schiff believes that the United States is close to being tapped out on debt, and very soon we will no longer be able to get any further loans, when in fact we will see our $17+ trillion debt expand to $20 or even $25 trillion before the U.S. government falls into default and can borrow no more.

In addition to blaming debt, Schiff also says our economic problems are due to a lack of domestic manufacturing, which we know is not the reason for our troubles—the falling bubbles are. Most industrial nations have seen the percentage of their gross domestic product (GDP) related to manufacturing decline substantially in the past 50 years. In addition, our manufacturing will increase when our currency is no longer manipulated against us. Manufacturing and productivity are not the same things. We can boost productivity without a huge increase in manufacturing.

In terms of his advice for wealth preservation, we agree that U.S. stocks are not a good place to put your money in the long term. But we also know that Schiff's recommendations to move out of U.S. stocks and into foreign stocks is the equivalent of jumping out of the proverbial frying pan into the fire. Comforters are often wrong in their investment advice, and their clients can lose a lot of money as a result. We know for a fact that foreign stocks will crash for the same reasons we know U.S. stocks will crash because we have an understanding of the larger forces that are driving this global multibubble collapse. Schiff, like many others, is missing this because he is a comforter, who doesn't see the bigger picture.

Additionally, Schiff says oil will be a good investment. We say demand for oil will fall after the Aftershock hits the world economy, making it a bad investment, except in the United States, where the price of oil will rise due to the falling dollar. He says gold is now in a bull market; we say gold hasn't even begun to hit its future bubble heights. He says to stay liquid, and keep your cash handy to pick up bargains in real estate and other distressed assets; we say it's far too soon for that. Please avoid all bargain hunting until *after* the dollar bubble pops. Again, we are basing all this, not on our intuition or lucky guesses, but on our detailed analysis of how the overall economy is evolving.

Actually, we are a lot more respectful of these successful authors than we sound here, but our point is that it is not good enough to just get some of this right, and then get a lot wrong because you are a comforter (probably unconsciously) and are looking to the past for causes and solutions. The economy is evolving, not going backward. Getting it partially right is not enough; you have to get most of it right, and you have to get it right *for the right reasons.*

Epilogue: Say Good-Bye to the Age of Excess

It's sad to see it all go. It was the party of the century and not just in the United States, but around the world as well. The Age of Excess was like no other time in U.S. history, and there will never be a time like it again because eventually we do learn from our mistakes, even if painfully so. And how quickly we will forget the good times and how good they were when faced with the "shock and awe" of the Aftershock that will end the Age of Excess. This epilogue is dedicated to reminding us how good the Age of Excess really was.

But where do we begin? There was so much excess. First, there were all the corporate executives and investment bankers, who made hundreds of millions of dollars making terrible business mistakes that destroyed the value of their companies. And better yet, the government bailed out their companies, while the executives kept all the money they made from making the decisions that destroyed their companies, and they got some nice bonuses to boot. And why not? The government could always borrow so much money, it really didn't matter. Why hold anyone accountable when we're all in this party together, right?

And let's not forget all the great Internet companies whose values kept going up, up, up, even though their revenues and profits did not. We knew they were worth a lot of money because sooner or later some other company was bound to buy them at massively overvalued prices. And why should the acquiring company worry about overvaluation? Their stock never suffered from their bad decisions; it just kept going up, up, up along with the rest of the stock market, despite terrible management.

That same party thinking worked wonders for private equity firms, the true masters of the universe. Their strategy was simple: always pay a higher price to buy a company than anyone else, and then just let the ever-rising stock market make you billions when you sell it later. Some private equity firms made billions just by taking themselves public because everyone on Wall Street knew that their strategy of buying companies at very high prices was foolproof.

Even folks on Main Street got to play at the party. Lots of credit cards and home equity lines of credit made everyday life very festive, indeed. We got to enjoy lots of big-screen TVs, the latest computers, and all sorts of new gadgets and gizmos at the party. And with retirement stock market accounts rising so rapidly, why not put everything in stocks, including our future Social Security? Remember that one?

Even if stocks didn't go up every year, you could always count on your home as a great investment. No matter how much the price went up, we just knew it would never, ever go back down very much. Market cycles worked only in the up direction, right? Even if your income didn't rise very much, the value of your house could easily double in a few years. We didn't entirely know why, but something really good must have been happening somewhere. Whatever it was, we didn't care. It was all part of the joy of the Age of Excess. In the Age of Excess, you didn't have to think too much about why things were so good—they just were.

Even better, in the Age of Excess, good jobs never, ever disappeared. If you lost one, you could always just hop onto another—like catching the next train leaving the station. And plenty of jobs meant you didn't have to waste perfectly good money by putting it in a savings account. Let those poor Chinese peasants, who made all the stuff we bought do all the saving. Besides, saving money was downright un-American. If you saved, you were hurting the economy. And look what happened when we finally stopped buying so much and started saving a little in late 2008—the economy really started to tank. If we had just kept spending as we did before, we'd still be doing just fine.

Speaking of which, don't forget that in the Age of Excess, patriotism means doing your part to help in a war. That certainly doesn't mean tax increases—in World War II, tax rates were as high as 75 percent. No, it actually means you need your taxes decreased for all of your suffering from high taxes. It also doesn't mean a draft or volunteering for the war. In World War II, over half of Congress volunteered for the war. In World War I, Charlie Merrill, the founder of Merrill Lynch, was so interested in volunteering for the war that he drove down from New York to Fort Myers in Washington to speed up his enlistment process. In the Iraq War, there were so many titans of Wall Street volunteering that they had to set up a separate sign-up window at the Pentagon! (Not really.)

Of course, patriotism also doesn't mean cutting your consumption to help out the boys fighting the war. No, what it means to be a patriot in the Age of Excess is to put those "We Support Our Troops" stickers on your car and drive to the nearest mall. In fact, to be even more patriotic, you should buy more cars to put more stickers on, especially if those cars are one of those hot new BMWs or Mercedes. Wow, now that's real support. To show how much we supported our troops, by 2008 we had purchased 35 million more cars than we had registered drivers. That's a lot of cars to put stickers on! If only we had done that in World War II, imagine the difference it would have made. But that wasn't war in the Age of Excess, where war has no cost.

And, finally, who could forget that in the Age of Excess, the government has no limit on how much it can borrow. If we hit a rough patch in the economy, we just convert to the bailout economy. Made a business mistake or a personal financial mistake? No problem; the government will just borrow money to bail you out. Bailouts are easy, and the government wouldn't think of raising taxes to cover bailouts when it can so easily borrow so much money at such low interest rates. That's just part of being the U.S. government in the Age of Excess. No money? No worries; the government can just borrow what it takes to tide us over. Is there any limit to what the government can borrow? Well, why worry about it? Something good must be happening to let the government borrow so much money. And that's after it has already borrowed $10 trillion and hasn't been able to pay back a penny of that debt. It's almost magical. But whatever it was, in the Age of Excess, you didn't have to think too much about why things were so good— they just were.

Too bad it had to end.

Appendix: Are the Bond, Stock, and Gold Markets Manipulated?

The possibility of market manipulation by governments comes up periodically from our readers, and so far we have mostly ignored the issue in our writings. It is sometimes brought up as a reason for short-term movements in the markets. This appendix will address three areas of potential government intervention or manipulation:

- Bonds
- Stocks
- Gold

Bond Market Manipulation

The Fed openly manipulates the bond markets, mortgage markets, and the foreign exchange markets. It also regulates and openly manipulates the banking markets. Open market operations, in which the Fed buys and sells Treasury bonds (money printing), clearly manipulate the bond markets. Money printing makes dollars plentiful, which keeps interest rates low. Without money printing, interest rates would likely rise and bond prices would decline.

When the Fed buys Freddie Mac and Fannie Mae mortgage-backed bonds, it is clearly manipulating the mortgage market and the entire bond market. In addition, by buying mortgage-backed bonds, the government is also manipulating home prices because buying these bonds keeps interest rates low and reduces the speed with which it forces banks to foreclose on mortgage holders. By saving Fannie Mae and Freddie Mac and by bonding mortgage-backed bonds, the government made mortgage money easier to find, and housing prices were kept much higher than they would have been otherwise.

The Federal Reserve also intervenes in the foreign exchange markets. It uses foreign currency swaps, where the Fed lends money to foreign central banks, to manipulate foreign exchange.

The Fed directly manipulates the banking market by making it easier for banks to profit by lending to them at very low interest rates and allowing them to lend to consumers at significantly higher interest rates. The Fed essentially lowers the banks' cost of goods sold—their "goods" being money. This also manipulates the value of their stock and their ability to raise more capital by making them more profitable.

Also, by manipulating the bond, foreign exchange, and banking markets, the Fed also indirectly, but powerfully, manipulates the United States and world stock markets.

All of this manipulation is being done to help stabilize the financial markets and thus stabilize the United States and world economy. Of course, if this manipulation also helps maintain asset price bubbles, then ultimately it is stabilizing short-term financial markets at the expense of long-term financial market stability. That's because, ultimately, these asset bubbles cannot be maintained. It is a micro version of the much larger macro problem of the Federal Reserve's printing money and Congress's borrowing massive amounts of money. It stabilizes the short-term economy at the cost of massive destabilization later.

Stock Market Manipulation

While the manipulation of bonds is done openly, the potential manipulation of stock markets, if it occurs, is done indirectly and has been a subject of great interest to conspiracy theorists for a long time. However, in the past few years, interest in possible government intervention in stock markets has become more widespread. The word *intervention* sounds better, but it means the same thing.

Not long after the first edition of *Aftershock* was published in late 2009, the topic of stock market manipulation jumped to the mainstream media when Charles Biderman, the president of Trim Tabs, a well-respected financial markets research firm, released a report saying that the huge increase in the stock market in 2009 was hard to explain based on the sources of funds moving into the market that normally drive up a stock market.

Trim Tabs made a common-sense analysis of the key flows of funds. An excerpt from their report, which details those flows of funds, follows:

> We cannot identify the source of the new money that pushed stock prices up so far so fast. For the most part, the money did not come from the traditional players that provided money in the past:
>
> - *Companies.* Corporate America has been a huge net seller. The float of shares has ballooned $133 billion since the start of April.
> - *Retail investor funds.* Retail investors have hardly bought any U.S. equities. Bond funds, yes. U.S. equity funds, no. U.S. equity funds and ETFs have received just $17 billion since the start of April. Over that same time frame bond mutual funds and ETFs received $351 billion.
> - *Retail investor direct.* We doubt retail investors were big direct purchases of equities. Market volatility in this decade has been the highest since the 1930s, and we have no evidence retail investors were piling into individual stocks. Also, retail investor sentiment has been mostly neutral since the rally began.
> - *Foreign investors.* Foreign investors have provided some buying power, purchasing $109 billion in U.S. stocks from April through October. But we suspect foreign purchases slowed in November and December because the U.S. dollar was weakening.
> - *Hedge funds.* We have no way to track in real time what hedge funds do, and they may well have shifted some assets into U.S. equities. But we doubt their buying power was enormous because they posted an outflow of $12 billion from April through November.
> - *Pension funds.* All the anecdotal evidence we have indicates that pension funds have not been making a huge asset allocation shift and have not moved more than about $100 billion from bonds and cash into U.S. equities since the rally began.
>
> If the money to boost stock prices did not come from the traditional players, it had to have come from somewhere else.

The phrase "somewhere else" is key. Their conclusion was that it was possible that the Federal Reserve had acted to directly manipulate the stock market and was responsible for much of the rise in 2009. They clearly indicated that they didn't have any direct evidence of this, and the evidence was only circumstantial. Hence, they lacked any real proof that would stand up in a court of law or public opinion.

Most people ignored the report as unimportant, even though Trim Tabs is widely used and respected. In fact, they were respected enough that CNBC interviewed them regarding the report. Trim Tabs has a good track record in calling the 2000 bear market and in calling the 2002 bull market. But they missed some of the 2009 bull market by having turned more bearish after the market had risen 40 percent. They said their research had shown that the normal sources of funds to buy stocks were declining and, hence, the bull market was nearing an end.

They were wrong, since the market moved up another 30 percent. Hence, the few people who commented on the report released in January 2010 felt it was partly sour grapes at having missed all of the bull market.

One of the few people who bothered to respond to the report was Barry Ritholtz, certainly no cheerleader, having authored *Bailout Nation* (with Bill Fleckenstein and Aaron Task). He is also one of the more interesting people on Wall Street. On his web site he made some key points against the Trim Tabs report. First, it would be very hard to cover up such large-scale operations over a long period of time. Second, if the Fed was trying to keep the market up over the last decade, it had sure done a bad job of it. Hence, he didn't give the report any credibility.

Barry took a lot of flak from his readers, many of whom strongly disagreed with him. It is also worth pointing out that the Fed may not be trying to boost the market long term. Instead, its intention would more likely be to save the market from the big collapse of what has been a historic and, we think, very bubble-ish 1,000+ percent increase in the Dow since the early 1980s.

The manipulation issue has also brought up the issue that had been raised before of whether the government has an informal plunge protection team (PPT). This would be a group of Fed, Treasury, and major bank officials who talk to each other when there is the threat of a major stock market plunge and work to prevent it or counteract a plunge once it happens.

This idea supposedly got going after the huge 20 percent stock market crash of 1987. In that case, as was well documented in a *Wall Street Journal* article written shortly after the crash, the problem the stock market faced was not Black Monday, when the market crashed 20 percent, but Terrible Tuesday, when the markets stopped functioning Tuesday morning after the crash.

The problem, specifically, was that the New York Stock Exchange's market makers had basically run out of capital and couldn't function. There was no market being made in such key stocks as IBM and GM. Market makers on the New York Stock Exchange had been somewhat thinly capitalized and were laid low by their huge losses on Monday and couldn't function on Tuesday.

A 20 percent drop in the stock market is a problem, but a dead stock market is a much bigger problem. So the Fed and Treasury basically stepped in and told the big banks to lend money to the major market makers, and they would back up the banks if they took any losses. Well, that did the trick. The banks lent the market makers the money they needed, and the stock had one of its biggest one-day rallies in history. Terrible Tuesday became Terrific Tuesday!

After that event, the PPT came into being as an informal group of the same people who worked together to save the market on Terrible Tuesday to deal with any Terrible Tuesdays in the future. Clearly, such direct intervention in the stock market had worked wonders.

Could this same type of thing have happened during the May 2010 flash crash? As further investigations have shown, the flash crash was primarily due to a series of down days culminating in a big down day—the day of the flash crash. It was accentuated by high-frequency traders, who do over 50 percent of the trading in the market now, exiting the market when it got too volatile. Of course, that's part of a broader problem of low volume and little long-term interest in the stock market. But, in many ways, the flash crash wasn't too different from Black Monday of 1987—a big bad day after a series of bad days.

The day of the flash crash had been going badly, but it got worse in the afternoon, partly due to a large trade by the Kansas City–based money management firm Waddell and Reed. After that, some large high-frequency traders pulled out of the market because the volatility was making it difficult for them to trade with any hope of making money. Thus, the flash crash began.

But why did it turn around so suddenly? Did the massive increase in volatility cause the high-frequency traders to come back in? That concept doesn't make sense—the higher volatility of the flash crash would seem likely to push them farther away from the market. Almost like the market makers of 1987, high-frequency traders exited the market because they didn't have the capital or didn't want to risk their capital in such a market. Thus, liquidity was drying up and the market was essentially dying. Seems like a perfect time for another intervention like the one in 1987. Only this time it was much quicker. They didn't act before a 20 percent decline and were able to stop the decline rather quickly and very sharply— a much better performance than 1987. But is it true? And wouldn't we have heard about it by now? You would think so, but it's difficult to be sure. The incredibly sharp turnaround had the telltale signs of a huge intervention.

However, all of the discussion of the flash crash in the media or by financial analysts was on why it went down so fast, not why it went up so fast. In fact, there was almost no discussion at all of why it went up so fast—that was considered normal and not worthy of discussion. The real question was what kind of technical trading error made it happen. Fat fingers? Dumb traders? Once the investigations showed it was not a trading error but a big market downturn accentuated by a large trade, people seemed to lose interest. And, again, no one asked why it went up so much so fast.

So we're back to Barry Ritholtz's question. Can something like stock market manipulation remain a secret? To answer that question, let's look at other recent financial community secrets. Enron and Bernie Madoff are obvious examples. However, both remained a secret even though there had been ample warning of problems to anyone looking at them closely. *Fortune* magazine saw something wrong in Enron, and Harry Markopolos (a Chartered Financial Analyst and Certified Fraud Examiner) actually wrote a report to the Securities and Exchange Commission detailing what he thought was going on with Bernie Madoff. So it wasn't a secret, but no one wanted to see it.

In the end, people want to see what they want to see. Even in nonfinancial areas this is true. In the movie *All the President's Men*, one of the editors at the *Washington Post* asked his fellow editors this question: If Watergate is true, why aren't any of the other newspapers like the *New York Times*, *Los Angeles Times*, and *Chicago Tribune* following it? Were staff members at the *Washington Post* the only ones who thought they knew the truth? It did seem hard to believe. But, often, even on big issues, people don't even ask the question.

Is Charles Biderman of Trim Tabs correct in thinking the Fed is intervening? We don't know for sure (and neither does he), but there are clearly a lot of reasons the Fed would want to see the stock market go up. A rising stock market has probably helped out the economy more than any other single positive element from 2009 to 2013. Certainly, it is the only part of our economy that has grown so rapidly. It has put more dollars into people's pockets than even all the borrowed money Congress has spent. It has certainly helped encourage the top 20 percent of our income earners who do over 40 percent of our consumer spending to get back into spending mode.

That puts a lot less pressure on the Fed to do other things like print more money via quantitative easing to boost the economy. You might say pushing up the stock market is probably one of the most cost-effective ways to spur the economy.

People who figure the Fed is manipulating the market mostly assume they are doing it by buying stock futures. That's part of the reason a lot of the upward activity in the market takes place overnight, and there are days when the market opens up with a huge increase despite a complete lack of significant good news. Of course, we really don't know how such manipulation could occur. It could also be via foreign intermediaries. But, again, we don't know the exact mechanism of how this might occur.

All of this could be explained by other factors. And, clearly, a key factor has been that cheerleaders want to see the market go up. However, that cheerleader spirit is also a key reason that manipulation works. With a very skeptical market, such periodic manipulation would fail because investors would not believe in it, so it is important that the cheerleaders keep the animal spirits high. To a more skeptical market, government manipulation of stock prices would not work. It might look more like Chinese manipulation of its currency—the currency shows a rock-solid movement up or down, based on what the government wants, with almost no volatility. It is fully manipulated all the time.

With the stock market heavily driven by cheerleaders, it doesn't take much manipulation to turn the market around from having a big fall. That's very different from manipulating the market all the time. Key manipulations done at the right time, like turning around the flash crash, greatly helps cheerleader psychology and would be relatively easy to perform.

And everyone wants to see them succeed, even non-cheerleaders. What could be better than a rising stock market and an improving economy? We'd certainly be the first ones to support it if we thought it would work in the long run.

It's only an issue if it is part of maintaining asset bubbles that are unsustainable. And in that broader context, it won't work. Even with a lot of manipulation, it will fail in the end, just as blatant Chinese manipulation of their currency will fail. That's one reason most countries don't manipulate their currencies to anywhere near the extent that the Chinese do. It's not just highly risky; such manipulation never works in the long run. It is just covering up an underlying problem—in China's case, it is a chronic trade surplus that China is using to boost its economy beyond what is economically sustainable. In our case, it is a series of asset bubbles that are unsustainable.

Lacking a smoking gun, stock market manipulation will remain a mystery. And few people will want to investigate because almost no one wants it to be true. Plus, they also hope that it will work.

And that mentality shows up in other ways, such as the lack of interest in a Fed audit. Even though it has received bipartisan support from congressmen as diverse as Republican Ron Paul and Democrat Alan Grayson, it didn't pass. It's almost as if people know the Fed has secrets that they don't really want people to know about. Is direct stock market manipulation one of them? If you don't ask, you'll never find out.

Well, that's probably not true. If the stock market melts down along with much of the economy, like the Enron and Bernie Madoff frauds, people will be mad, and it's likely they will ask these questions, and we will likely find out. But, of course, at that point it will be too late.

This is why we are awarding the ABE Intellectual Courage Award to Charles Biderman, president of Trim Tabs. Not because we think he's right. We don't know. But he did ask the question. And, at this point, that's what's important. He is a long-time well-respected financial analyst who has made good calls in the past, and he backed up his question with good research and exposed himself to ridicule for asking a reasonable question nobody else wants to ask. He is also a Wiley author—a blatant plug for our excellent publisher, which, by the way is a great example of a company that can survive the ups and downs of the American economy and still thrive. They were founded in 1807. That's over 200 years of surviving and thriving—not bad at all.

Gold Market Manipulation

Clearly, the price of gold is not as big a concern for the government as is supporting the stock market. However, there is a link between gold and stocks. When investors turn to gold, money is pulled out of stocks and bonds. As long as gold doesn't rise too much, there isn't much to worry about, especially in a nonbubble economy, because U.S. investors favor stocks and bonds over gold.

But gold presents a real problem for those who want to protect stocks and bond prices in a bubble economy that is beginning to fall. Rising gold prices are very dangerous when the government is trying to maintain the other asset bubbles. By pushing the price of gold down, investors are left with few legitimate alternatives other than the traditional markets, which helps maintain those bubbles.

The manipulation of gold is more obvious in Europe than in the United States. European central banks perform the most active and open buying and selling of gold by governments. European central banks have been selling gold for many years to keep the price in check. They have agreed to sell up to about 500 tons of gold a year. This agreement is in effect today, but in recent years very little gold was actually sold, whereas in past years the amount of gold sold was often close to the agreed-upon figure. Large sales of gold naturally push or keep the price of gold down.

The type of manipulation that most people are concerned about would be attempts by the U.S. Federal Reserve to push the price of gold down. One potential way to manipulate the price of gold is through gold swaps.

Gold Swaps

Governments have two ways to depress the price of gold with gold swaps. The first way is for two central banks to literally swap large amounts of gold with each other with the objective of doing nothing more than muddying the accounting waters, which helps to slow down rising gold prices.

A second type of gold swap involves only one central bank's gold reserves, which are lent for currency to another central bank. The real problem with this tactic is that the banks consider these swaps to be collateralized loans, and thus they don't appear on their balance sheets. No one knows for sure just how much gold and silver the Fed and other central banks have lent to each other in this way, but it would be worth taking a closer look if we could. A serious audit of the Federal Reserve would be a big step forward.

Gold Sales

Another way the price of gold can be manipulated is by the potential sale of gold by the Federal Reserve. If it occurred, this would be a dramatic step for the government and generally hasn't been taken seriously in the financial community.

However, more recently, gold has taken some remarkable falls in some very short periods of time, usually right after a large amount of gold has been dumped on the market in a very short time such as in April 2013. This kind of not-for-profit sale is highly suspicious. If a private (nongovernment) seller did have that much gold to sell, they would want to do so at a profit and therefore it wouldn't make much sense to dump it all at once and depress the price. To maximize potential profits, a private seller would naturally want to spread out the sale over time in order to not depress the price of gold and therefore get the best price possible. In fact, there is a whole industry of companies who specialize in helping larger investors pace out the sale of their assets in smaller increments in order to maximize their gains. But if the goal is not to get the best price possible, but to make gold prices fall, then selling a very large amount over a very short time makes sense.

In an article for Sharps Pixley in April, Ross Norman, a former gold trader for NM Rothschild & Son and for Credit Suisse, described the especially unusual circumstances that led to gold's fall in April 2013:

> The gold futures markets opened in New York on Friday 12th April to a monumental 3.4 million ounces (100 tonnes) of gold selling of the June futures contract . . . in what proved to be only an opening shot . . .
>
> Two hours later the initial selling, rumoured to have been routed through Merrill Lynch's floor team, [was followed] by a rather more significant blast when the floor was hit by a further 10 million ounces of selling (300 tonnes) over the following 30 minutes of trading. This was clearly not a case of

disappointed longs leaving the market—it had the hallmarks of a concerted "short sale," which by driving prices sharply lower in a display of "shock & awe"—would seek to gain further momentum by prompting others to also sell as their positions as they hit their maximum acceptable losses. . . .

While we don't have definitive proof, events like the one described here are a strong indication that governments are manipulating the price of gold. Note that the sales in question are of futures contracts (paper gold) and not physical gold. Selling physical gold in such large quantities in a short amount of time is much more difficult, and the more manipulation the government engages in, the more it drains the government's resources to continue manipulating in the future. Those interested in the specific details about how gold price manipulation might work should take a look at an online article by Paul Craig Roberts and David Kranzler that makes a compelling case for the government's potential role in the April 2013 gold price drop. Both authors of "The Hows and Whys of Gold Price Manipulation" are highly credentialed. Roberts served as Assistant Secretary of the Treasury for Economic Policy, associate editor of the *Wall Street Journal*, columnist for *Business Week* and *Scripps Howard*, and has held many university appointments. Kranzler traded high yield bonds for Bankers Trust for a decade. In the short term, manipulation can push the price down even while demand remains high. However, once gold is moving strongly upward, manipulation may not cause the price to fall; it may simply reduce the speed at which the price of gold rises.

Market Manipulation Summary

The fact that there are such indicators that the government has been manipulating the gold market is significant. It's a very unusual step, more complicated than behind-the-scenes manipulation of the stock market, and certainly more complicated than intervening in the bond market.

Terms like *moral hazard* no longer even exist in the government's vocabulary. As we have said before, that mentality has changed so much that we predict that almost anything that gets into trouble and might threaten the stability of the economy and its asset bubbles will likely be deemed necessary for a bailout, no matter who benefits or whose responsibility it was.

If anything, manipulating the stock market would fit right into what has become an increasing willingness on the part of the government to use its printing and borrowing powers to shore up the economy short term and a tremendous willingness to maintain asset bubbles.

Investment Impact

Long term, if manipulation exists, it will have no impact on the Aftershock scenario other than to make the meltdown that much bigger. Short term, it will certainly have an impact in forestalling the Aftershock, just as the government's other measures of borrowing and printing money will forestall the Aftershock, as we have discussed previously.

Short term, any manipulation certainly makes it harder to time the market. That's part of what manipulation is trying to do. In foreign currency manipulation that is the key impact of manipulation, the central bank manipulates the market in part to scare off manipulators from attacking a currency. A central bank does this with well-timed purchases and lots of mystery surrounding their exact purchases and the timing of those purchases. The central banks want to make the market participants sweat big time and hopefully cause them huge losses if they go against the central bank.

Of course, we don't recommend that most investors try to time the markets too closely. We strongly suggest, for the reasons we mentioned in the book and the reasons we have mentioned in the past, that you make long-term deliberate decisions on where to put your investment capital. You can move short term with the bubbles, but always remember that they are bubbles and your profits depend on your not being in those markets when the bubbles pop.

To make comments on the material in this appendix or enter a discussion thread, please visit our web site at www.aftershockeconomy.com/appendixcomments.

Bibliography

Altman, Daniel. "Uncle Sam, Deadbeat Debtor?" *New York Times,* July 23, 2006.

Athanasoulis, Stefano, and Robert J. Shiller. "The Significance of the Market Portfolio." *Review of Financial Studies,* 13, no. 2 (2000): 301–29.

Athanasoulis, Stefano, and Robert J. Shiller. "World Income Components: Discovering and Implementing Risk Sharing Opportunities." *American Economic Review* 91, no. 4 (2001): 1031–54.

Baker, Dean. "The Menace of an Unchecked Housing Bubble," *Center for Economic and Policy Research,* March 16, 2006. www.cepr.net/index.php/op-eds-&-columns/op-eds-&-columns/the-menace-of-an-unchecked-housing-bubble/ (accessed October 19, 2006).

Ballinger, Kenneth. *Miami Millions: The Dance of the Dollars in the Great Florida Land Boom of 1925.* Miami, FL: Franklin Press, 1936.

Batra, Ravi, ed. *The Great Depression of 1990: Why It's Got to Happen, How to Protect Yourself.* New York: Simon & Schuster, 1987.

Berman, Dennis K. "Fistfuls of Dollars Fuel the M&A Engine." *Wall Street Journal,* January 3, 2006.

Biderman, Charles, and David Santschi. *Trim Tabs Investing: Using Liquidity Theory to Beat the Stock Market.* Hoboken, NJ: John Wiley & Sons, 2005.

Blinder, Alan S. and Janet L. Yellen, *The Fabulous Decade: Macroeconomic Lessons from the 1990s.* New York: Century Foundation Press, 2001.

Bohm-Bawerk, Eugen Von. *Capital and Interest,* 3 vols (1884 and 1889), trans. G. D. Huncke and H. E. Sennhole. South Holland, Illinois: Libertarian Press, 1959.

Bonner, Bill, and Addison Wiggin. *Empire of Debt: The Rise of an Epic Financial Crisis.* Hoboken, NJ: John Wiley & Sons, 2006.

Bruno, Michael, and William Easterly. "Inflation Crises and Long-Run Growth." *Journal of Monetary Economics,* 41(1) (1998): 2–26.

Buffett, Warren E. "Chairman's Letter to Shareholders." Berkshire Hathaway, Inc. 2005 Annual Report.

Bulgatz, Joseph. *Ponzi Schemes, Invaders from Mars, and Other Extraordinary Pop Delusions, and the Madness of Crowds.* New York: Harmony, 1992.

Case, Karl E., Jr., and Robert J. Shiller. "The Efficiency of the Market for Single Family Homes." *American Economic Review,* 79(1) (March 1989): 125–37.

Cassidy, John. *Dot.con: How America Lost Its Mind and Money in the Internet Era.* New York: Perennial Currents, 2003.

Celente, Gerald. *Trends 2000: How to Prepare for and Profit from the Changes of the 21st Century.* New York: Hachette Book Group, 1997.

Clements, Jonathan. "The Debt Bubble Threatens to Derail Many Baby Boomers' Retirement Plans." *Wall Street Journal,* March 8, 2006.

Cooper, Jim. "A Truer Measure of America's Ballooning Deficit." *Financial Times* (London), May 1, 2006.

Coronado, Julia Lynn, and Steven A. Sharpe. "Did Pension Plan Accounting Contribute to a Stock Market Bubble?" Washington, D.C. Board of Governors of the Federal Reserve System, Finance and Economics Discussion Series No. 2003-38, 2003.

Cutler, David, James Poterba, and Lawrence Summers. "What Moves Stock Prices?" *Journal of Portfolio Management*, 15(3) (1989): 4–12.

"Danger—Explosive Loans." *BusinessWeek*, October 23, 2006.

Delasantellis, Julian. "U.S. Living on Borrowed Time—and Money." *Asia Times Online*, March 24, 2006. www.atimes.com/atimes/Global_Economy/Hc24Dj01.html.

Dent, Harry S. *The Roaring 2000s: Building the Wealth & Lifestyle You Desire in the Greatest Boom in History.* New York: Simon & Schuster, 1998.

Dent, Harry S. *The Great Depression Ahead: How to Prosper in the Crash Following the Greatest Boom in History.* New York: Free Press, 2008.

Dent, Harry S. *The Great Crash Ahead: Strategies for a World Turned Upside Down.* New York: Free Press, 2011.

Duncan, Richard. *The Dollar Crisis: Causes, Consequences, Cures.* Hoboken, NJ: John Wiley & Sons, 2005.

Easterlin, Richard. "Does Economic Growth Improve the Human Lot?" *Nationals and Households in Economic Growth: Essays in Honor of Moses Abramovitz*, Ed. Paul David and Melvin Reder. New York: Academic Press, 1974.

Eichengreen, Barry. *Golden Fetters: The Gold Standard and the Great Depression:1919–1939.* New York: Oxford University Press, 1992.

Einhorn, David. *Fooling Some of the People All of the Time: A Long Short Story.* Hoboken, NJ: John Wiley & Sons, 2008.

Evans-Pritchard, Ambrose. "SocGen Crafts Strategy for China Hard-Landing." *The Telegraph.* January 20, 2011. www.telegraph.co.uk/finance/china-business/8272388/SocGen-crafts-strategy-for-China-hard-landing.html (accessed February 16, 2011).

Fergusson, Adam. *When Money Dies: The Nightmare of Deficit Spending, Devaluation, and Hyperinflation in Weimar Germany.* New York: Public Affairs, 2010.

Fisher, Irving. *The Nature of Capital and Income.* New York: Macmillan, 1906.

Fisher, Irving. *The Stock Market Crash— and After.* New York: Macmillan, 1930.

Fisher, Irving. *The Theory of Interest.* New York: Macmillan, 1930.

Friedman, Milton. *Money Mischief: Episodes in Monetary History.* New York: Harcourt Brace Jovanovich, 1992.

Froot, Kenneth, and Maurice Obstfeld. "Intrinsic Bubbles: The Case of Stock Prices. *American Economic Review*, 81 (1991): 1189–1214.

Galbraith, John Kenneth. "The 1929 Parallel." *Atlantic Online*, January 1987, www.theatlantic.com/doc/198701/galbraith.

Galbraith, John Kenneth. *The Affluent Society.* New York: New American Library, 1995.

Galbraith, John Kenneth. *The Great Crash: 1929*, 2nd ed. Boston: Houghton Mifflin, 1954.

Glover, John and Joe Brennan. "Greek, Irish Banks Force ECB to Print More Money: Euro Credit," *Bloomberg.* February 16, 2011. www.bloomberg.com/news/2011-02-16/greek-irish-banks-force-ecb-to-print-more-money-euro-credit.html (accessed February 16, 2011).

Gordon, Robert J. "U.S. Productivity Growth Since 1879: One Big Wave?" *American Economic Review,* 89, no. 2 (1999): 123–28.

Gross, Daniel. *Pop! Why Bubbles Are Great for the Economy.* New York: HarperCollins, 2007.

Gross, William H. *Everything You've Heard About Investing Is Wrong.* New York: Times Books, 1997.

Heilbroner, Robert J. *The Worldly Philosophers: The Lives, Times, and Ideas of the Great Economic Thinkers,* 7th ed. New York: Simon & Schuster, 1999.

Heilbroner, Robert, and William Milberg. *The Crisis of Vision in Modern Economic Thought.* New York: Cambridge University Press, 1995.

James, Harold. *The End of Globalization: Lessons from the Great Depression.* Cambridge, MA: Harvard University Press, 2001, 125 and 142.

Janszen, Eric. *The Postcatastrophe Economy: Rebuilding America and Avoiding the Next Bubble.* New York: Penguin Group, 2010.

Jung, Jeeman, and Robert J. Shiller. "Samuelson's Dictum and the Stock Market." *Economic Inquiry,* 2005.

Katona, George. *Psychological Economics.* New York: Elsevier, 1975.

Keynes, John Maynard. *A Tract on Monetary Reform.* London: Macmillan, 1923.

Keynes, John Maynard *The General Theory of Employment, Interest and Money.* New York: Harcourt Brace & World, 1961.

Kindleberger, Charles P. *Manias, Panics and Crashes: A History of Financial Crises,* 2nd ed. London: Macmillan, 1989.

Kindleberger, Charles P., and Robert Z. Aliber. *Manias, Panics and Crashes: A History of Financial Crises,* 5th ed. Hoboken, NJ: John Wiley & Sons, 2005.

Krugman, Paul. *The Great Unraveling: Losing Our Way in the New Century.* New York: W. W. Norton & Company, 2004.

Krugman, Paul. *The Return of Depression Economics and the Crisis of 2008.* New York: W. W. Norton & Company, 2009.

Krugman, Paul. "How Fast Can the U.S. Economy Grow?" *Harvard Business Review,* 75 (1977): 123–29.

Lewis, Michael. *Panic: The Story of Modern Financial Insanity.* New York: W. W. Norton & Company, 2009.

Lewis, Michael. *The Big Short: Inside the Doomsday Machine.* New York: W. W. Norton & Company, 2010.

Lindert, Peter. *Growing Public: Social Spending and Economic Growth Since the Eighteenth Century.* New York: Cambridge University Press, 2004.

Lowenstein, Roger. *Origins of the Crash: The Great Bubble and Its Undoing.* New York: Penguin Press, 2004, 2.

Lucas, Robert E. "Asset Prices in an Exchange Economy." *Econometrica,* 46 (1978): 1429–45.

Mandel, Michael. "Bubble, Bubble, Who's in Trouble?" *Business Week,* June 15, 2006.

McGrattan, Ellen R., and Edward C. Prescott. "Is the Stock Market Overvalued?" *Federal Reserve Bank of Minneapolis Quarterly Review,* 24 (2000): 20–40.

Meltzer, Allan H. "Monetary and Other Explanations of the Start of the Great Depression." *Journal of Monetary Economics,* 2 (1976): 455–71.

Nima. "Inflation & Money Supply in China," *EconomicsJunkie.* November 18, 2010. www.economicsjunkie.com/inflation-money-supply-in-china/ (accessed February 16, 2011).

Perkins, Edwin J. *Wall Street to Main Street.* Cambridge, UK: Cambridge University Press, 1999.

Posen, Adam S. "It Takes More than a Bubble to Become Japan." *Institute for International Economics Working Paper No. 03-9,* October 2003.

Powers, Bill. *Cold, Hungry and in the Dark: Exploding the Natural Gas Supply Myth.* Gabriola Island, BC Canada: New Society Publishers, 2013.

Prechter, Robert R. *At the Crest of the Tidal Wave: A Forecast for the Great Bear Market.* New York: John Wiley & Sons, 1995.

Prechter, Robert R. *Conquer the Crash: You Can Survive and Prosper in a Deflationary Depression.* Hoboken, NJ: John Wiley & Sons, 2003.

Pressman, Steven. *Fifty Major Economists,* 2nd ed. New York: Routledge, 2006.

Pressman, Steven. "On Financial Frauds and Their Causes: Investor Overconfidence." *American Journal of Economics and Sociology,* 57 (1998): 405–21.

Reich, Robert B. *Aftershock The Next Economy and America's Future.* New York: Alfred A. Knopf, 2010.

Reich, Robert. "The Sham Recovery," *The Huffington Post,* March 12, 2010. www.huffingtonpost.com/robert-reich/the-sham-recovery_b_497439.html (accessed February 16, 2011).

Reinhart, Carmen M. and Kenneth S. Rogoff. *This Time Is Different: Eight Centuries of Financial Folly.* Princeton, NJ: Princeton University Press, 2009.

Rickards, James. *Currency Wars: The Making of the Next Global Crisis.* New York: Penguin Group, 2011, 2012.

Romer, Christina. "The Great Crash and the Onset of the Great Depression." *Quarterly Journal of Economics,* 105 (1990): 597–624.

Rosenberg, Yuval. "The Boomer Bust." *Fortune,* June 19, 2006.

Roubini, Nouriel, and Stephen Mihm. *Crisis Economics.* New York: Penguin Press, 2010.

Samuelson, Robert J. "A Financial 'Time Bomb'?" *Washington Post,* March 12, 2003.

Samuelson, Robert J. *The Good Life and Its Discontents: The American Dream in the Age of Entitlement, 1945–1995.* New York: Crown, 1995.

Samuelson, Robert J. *The Great Inflation and Its Aftermath: the Past and Future of American Affluence.* New York: Random House, 2008.

Saxonhouse, Gary R., and Robert M. Stern. *Japan's Lost Decade: Origins, Consequences and Prospects for Recovery.* Massachusetts: Blackwell Publishing Ltd, 2004.

Schiff, Peter D., and Andrew J. Schiff. *How An Economy Grows and Why It Crashes.* Hoboken, NJ: John Wiley & Sons, 2010.

Shiller, Robert J. "Measuring Bubble Expectations and Investor Confidence." *Journal of Psychology and Markets,* 1, no. 1 (2000): 49–60.

Smith, Adam. *The Money Game.* New York: Vintage Books, 1976.

Soros, George. *The New Paradigm for Financial Markets: The Credit Crisis of 2008 and What It Means.* New York: Public Affairs, 2008.

Stovall, Sam. *The Seven Rules of Wall Street.* New York. McGraw-Hill: 2009.

Summers, Lawrence H., and Victoria P. Summers. "When Financial Markets Wore Well: A Cautious Case for a Securities Transactions Tax." *Journal of Financial Securities Research*, 3, no. 2–3 (1988): 163–88.

Taleb, Nassim Nicholas. *The Black Swan: The Impact of the Highly Improbable.* New York: Random House, 2007, 2010.

Turk, James. *The Coming Collapse of the Dollar and How to Profit from It: Make a Fortune by Investing in Gold and Other Hard Assets.* New York: Currency, 2004.

Vittachi, Nury and Marc Faber. *Riding the Millennial Storm: Marc Faber's Path to Profit in the New Financial Markets.* Singapore: John Wiley & Sons, 1998.

Wanniski, Jude. *The Way the World Works*, 2nd ed. New York: Simon & Schuster, 1982.

Wiedemer, James. *The Homeowner's Guide to Foreclosure: How to Protect Your Home and Your Rights*, 2nd ed. New York: Kaplan Publishing, June 3, 2008.

Wiggin, Addison. *The Demise of the Dollar . . . and Why It's Great for Your Investments.* Hoboken, NJ: John Wiley & Sons, 2005.

Will, George F. "Guaranteed Collisions." *Washington Post*, May 15, 2005.

"World Finance: The Coming Storm for Banks." *The Economist*, February 20, 2004.

Index